My Life
in
Natural History

by
Walter J. Breckenridge

1903-2003

Compiled and Edited
by

Barbara Breckenridge Franklin
and
John J. Moriarty

2009

Special Publication
of
J.F. Bell Museum of Natural History

Sponsored
by
Minnesota Ornthologists' Union
Minnesota Herpetological Society
Minnesota DNR Nongame Wildlife Program
Breckenridge Chapter of Izaak Walton League

ISBN 978-1-885209-59-7

W J Breckenridge

Portrait
Walter J. Breckenridge
March 22, 1903-May 22, 2003
by
Murray Olyphant 1987

Dedication

This book is for all who see the beauty of the natural world and care for it,
but especially his nine great grandsons:

Cole and Sam Bates-Norum

Samuel and Christopher Breckenridge

Turner Norum

Thomas and John Quello

Breck and Jacob Schwietz

Table of Contents

PREFACE

When I began to transcribe my father's autobiography over ten years ago, I had hoped someone who knew publishing would materialize out of the blue to take the project a step further and actually make it appear in print. The experience of reading the story word for word as I unraveled his manuscript was both fascinating and daunting. Beginning in his totally unintelligible scrawl, eventually recording it on a little Royal portable typewriter, and finally graduating to a "real word processor" at the age of 90, he still didn't quite get the hang of "word wrap" or even computer files. Consequently, much of his work was incorporated in three or four places, and every line had to be read to eliminate returns at the end of each line. But the story itself provided an invaluable insight into his life, his thinking and his devotion to the natural world.

Growing up in his world at the Brackens, we took so much for granted. The wildlife outside our windows and the birds sharing their meals with us were a way of life. Where else would you find baby wood ducks paddling through the ice cream plates and the flower arrangement to entertain guests after dinner?

It has been a long road, but at last one of Daddy's friends and fellow natural historian, John Moriarty, DID materialize with an offer I simply couldn't refuse. "How are you coming on your father's book?" he asked. "I have some suggestions for getting it published." I leapt at the chance, and finally it is becoming a reality, too late for Mother and Daddy to see, but as a tribute to their lives and to his art.

In editing his autobiography John and I have tried to organize Daddy's stories in a clear and concise manner while still preserving his voice in the telling. We hope that you will remember him or get to know him through this book.

Barbara Breckenridge Franklin
The Brackens
Brooklyn Park, MN

August 2009

FOREWORD

Walter Breckenridge ("Breck") was a humble man who embodied the Bell Museum's mission of connecting people to nature. Throughout his long association with the Bell Museum, and especially during his 13-year tenure as Director, he inspired people to be conscientious stewards of their natural resources. He also nurtured the careers of undergraduate and graduate students.

My personal life intersected for the first time with Breck in 1973. As an undergraduate premed student at the University of Minnesota, I was coming to the stark realization that I didn't want to be a medical doctor. I wondered if my long-term interest in birds could somehow be translated into a career in ornithology. Someone (I don't recall who) suggested that I contact Breck at the Bell Museum. When I reached him at his home, he kindly explained that he had retired and encouraged me to contact Dr. Dwain Warner, Curator of Birds. After a brief meeting with Dwain, I ended up majoring in zoology, followed by a Ph. D. at the University of California - Berkeley. Later, while I was a professor/curator at the Museum of Natural Science at Louisiana State University some exciting news from Minnesota trickled south.

As a testament to the respect and admiration many held for Breck, his friends and admirers had established an endowment to create the Breckenridge Chair in Ornithology in the Bell Museum, my academic "birthplace." Eventually, I was honored to become the first holder of the Breckenridge Chair. My contact with Breck had now come full circle - the young undergraduate Breck encouraged to pursue a career in ornithology ended up being appointed the first Breckenridge Chair in Ornithology.

Upon returning to Minnesota, I would come to find out for myself what a wonderful man Breck was through our occasional personal visits and now, through his autobiography. I was surprised to learn that he and I have had many parallel career and life experiences, and it is fascinating to read about his. His writings provide an interesting glimpse into life in rural Iowa in the early 1900s, life as an undergraduate student, and his dual career as museum worker and graduate student. His notes from the field expeditions are important because they reveal the true nature of field expeditions. Field expeditions often sound glamorous - but typically involve long hours and sometimes tedious work. I doubt anyone will find the accounts of the Arctic expeditions boring. In fact, they are among the more page-turning parts of the autobiography. And if you've ever contemplated a driving trip through western North America, the itinerary Dorothy and Breck followed on their "Second Honeymoon – 1934" would be a great model.

I will let the reader discover all that his autobiography offers, but I would highlight two important parts of Breck's influence. The first highlight involves the short section on his "Audubon" lectures. Over several years, Breck gave at least 595 lectures in all but two of the lower 48 states to a combined audience of nearly 100,000 people. These lectures were illustrated with his path-breaking natural history movies. These movies, which he narrated as they played, were a huge success. Sunday afternoon lectures at the Bell

Museum, also accompanied by his movies, were an important event for many. Breck had a huge impact on an immense and diverse audience.

The second important contribution of Breck's was his recognition of the huge problem created by human over-population. Ahead of his time, Breck wrote numerous articles about the perils of overshooting our environment's "carrying capacity", and he did so with authority, clarity and elegance. Unfortunately, like most attempts to sound the alarm about human overpopulation, it will probably take catastrophic events to make people appreciate the wisdom in Breck's message.

One of my last encounters with Breck was during a talk I gave at his home chapter of the Izaak Walton League. After my presentation, Breck announced that he and Dorothy were moving from their home on West River Road to a senior's condominium. To lighten the moving load, he had brought a number of his paintings, most of which were not finished because they didn't pass muster with his artistic side. Even though they were in various stages of completion, they seemed like masterpieces to the audience! Ever modest, Breck laid them out on a table and asked that for each painting you took, you donated a dollar to his local IWL chapter. A dollar -- for a Breck original! My initial reaction was to back my car up and take them all!! There was a controlled panic as we all sorted through and claimed our treasures. Best $3 I ever spent! My only regret is that I never asked him to sign his unfinished painting of a tropical solitaire from Central America, but that is part of its charm to me. That painting has hung in our home for over a decade and is a permanent fixture.

Breck wasn't the richest of men, but he had at least two qualities that cannot be bought: absolute class and an absence of ego. I am sure that for my one story, there are numerous others to be told of how someone's life was positively changed by Breck's influence. The world needs more people like Breck. His autobiography shows us why.

Robert M. Zink
Breckenridge Chair in Ornithology
Bell Museum
University of Minnesota

August 2009

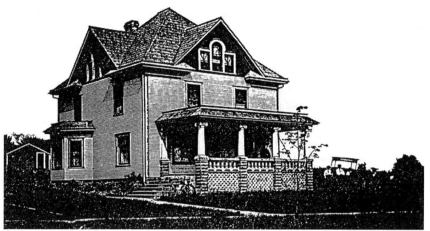

Chapter 1: Boyhood

Childhood home on Jackson Street in Brooklyn, Iowa

Breck at four years old

When I first began this writing project I did not consider writing what would be called an "autobiography." I simply intended to reproduce a number of my better paintings with a page of text for each explaining something of the situation that led up to the painting of the picture. After writing a few of the possible scripts they became more and more expanded until they took on the character of a real autobiography, which it now has turned out to be.

My recollections of my life ninety odd years ago are very sketchy with only a few occurrences that might illustrate the somewhat primitive conditions we experienced during those early 1900 years.

Regarding my very early years in the small town of Brooklyn in east-central Iowa, I have only a few vivid recollections. I recall that we had an outdoor privy reached by a wooden walkway that rendered winter use a very chilling experience. This, of course, meant chamber vessels in our bedrooms. We did have a town water system providing drinking water, but for washing, a cistern gathered soft water from the roof that was brought up to the kitchen by a squeaky hand-operated pump. A somewhat twisted catalpa tree in our front yard was easy to climb and a rope-swing hung from one of the larger limbs that gave me lots of swinging fun either by myself or by being pushed by one of my two older brothers.

We had no preschool or kindergarten. I started school in the first grade at five years of age. There we had some single desks but most were double-sized where we boys

1

hated to be seated with a girl. We wrote on slates with slate pencils and erased the writing later with a damp cloth.

My earliest remembrance of automobiles was while we were living only a couple of blocks from Dad's hardware store when we often ran to the window to see a car going by. Horses would often shy away from a car passing nearby or even run away when frightened by a car. Less than a dozen makes of cars were seen on the roads and my brothers and I could identify all of them very easily as they were so different in shape. Some of these early makes were Maxwell, Saxon, Studebaker, Overland, Buick, Reo, Metz (chain driven), Regal Underslung and a few with high buggy-like wheels that had no names I can recall. Fords appeared later.

We considered my cousin, Glen Hall, to be a rather reckless young fellow. On one occasion I recall riding with him in his parents' Overland sedan. On an especially smooth stretch of country road he stepped on the gas and reached 37 miles an hour. This was the fastest I had ever ridden in a car. Little did I realize then that I would still be living and driving my car at age 93 and not too surprised to find myself stepping too heavily on the gas and hitting 75 miles an hour. In those early years when we boys wanted to comment on something going remarkably fast we would say it was going "like 60."

Dad had no car until we moved to our new house on the north edge of the town. There he had built a rather large chicken house one end of which was later rebuilt into a garage for the Buick touring car, which we must have bought in about 1910. My first personal car was a small sort of a pickup Ford truck roadster that Dad had been using for running errands at the store. I bought this from him just after my graduation from college to supply me with transportation to Minnesota on my first job at the Museum. It was hand cranked where one first had to retard the spark on the steering wheel, then pull out a wire loop in front just below the radiator to choke the carburetor, then give the front end crank a few vigorous

turns (sometimes many) to get the motor going. Occasionally the motor would kick back prematurely and jerk the crank out of your hand. It was not unusual for owners of Model T Fords to suffer broken arms just above the wrists when this kickback occurred. Later I installed an in-the-car starter just below the steering wheel, which I pulled on vigorously to start the motor. Windshield washers were hand operated. And starting these early cars on cold winter mornings is a whole story in itself.

Just about a block from our home in Brooklyn was a blacksmith shop where we could often hear the pounding of his hammer on the anvil as he shaped horse shoes to fit the horses' hoofs. We often stood around in his shop to watch him pumping the bellows that kept the coke fire for heating the shoes and to see the sparks fly as he pounded them into shape. I often wondered why the horses tolerated him fitting the hot shoes on their feet, not realizing that the outer layer of their hoofs were like finger nails – without nerves to register pain.

There are four shops in Brooklyn that cling in my memory because of their distinctive odors. One was the blacksmith shop, and Dad's harness shop is described in the next chapter. Number three was the tiny laundry squeezed in next to the grocery store at the north end of the town's business district. It was operated by a Chinaman named Fong Soon. He had no family and returned to China for a visit occasionally. He was especially skillful in laundering, folding and wrapping shirts for his customers. The steamy atmosphere carried the odor of the particular soaps he used. I recall we invited him for dinner at our home when I was a very small youngster. Mr. Soon finally went on a visit to China and never returned. Shop number four was a small cobbler shop run by an elderly bachelor, Johnnie Schmidt. He often would ask what our names were and was much amused when we called our parents by their first names, Rob and Bessie. The special odor in that shop was from the heavy leather he used in repairing the soles of the shoes.

We frequently celebrated certain occasions that were looked forward to with great anticipation. On birthdays we would expect Dad to bring home an angel food cake with ice cream from "Tet Neff's" bakery. When Christmas was approaching my older brothers, Robert and Harold, and I would spend days poring over book catalogues to decide what books we would like Santa Claus to bring us on the night before Christmas. There was no bookstore in our town. Then on Decoration Day (as we called Memorial Day) we would take the long solemn walk to the IOOF Cemetery over a long elevated wooden sidewalk that spanned a marshy place to visit and place flowers on Esther's grave. She was the sister I never knew since she died at only eight years of age in 1903, the year I was born.

In 1908 when I was five years old my parents built a large white-pillared home on the north edge of town. Just a block south of this home was an east-west highway called the River-to-River Road, so called because it ran across Iowa from the Mississippi on the east to the Missouri on the west. The highway was marked only by signs painted on telephone or fence posts. It was neither paved nor graveled and the dust in summer became almost ankle deep causing passing cars to throw up dense clouds of dust. People traveling any distance wore light, full length coats referred to as "dusters." As might be expected, the city mothers complained vociferously until the city fathers decided to settle the dust with the application of used motor oil. A few main streets finally were paved and this we thought was wonderful but surely the time would never come when the roads between towns would be paved.

In our new modern home, heating problems did not involve electricity, oil or gas, but wood and coal. One room in the basement was the furnace room. A brick wall separated the furnace from the coal bin. A sturdy team of draft horses pulled a heavy wagonload of coal up to the north side of the house and the coal was hand shoveled down a heavy metal chute into the coal bin – always a dirty, dusty job. In order to start the furnace wood kindling was needed. All of the merchandise for Dad's hardware store came in wooden boxes or crates. These containers were delivered to the house by dray wagon. Knocking apart the boxes and chopping them into kindling lengths was a regular job of my two older brothers, while I pulled the nails from the kindling. The kindling was then tossed into the basement and stored under the stairs adjacent to the furnace room. All this material and effort was expended in order to keep us warm in winter. Cooling us in summer consisted simply of opening the windows.

A question often asked of me is "How did you become so interested in Nature? Did any one person guide your interest into this field?" I have thought about this a good deal while writing my autobiography and no one stands out as that person. I recall asking various people for information about Nature, such as the name for the large black bird with a bright yellow head that I found present but not common in the marshes and ponds in our area. I approached my friendly, attractive redheaded eighth grade teacher, Lois Beers, for the answer but found she knew little or nothing about the bird. But her reply was, "We'll just call it a 'yellow-headed blackbird' until we find out." This, of course, has always been the widely accepted common name of the bird.

Then there was the small, inconspicuous songbird I found commonly perched on fences or telephone wires. I had no bird book nor could I find one in the school or public library but in our huge unabridged dictionary was a series of black and white pictures of birds and I decided to call it a "linnet." When my parents found how curious I was about birds, they got me a pocketsized copy of *The Bird Book* by Chester Reed where my bird turned out to be a "dickcissel."

Such experiences convinced me that my interest must have originated from "spontaneous generation," not from any similarly interested adult. However, I have concluded that our aging bay carriage horse Major,

Maj for short, was intimately involved. My parents were not farmers but they did keep this friendly horse, given to Mother by her parents as a means of transportation. Since we lived in a small town (population 1200) and Dad's hardware store, the grocery store and school were close by we did not need any means of transportation other than our feet and bicycles. For distant travel we had trains, but Mother had several sisters and brothers who lived on farms some distance from town that we were anxious to keep in touch with. So to serve our needs for middle distance travel we boarded Maj in a local stable together with a "surrey with a fringe on top." Occasionally early on a Sunday morning, my two older brothers and I enjoyed accompanying Dad to the stable to watch him get the harness from its peg and throw it over Maj's back, fastening all the buckles and backing him between the shaves of the surrey. Then we would drive home to pick up Mother and the picnic basket.

When we took off, it was not in a car at 50 to 60 miles an hour but at Maj's walking speed of 3 to 4 miles an hour, for the two hour drive to Uncle William Hall's farm. It was no doubt on these quiet country rides that I had some of my first contacts with wild flowers, butterflies and birds. At first I was too small to be permitted to ride on the steps of the surrey, but my brothers enjoyed the chance to jump off to pick flowers, chase ground squirrels or to run ahead and wait for the surrey to catch up. Later I competed with them for the fun. I remember that at that time there were Osage orange hedges that served the farmers as fences before wire fences were widely used and where road cuts were made in the hills, the bright yellow Osage orange roots appeared out of the eroded banks. And we often were disappointed that the huge green fruits of these trees were far too bitter to be eaten.

No doubt these leisurely country rides stirred my interest in Nature. One of my earliest sketches was of a meadowlark (Plate 1). My concern for it came later. Early in life I came to realize that in my Iowa setting humans had eliminated many native plants and animals: a practice I would now refer to as mono-culture of only those crops of direct value to humans. Forested areas in Iowa were greatly altered, but in spite of all these disturbances, I often visited them to learn about the lives of the natural life still to be found in these so-called "Natural Areas." The little border of trees growing along Big Bear Creek in which there was a small thicket that we called "The Jungle" and a limited forested area known as "Kent's Woods" five miles north were my boyhood wildernesses. There were no nature centers or state parks available to me.

PIONEER TONSILECTOMY

I had been having repeated sore throats when at the age of 14 or 16, the doctor mentioned to my parents that I should have my tonsils removed some time soon. A few days later I thought I might as well have it over with so I simply walked into Doctor Ringena's office and told him I wanted to have him take out my tonsils. So with no nurse present he sat me into his operating chair and started cutting. I actually held one of his tools in place to help with the operation. However, after getting the first one out he decided we should have help on the second one so we called my Dad from the store down the street and he came up and acted as nurse for number two. What a contrast to the hospital tonsillectomies of today! Some years later, while I was in college I believe, I was having a routine physical examination and the doctor commented, "What a neat tonsillectomy you had." When I explained how it was done he told me that not having an anesthetic caused me to tighten up my throat muscles. That made the tonsils stand out so the surgeon could determine exactly where to make the cuts for a neat job.

GREAT LAKES TRIP

I believe it was when we three boys, Walter, Harold and Robert, were 8, 11, and 13 years old that the family embarked on an extended tour of the Great Lakes. We took the train to Duluth where we boarded the passenger ship the "Tionesta" and set out across

Lake Superior. At Sault Ste. Marie, Michigan we had the exciting experience of passing through the huge locks that lowered our vessel quite a number of feet to the level of Lake Huron. Crossing Huron we encountered a bit of heavy weather and I recall getting very seasick. But on landing in Detroit and getting my feet on solid ground again, I was soon O.K. While there we visited Belle Isle Park and my only recollection of the park was that all of the squirrels there were jet black, the first black squirrels I had ever seen. They were, of course, a melanistic form of the ordinary gray squirrel. Nearly all the details of our long voyage across Lakes Superior, Huron and Erie have been lost in the fog of the 88 years that have passed since that experience. But this first long trip away from home was a wonderful break in my rather sedentary life in little Brooklyn.

BICYCLES

Distances around Brooklyn were quite ideal for us to use bicycles a good deal. But one bike I used a lot was retired for a period of time on a Saturday afternoon. Horses and buggies together with a few cars made for heavy traffic that particular day in the business district when I was riding my bike home with a package under my arm. For some reason I cut across the traffic and a car hit my hind wheel, throwing me to the ground and running over the hind wheel. I was not hurt but I was really upset when I saw what a wreck my nice bicycle was. I carried it up onto the sidewalk in front of Dr. Ringena's office and ran down the street to Dad's hardware store. There I located Mac Mcgregor, one of Dad's shop workers, who came to help me carry my mangled bike back to the shop. I'm sure that cycle today would be considered totaled and a new one gotten to take its place. But then we located a usable wheel from another traffic victim, pounded the frame back into shape and I got a few more seasons' use from it.

BUTTERFLIES

Soon after moving to our new home on the outskirts of town I accidentally found a new hobby. Only a stone's throw from home I found a farmer's large clover field, which was attractive to many species of colorful butterflies. I captured a few with my cap and became intrigued with their colorful patterns. Neither our school nor town library had any book on butterflies so when I saw in a magazine an ad to purchase certain species, I answered the ad and got a small booklet with several species shown in black and white illustrations but with only their scientific Latin names. These I soon learned before I found that they had common names and I still remember many of those names. Following instructions in the ad I got some calcium cyanide from the drug store (certainly not today) and made a butterfly-killing jar. I then mounted the insects in a grooved board and when they dried I put them in glass-covered cardboard trays padded with cotton called Riker mounts. Napthaline crystals (mothballs) were buried in the cotton to ward off insects that were prone to destroying the butterfly bodies. I'm afraid the collection has long since disappeared but my interest in them still persists and I have only recently made numerous watercolor paintings of butterflies with the larva and chrysalis depicted with the food plants shown.

Thinking back into the often-dark corners of my boyhood memories, I find I still remembered collecting an especially colorful butterfly, which I identified as a gulf fritillary. This was listed as a southern species, a few individuals of which might wander north (how far north was not stated). But since I had seen just one individual, I must have been near the northern edge of its range. Recently I began wondering if I had taken a species really rare in Iowa, so I began browsing through my library of butterfly books to see if their ranges were given. I even remembered its scientific name, which at that time was Dione vanilli. This name no longer appeared in the literature. Its genus had been changed to Agrults, but vanillae had been retained as its species name. I was a bit disappointed to find the species appearing on a Minnesota list, but it was regarded as very rare this far north.

My specimens had long since disappeared, but I found excellent reproductions in my books so I undertook making a watercolor painting of my rare find. Since I had collected it in a clover field, I appropriately painted it perched on a clump of blossoming red clover plants. I had hoped to include the larva and chrysalis, but I have not, as yet, been able to find any illustrations of these developmental stages of my memorable gulf fritillary.

TAXIDERMY

One teenage incident that I later realized was to be quite significant in my future was when Dad brought home a very beautiful but dead specimen of a prairie chicken. We couldn't just pick off the feathers and cook and eat this bird. How I would like to preserve it! But how? Actually Dad was not a hunter but the owner of a hardware business. He was friendly with many of his farmer customers and one apparently had learned that he had a son who was interested in birds. It was he who brought in the prairie chicken that had been killed flying into a telephone wire. On handling the bird I was naive enough to wonder if birds had skin tough enough to be removed without losing the feathers.

After showing the bird to a neighbor boy, we decided to pool some of our meager assets and sign up for a correspondence course with the Northwestern School of Taxidermy, which we had seen advertised in a magazine. Thus taxidermy became my free time hobby throughout my high school years. An interesting incident took place when I was in need of a specimen on which to practice skinning and mounting a bird. I knew that a flock of grackles could usually be found in an old orchard back of our home. I took my 410-gauge shotgun and went grackle hunting. While looking for a good plumaged specimen, I noticed a small flock of crows flying toward the orchard and hoping I might even get a crow for my practice, I hid behind a tree and waited for them to get within good range of my little shotgun. Then without my firing a shot one of the birds fell dead at my feet. I couldn't have been more surprised

or puzzled over such a fortunate development. I wondered, "Could it possibly have been shot by some hunter with only a single shot entering the lungs causing it to collapse some time after actually being hit?" I was not an expert at performing autopsies but on skinning the bird I found no injury that might have resulted in its death. My only explanation for the incident was that the Fates were actually steering me toward museum work as my lifetime vocation.

I followed my taxidermy hobby all through high school and by the time I graduated I had a collection of about 60 mounted specimens of birds and small mammals. I puzzled over what to do with the collection until another unexpected thing happened. My senior class presented a class play that netted them a few dollars. And when the time came to dispose of the money, someone suggested that they use it to build a couple of glass-fronted cases to house my collection. I was, of course, very pleased at the suggestion so I donated it to the school to aid in their nature studies in biology.

TRAPPING

Before I was permitted to use a gun I took up trapping muskrats along Big Bear Creek a half-mile north of my home. I pored over fur prices of F.C.Taylor & Co in St. Louis where I marketed my furs. I read articles and books about pioneer trappers and Indians trapping beavers, raccoons, martins, fishers, bobcats and foxes. I dreamed about someday running my own trap line in the northern wilderness but the only furbearers I could hope to get were muskrats. Skunks were available to me but the odor, "Ick!!! What about the odor and going to school?" I read about how trappers considered how difficult mink were to trap. I knew they occurred in small numbers along Big Bear Creek and I developed a real ambition to outwit just one to prove my skill as a trapper. Every time I found mink tracks, I prepared a carefully baited set. One evening I made what I felt was an extra promising set at hole in the ice. Before school the next morning I hurried down to the creek to check my success. As I came over the bank

6

in view of the set, I was really jubilant to see a fine dark mink crouched in the shallow water obviously caught in my trap. Running down the bank to retrieve my prize I saw him dive into the water. I was not particularly concerned since I knew I could pull him back with the staked chain attached to the trap. But HORRORS! To my terrible disappointment the mink had pulled the stake out in his last great effort to escape and both trap and mink were gone. In desperation I rolled up my sleeves and repeatedly reached down into the freezing cold water under the ice hoping to find that the trap chain had become entangled in some roots and I could retrieve my loss. But no success! I probably actually sat down and cried but I remember well that this was by far the keenest disappointment I had ever experienced in my, then, short life. For some time afterwards I was deeply depressed to think that I had been responsible for the death of a beautiful mink, the pelt from which I could get no benefit.

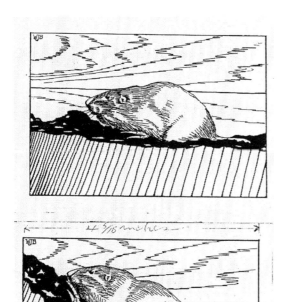

"We got ten cents apiece for trapping pocket gophers." (pen & ink)

Quite a different type of trapping was one of my efforts to make a little more money for my college education. I trapped pocket gophers in local farmers' pastures. Pocket gophers were small, expert digging rodents that burrowed in the ground throwing up small piles of dirt at intervals all along their burrows. This damaged the productivity of the pastures and the farmers were anxious to get rid of them, so my brother Harold and I had no trouble getting permission to trap in their land.

Our technique was to dig down with a small spade to get to the burrow and then to set a small, number zero steel spring trap in their runway. Then we covered the trap with a shingle to darken the burrow to keep the animal from seeing the trap. The trap was then staked securely with the chain attached to the trap. We carried a notebook where we recorded the location of each trap by counting the number of fence posts in two opposite directions. These animals had very distinctive front paws with very long claws for digging. These we cut off and kept in a small pocket-sized tobacco can filled with salt to preserve them throughout the trapping season. They were then taken to the county auditor who paid us ten cents a piece for them. Not a very remunerative activity, but it gave us something to do and it satisfied our hunting instinct presumably inherited from our "hunter gatherer" ancestors. The illustration here is from my first published work, which appeared in *The Journal of Mammalogy,* 1929.

INDIANS

While still a youngster I developed a great interest in Indians. At that age my favorite author was Ernest Thompson Seton. His *Two Little Savages* I read time after time. No doubt Dad generated this interest. As a young man he had worked in the lumber camps in northern Minnesota where he had considerable contact with the Ojibwa Indians. His duties saw him traveling in the woods using Indian birch canoes in summers and Indian snowshoes in winter. He kept a record book of some of his surveying data and in the back of it he recorded over 300 words and phrases of the Ojibwa language. These I read repeatedly and I still remember some of them. My next-door neighbor, Ralph Dayton, and I often played Indian and we gave each other Indian names. Mine, as I recall, was "Shoo-Ne-ah-Wauhgauze" meaning Silver Fox. Many Indians at that time were still living extensively by trapping furbearers. In fact, a small band of Musquauke Indians from the Tama "Reservation" 20 miles to the north, occasionally visited my hiking grounds along Big Bear Creek to trap muskrats and mink. I was thrilled when once I found a dome-shaped wickiup of poles left by these Indians. The frames had supported cattail mats to form their temporary shelters, much as we then used canvas tents. My reaction to this was "Gee, to think that real Indian trappers have been living and trapping right here where I have been hiking."

BIRDS

While I was still in grade school, I studied the small bird guide my parents had bought me so repeatedly that when I would see a bird that was new to me I would recall its name immediately from having seen its picture. I had no binoculars at that time and in fact, I felt that it was cheating to use them. I contended that one should stalk the birds sufficiently close to get the characters

Breck studied the great horned owl as a boy (pencil sketch)

needed for identifications. I finally admitted that binoculars were really quite essential for correct identifications. My first pair was heavy cast iron binoculars that were surplus from World War I.

One of my boyhood contacts with owls involved the largest of these birds, the great horned owl. A pair of these big raptors inhabited a limited strip of woods along Big Bear Creek only a half mile from my home. After taking up taxidermy as my hobby, I had to have subjects with which to work and a great horned owl would have made an exciting subject. I made numerous attempts to get one of the pair with my little 410-gauge shotgun, but the bird always detected me before I could get within range of it and I never did get one for my collection. I finally decided that it would be more fun to watch the activities of the pair rather than to shoot them. Not long afterwards I located the nest of the birds. The most rewarding of my observations was how early in the season they began nesting. Once I climbed to the nest early in January and found that three eggs had already been laid and were soiled and nest stained indicating that the first one must have been laid back in December. This predated our Minnesota records considerably since we usually look for them to have eggs by Washington's Birthday, February 22. At that time I was not familiar with the literature, but this could have been a record for the early egg laying for this species in mid-Iowa.

While working in my Dad's hardware store in summer, a customer brought me a slightly injured great horned owl. I nursed it back to health and was taking it into the field to release it. I was carrying it under my arm and holding its feet and powerful talons tightly in my hand. In climbing over a fence I swung my leg up and over the top wire giving the bird the chance to grab my thigh which it did with a vengeance and I had considerable difficulty prying it loose from my bleeding leg.

RECREATION

In winter one of our teenage recreations was the somewhat dangerous sport of hopping bobsleds. Most local farmers would drive their teams of horses pulling the heavy bobsleds to town for shopping in the morning and return in the afternoon. About noon some would already be returning out from town, giving us a chance to catch a ride out into the country. We would stand on the heavy runners and hold onto the sled body. Some farmers would object to our hopping onto their runners while others had no objection but smiled and warned us to be careful. During the noon hours some would still be heading into town giving us the chance to get a ride back home. Sometimes we would take our sleds along and if we failed to get a ride back we could at least slide down any hills enroute in order to shorten the long walk back.

Ralph often hiked the Big Bear Creek area with me. A still smaller tributary of this creek we called Stoney Creek led us along its wooded borders into quite a wild, wooded area. There we chose a spot and dug away the soil at the base of a steep bank to form a cave-like shelter. Then, with some poles embedded above the excavation, we constructed a roof shelter to form quite a cozy little hut we treated as our home while exploring the surrounding areas.

While in grade school our favorite sports at recess involved a great deal of physical activity. TV of course hadn't even been thought

Public school in Brooklyn, Iowa

of at that time. One of these games we called "Blackman." Where the name originated is still a question, but there was no racial reference, I'm sure. In this game two "safe zones" were designated about 20 to 30 feet apart. Contestants would try to run between these safe zones without being tagged by one designated as "it." If one was tagged, that youngster became "it" and the "it" person became just another contestant.

Another popular game was called "One and Over." The game began by having each contestant make a long jump from a given mark. The one with the longest jump then told the shortest jumper to put his hands on his ankles in "leapfrog" fashion and stand a few feet beyond the base mark. The longest jumper then leapfrogged over the youngster designated as the "down" person, who then moved ahead to where the pacesetter's heel landed. The pacesetter then called the next jump an "over" if he felt he could leapfrog over the "down" person in a single jump. If it was too long for that he called it a "one and over" and when still farther it became a "two and over." If one of the competitors was able to make this in one jump instead of the two, the pacesetter then would have to take the place of the "down" person and he would become the pacesetter and pacesetting would begin again. It was in this game that I began realizing that I had some ability at long jumping. This served me well in high school and later in college.

While in high school I had only a mild interest in athletics. I competed in several track events, but was especially good in the broad jump (now called the long jump). I won in this event in a number of inter-school meets with jumps of between 19 feet and 20 feet and later in college I made a jump of 21 feet. Our school had teams only in baseball, basketball and track. I did fairly well in baseball and track, but was too small to compete in the more strenuous contact sports. During the winters while in high school I tended the coal-burning furnace in Dad's hardware store. In the early morning hours I would run the four or five blocks to and from the store to keep in training for track.

Professional sports were unimportant to us, since my recollection is that baseball was the only professional league in existence at that time and we were so far removed from any large cities that had teams we felt no allegiance to any one. Professional football, basketball, or hockey had not come into existence in my early years.

During several of our cold, snowy winters, my parents vacationed for a week or two in Florida. On one of these trips Dad was stricken with rheumatism and was brought home on a stretcher. He soon recovered almost completely but had minor recurrences of the problem in later years. During their absences on these trips, Mac Mcgregor, one of Dad's employees, and his wife, Effie, were called in as family sitters. We boys enjoyed their coming immensely since they were lots of fun and did a great job tending the house as well as boy sitting.

CHAUTAUQUAS

The arrival of the Chautauqua in our town of Brooklyn, Iowa was one of the highlights of our summer season. It was a successful combination of education and entertainment available to small towns everywhere. Several companies had originated these programs. While still in high school I learned that the Acme Chautauqua Company hired students for the summer. Their duties were to erect the big tents and the canvas walls surrounding it; take care of the tent while on location; sell tickets and conduct simple entertainment programs for the youngsters for an hour or two during the mornings. The afternoon and evening programs were for the general public. I along with a school chum, Theral "Toots" Crider, applied for and got jobs with the Acme Company whose circuit visited southern Minnesota, Iowa and eastern Kansas and Nebraska. The two of us were separated, each with a different program unit that leap-frogged over each other from town to town throughout the summer season. The job proved to be a really husky physical experience: unrolling the big canvases, driving many big three foot stakes with a twelve pound maul and learn-

ing how to tie the wall and tent ropes firmly enough to withstand any storms that might occur. Mr. Carpenter, the director of my unit, and some local helper assisted in the heavier part of the work. I slept on a cot in the tent draped with mosquito net in order to be available in any emergency. Yes, mosquitoes were a problem and the people attending the programs seated on plank seats often lighted smudges to discourage the insects. I think repellents were just coming into wide use at that time.

I usually looked up a local person interested in birds at each stop so I could do some hiking during off-hours. I recall one particularly good time we had swimming and diving in a deep abandoned quarry pit. And at Colony in eastern Kansas, some oil wells were being drilled and one had just hit a natural gas pocket. It roared so that it was hard to converse nearby and putting my hand in the cold jet of gas, it was blown sky-high in spite of all my efforts to hold it in the jet. I recall contacting a sturdy high school student, Adrian Wruke, in Minnesota Lake who took me out on a very productive bird walk. Many years later he surprised me when he walked into my office in the Bell Museum for a chat about all that had happened in the intervening years.

During my early teenage years I was a Boy Scout but we had problems keeping a Scout Master for periods long enough for me to gain first class rank and begin getting merit badges so I never became an Eagle Scout. One Scout activity that my brother, Robert, and I got lots of fun out of was communicating in codes. We became quite proficient with our semaphore signaling such as sailors used on ships in those days. We also had numerous ways of utilizing the Morse code. For instance, we could look north from our backyard across the Big Bear Creek Valley to a hilltop about a mile away. One evening Robert rode his bicycle over to that hilltop and lighted a small campfire. Then by holding up a blanket to conceal it from me, he sent dot and dash messages to me in our backyard. I don't recall whether or not we qualified for a merit badge, but we enjoyed very much our accomplishments in that field.

Even though I could not actually qualify for merit badges I recall attempting to meet the requirements for archery badge. One of the requirements was to make a bow and arrow that would shoot 150 yards. Hickory was a choice wood for bows, but I knew that Osage orange was very strong and flexible. However, I searched in vain for a branch long and straight enough from either of these woods. I eventually found that a local shop that repaired wagons and buggies had long squared hickory strips for buggy reaches (the poles used to connect the front and rear axle assemblies.) This served my purpose ideally so I made a fine five-foot bow and notched the ends for the string. This I made by twisting several strands of linen cord that Mr. Waldorf, the harness maker who worked in Dad's harness shop, used. The arrows I split from lightweight redwood and attached chicken feathers to guide their flight. And I created a wrist guard to protect my wrist from the snapping cord when an arrow was shot. I was quite proud of my archery equipment but, at my age of only 12 or 13, I failed to quite make the 150-yard requirement for the merit badge.

Bill Gloe and Breck located this burled elm tree

Another project I recall was attempting to carve a pioneer drinking cup out of a small tree burl. Along Big Bear Creek we found an elm tree with an enormous burl several feet across that completely encircled the huge trunk shown in the accompanying photo of my chum, Bill Gloe, and me. Just above this huge burl was the small one I had been looking for. We sawed it off and I undertook hollowing it out but found the wood extremely hard. When only half done I laid it aside with the idea I would finish it sometime when I had more time and energy. Believe it or not, I preserved it and actually finished it just 80 years later and it is still hanging in my studio to show my friends.

PETS

"A youngster should never grow up without a dog." My parents must have heard this comment and saw that I had a pet fox terrier soon after we moved to the new house

The pioneer drinking cup Breck carved from an oak burl

on the outskirts of town. I recall that Dad located a family raising fox terriers in Pella, Iowa, a Dutch community about forty or fifty miles from Brooklyn. I was really thrilled when the little fellow arrived as a recently weaned puppy, white with a few scattered black spots. We built a small kennel under the back porch with a hanging piece of carpet as a door where he could come and go to its cozy shelter whenever he chose. We gave him the name "Rex" meaning "king" and he occupied a really royal place in our household for several years. He was big for a fox terrier and reasonably well behaved but there was no obedience school in our small town.

Rex and I enjoyed our companionship immensely chasing rabbits and ground squirrels and, more restfully, lying in a hammock together, sleeping on the porch. I must have been about 11 years old when I wrote an *Autobiography of Rex.* It was in the form of twenty 5 by 8 inch pages written on both sides, bound by heavy brown paper and tied with a brown ribbon. The penmanship was very legible – more so than mine today. It was full of incidents such as: "One day I went upstairs to take a nap but I chewed a hole in the comforter and picked out the cotton so I am not allowed to go upstairs for my nap any more."

Our neighbors, too, liked Rex but unfortunately the boy who delivered our groceries with his horse and spring wagon thought it was fun to tease him with his buggy whip. This soon developed well beyond just fun. Before long the boy refused to deliver our groceries for fear of Rex who became quite vicious whenever the grocery wagon approached our house. This led to further unfriendly behavior on Rex's part and we were finally forced to give him a new home at my Uncle William Hall's farm. But this did not have a happy ending. Uncle William and his son, my cousin Glen, raised hogs as a major part of their farming activities. When they found that Rex had killed several young pigs they were forced to dispose of my friendly little pet much to my sorrow when I learned about it.

Another pet I remember was a small yellow canary. Mother had enjoyed having one when she was young and living with her parents in Davenport, Iowa. She was the member of the family that induced us to get little "Dickie." He was not a good singer but I am sure Mother enjoyed his hopping about and chirping in his little brass cage. This was before TV and radio provided entertainment for housewives while confined with household duties. It was my responsibility to attend to Dickie; to clean his cage and to see that his food and water dishes were kept filled. Dickie was with us for several years but I do not recall just what happened to the little fellow.

Saw-whet owl on bur oak

Chapter 2: College Years

All through high school, 1917-21, I pondered much over how I could make a living from my interest in nature. I finally concluded in a preliminary way that forestry would be the best field in which to do this. While still debating the best college course for my training, I was lucky to hear the speaker at our high school graduation exercises, Professor Homer Dill, Director of the Natural History Museum at the University of Iowa and professor of a museum training curriculum. His comments on the museum field appealed strongly to me and at his invitation, I visited his institution and immediately decided to register in his courses. Natural history museums aim to educate the public to be concerned about the preservation of the natural environment. This was exactly what I had in mind as my aim in life but I did not want to be a teacher. Museums would allow me to exercise my technical leanings toward creating exhibits that would do the teaching for me. I realized that museums were few and far between and it would be a gamble to find a good paying position in this field. However, I decided to put all my eggs in one basket and train myself in this narrow field. Professor Dill gave a series of courses in museum preparation. He had recognized my rather advanced skill at mounting birds and mammals and I was much pleased when he suggested I delay my actual class work toward graduation by a year while I acted as his assistant in training his students in

taxidermy. This also gave me a year's income to help pay for my additional years of college training. I took up my sophomore courses the following year.

Bill Coultas was another of Professor Dill's students who often went afield with me to collect specimens both for the museum and for our own practice in taxidermy. Bill had a somewhat abnormal gait in his walking that puzzled me at first until he explained why. He was in the Navy during WWI and was assigned to the crew of a destroyer whose duty was hunting down submarines that were taking their toll of our troop ships crossing to the European war zones. Bill had his shift at spotting submarines from the "crow's nest" one stormy day when the pitching destroyer tossed him bodily out of his lofty perch and instead of dumping him into the dangerously rough sea with minor chances of rescue, he landed on the deck, I hesitate to say 'fortunately' since he broke both legs in the fall. They eventually healed but not quite aligned properly – thus his unnatural gait. He was still perfectly mobile, of course, and capable of paddling a canoe and shooting a shotgun.

IOWA RIVER ACCIDENT

During that year without classes I undertook some local field work that included an early spring - ice still on the river - canoe trip with

Bill on the Iowa River. We hoped to get some fine plumaged ducks for the museum collections.

"Glub! Glub! Grab that paddle and hang on!"

Bill and I came up from the chilling depths of the icy river sputtering and wheezing and wondering just what had happened. The paddle got away, but both of us on one side of the overturned canoe soon had it rolling. I splashed around the stern to the other side and steadied it upside-down with just a bubble of air buoying it up. Clinging to the keel strip we both wore silly grins in spite of our perilous situation. Neither river bank looked close enough for us to venture swimming since we had grave doubts about our ability to keep afloat at all away from our canoe in our heavy Mackinaw coats and hip boots full of water.

With huge ice cakes still lining the shore, we would have to make it in a very short time or we never would. "With that bend ahead I'm sure we'll drift near enough to shore to make it," was my optimistic prediction. Of course that did happen, or we wouldn't be here telling about this chilling experience of some enthusiastic but highly inexperienced young naturalists. All this took place many years ago, when one learned canoeing by experience, not by planned safety courses that were shepherded by competent Red Cross approved instructors.

But back to the overturned canoe. Bill and I, as students in museum training, had been given permits to take some specimens of ducks in spring in their bright breeding plumages for the museum collections at the University of Iowa. We had launched our canoe several miles up the Iowa River just after the spring breakup of the ice to collect a few such specimens. Just as we rounded a bend in the river, a small flock of blue-winged teal towered up from near shore. I, in the bow of the canoe was delegated to do the shooting, but Bill, momentarily forgetting his assignment of steadying the tiny tipsy craft, let fly with his 12-gauge shotgun just as I shot. The dual recoil, just as might

have been predicted, flipped the canoe so fast we hardly knew what was happening. Fortunately the one other canoe taking the trip that day was behind us, and their paddlers put on full steam when they saw our predicament. As our canoe rounded the next bend it drifted near enough to shore that we took a chance and found that even with our heavy winter clothes we could swim. We made shore all right and scrambled up the muddy bank where we ran along, keeping our canoe in sight until our friends could retrieve it and the paddles. Enroute the water began draining out of my clothes, and my body began warming up a tiny bit. Then I encountered a narrow ditch draining into the river. Already saturated I decided to simply wade across the ditch, but to my chilling surprise, it was unexpectedly several feet deep, and I plunged in again up to my neck. I had to drain out my clothes and warm up all over again. We soon built a fire with the dry matches our rescuers provided, and, stripping off our soggy clothes we toasted by the fire as best we could while at least our underwear partially dried out. Besides learning a lesson on how not to hunt from a canoe, we lost two shotguns and a camera, but not our binoculars, which were hanging around our necks throughout the entire experience. I remember that my parents never learned about this hazardous escapade until a number of years later.

SAULT STE. MARIE EXPERIENCE

One summer during my college career at the University of Iowa, I spent a month cleaning and cataloging a collection of mounted bird specimens for the high school biology department in Sault Ste. Marie, Michigan. On weekends I regularly visited an island in Saint Mary's River, which connected Lake Superior and Lake Huron, with two very enthusiastic birders, a dentist, Dr. Karl Christofferson, and a banker who was an ardent birdbander, M. J. Magee. The enormous canal with locks carrying huge freighters between the lakes was of great interest.

Professor Homer Dill preparing a moose for a habitat group at the University of Iowa (1925)

Bill Coultas & Breck worked together as museum students at the University of Iowa (1925)

Breck often went birding with M. J. Magee & Karl Christofferson at Sault Ste. Marie (1924)

Of even greater interest to us was the long sandbar built up by dredging operations to keep the canal navigable for the big ships. Along this sandbar we located numerous pairs of spotted sandpipers that found ideal nesting and feeding habitat there. The birds were just hatching their young during my visit and as with all the shorebirds, the newly hatched young were already actively running about feeding. At our approach they hid very effectively in the coarse vegetation and moved about only when the parent birds gave the all clear signal for them to reappear and go about feeding. We soon found that if we approached and sat down quietly for some minutes the mother bird would eventually give the all clear signal and the young would soon reappear nearby. Once we spotted them we could easily catch the still downy youngsters. Even at that early age the young had well-developed legs that would carry bands placed loosely enough as not to become too tight when they matured. Thus Dr. Christofferson and I spent a good many evenings banding. By the end of my stay we had successfully banded 77 young sandpipers, a record no doubt unsurpassed by any other banders in the country.

On weekends we often went birding on Saint Mary's Island. Once while we were eating lunch, Magee called my attention to a bird singing nearby and asked if I knew what it was. I did not and on investigating I found it was an adult male winter wren. I was amazed, and I still am, at such a tiny bird being able to produce such a long uninterrupted passage of really brilliant musical notes. On this same hike we spent considerable time searching in vain for the nest of a rare yellow-bellied flycatcher we had spotted while not realizing that it nested on the ground.

Mr. Magee had made the acquaintance of the captain of one of the ore boats carrying iron ore from Duluth to Cleveland, Ohio. On stopping one day to pass through the locks, the captain called Magee telling him that an owl had alighted on his ship while well out in Lake Superior and he was sure Magee would like to band it. Wondering what species it

might be, Magee hurried down to the locks for the bird, which proved to be a beautiful saw-whet owl. He banded it and, thinking that I might like to see the bird before he released it, he called me. I had never seen the species so I was glad to photograph the bird and the chapter heading sketch is the result.

COLLEGE ATHLETICS

After registering at the University of Iowa in the fall of 1921, I worked hard at my studies and in the first semester I got excellent grades. I did not want to become known as a "book worm" so in the spring of my freshman year I tried out with the track squad and won my freshman numeral in the broad jump and 100 yard dash. In my sophomore year I recall competing in a dual meet with Minnesota where I made my best long jump of a small fraction of an inch short of 21 feet –a fair jump, but not a big point winner.

During my second year at Iowa U I did not register for courses but acted as Prof. Dill's assistant. During the winter of that year I attended a gymnastic meet and was much impressed with how much fun it would be to be able to compete in that sport even though I had no gymnastic training in high school. So during my sophomore year along with my track work, I began working out with the gym squad. There were no intercollegiate gymnastic meets scheduled during the first semester of that year, so by hard work during my first semester I gained a spot on the gym team and actually competed in the second gymnastic meet I had ever seen. It was great fun learning new stunts on the various apparatus but I specialized in tumbling (now called floor exercise) and the high or horizontal bar. I remember lying awake at nights thinking about how I could control my movements in going from one position to another and deciding which could be combined best for a smooth continuous performance. I did this especially for the high bar, thinking a series through to get the right approach to the exciting flyaway somersault dismount for a well-positioned landing. On some of the more hazardous stunts we put a strong belt around our waists with ropes attached on the sides for the coaches to rescue us if we appeared to be landing on our heads rather than on our feet.

The Iowa gym squad had only three intercollegiate meets in my junior year (1924-25) and, as I recall, I won first in at least two of them in my event of tumbling. Then in the Big Ten Conference meet, I tied with a Minnesota gymnast for first place but won the first place medal on the toss of a coin. Actually some observers told me that I tied with the Minnesota gymnast who did a rather remarkable feat of strength, the exact nature of which I do not recall, but that my form and continuity were what won me the event. No doubt it was due to this that I was elected captain of the gymnastic team for my senior year. I must admit I was quite proud of a statement that appeared in the University yearbook, the 1927 Hawkeye. In commenting on the gymnastic activities it stated that the team was "Captained by Walter Breckenridge, unquestionably the best tumbler in the Big Ten Conference."

My muscular thighs must have been responsible for my ability to perform especially high, continuous series of handsprings and somersaults ending in a twister somersault. I recall that while warming up for competition in a dual meet with Illinois at Urbana, I succeeded in executing a series of four or five successive somersaults without touching my hands to the mat. I don't know just why I never attempted this in competition. In fact I now feel confident that I could have performed a double somersault, had my coaches suggested that I try it. To my knowledge, no one in the Conference at that time had ever executed this difficult maneuver.

I was also quite proud of the following paragraph that appeared in the University annual, The 1927 Hawkeye, in the report on the Gym Team's activities:

"Scholarship has always been emulated in Iowa athletics but for once it spelled disaster. With the reformed system of honor grading instituted just as the season was underway Breckenridge found himself graduated and was consequently unable to compete with his team. Coaches and men were disconsolate. They whispered the seemingly irreparable loss to one another as they chalked their hands for another try at a particularly stubborn exercise and wondered what could be done."

Actually what happened was that during the first semester of my senior year, the University Administration passed a ruling that awarded additional credits toward graduation for A and B grades. My scholastic record had already gained me election to Phi Beta Kappa, the honorary scholastic fraternity in my junior year, an honor usually attained only in one's senior year. If I accepted these credits and graduated early, I would not be able to compete in gymnastics. However, at the end of the first semester I had already accepted the appointment as preparator at the Museum of Natural History at the

Breck as gymnastics team captain at University of Iowa (1926)

University of Minnesota. This was a very choice position I had been overjoyed to receive at a time when such positions were very much at a premium. If I graduated in January 1926, I could then devote my full time throughout the second semester to perfecting several techniques in museum preparation under Professor Dill that I felt I needed to assure my success in my new job. Even though I regretted missing the excitement and possible honor of further athletic participation, I looked ahead and chose to graduate early.

WARTIME ACTIVITIES

As far as military experience goes, I never was in any active military unit. I was lucky in that I fitted in between both World Wars. I was 16 years old when the First World War ended and I was 41 and married with two small children when the U.S. entered the Second World War.

The uproarious celebrations of the signing of the November 11, 1918 Armistice, however, nearly landed Bill Gordon and me in trouble. The welcome news of its signing must have reached us in Brooklyn, Iowa during the night since I recall hearing bells and whistles disturbing our sleep on that memorable morning as people got up early to celebrate. Bill and I decided to add our bit to the noisy acclaim. If we could get into the Presbyterian Church we could ring the bell. We found it accessible and Bill began pulling the rope that began ringing the huge bell in the tower. I'm still not sure just why I decided to climb the tower since it was already ringing, but I did, and I noticed the tolling lever used when slow ringing suited certain occasions. So I gave the bell a pull and it swung into action just as it reached a peak of its ringing. The lever caught it as it swung back and unexpectedly lifted it completely off its supports. Fortunately it did not go crashing down through the supports of the tower but it simply settled quietly down on the platform on which its supports rested and, of course, it stopped ringing. Bill and I lost no time scurrying out to disappear among the village noise makers hoping that no one saw

us leaving the church. Apparently no one did and for some time afterwards the church fathers questioned as to who was guilty of disabling the church bell. It was years afterward before Bill and I revealed our role in the mishap.

A few years later, when I enrolled in the University of Iowa, I had a couple of years of required military training but I chose not to enlist in advanced officer training (ROTC). When the U.S. entered World War II, I felt I should contribute to the war effort beyond selling Liberty Bonds so I joined my neighbor, George Lange, in enlisting in the State Guard. We devoted two evenings a week to that training as well as 2 weeks of summer training at Camp Ripley. In this service I enlisted as a buck private, of course, but I advanced rather rapidly through corporal, sergeant, second lieutenant and first lieutenant and was offered company commander rank just as the World War ended. Feeling that the National Guard would soon become reestablished in our area I resigned from further service in the State Guard.

I had no trouble as to just what to do during my summer vacations when studying at the U. of Iowa since Dad owned and managed a small hardware business in my hometown of Brooklyn, Iowa. I joined his staff for a considerable variety of jobs that brought me some funds for my college expenses and I learned a good deal about the work I did. Usually I worked under experienced technicians. For instance, Dad had a skilled tinsmith who did a variety of metal work such as soldering leaky pails or other utensils and making sheet metal ducts for house heating. I learned some of his skills while working under him. Another of his workers was an experienced plumber and from him I learned to cut and thread metal pipes. A harness maker ran a shop as part of Dad's business and I always liked the unusual odor of leather and wax that permeated the atmosphere of his shop. From him I learned to make "waxed ends" as he called them. These were long strands of strong linen thread heavily coated with a special type of black wax with a large needle attached to each end. I usually found him straddling a tall stool-like chair, as it might be called, with a pair of huge wooden jaws built in at the end that opened, closed and locked by a foot pedal. These held the pair of leather straps to be sewed tightly together for him to pierce with a strong metal awl. The two needles were then pushed through the hole each in an opposite direction. These were then tightened and the process repeated in the next awl hole producing a strong double-stitched binding of the leather parts together, sufficient to withstand the strains that huge draft horses put on their harness while working in the field.

Rough-legged Hawk

Chapter 3: Museum Work

EARLY HISTORY OF THE BELL MUSEUM

In 1989 I was asked to reminisce briefly on the early history of the Bell Museum. When I realized that I first joined the staff of the museum in June of 1926, sixty-three years before, I presumed that some of my experiences might be regarded as early history. However, I prefaced my remarks with a few facts on the really early history, which began a little over a century ago.

The Museum actually began when the Minnesota Legislature established a Geological and Natural History Survey for the state in 1872 with N.H. Winchell, a geologist, as its director. Little happened for a few years, but in 1890, Henry Nachtrieb was placed in charge of the zoological section of the Survey, which included the Zoological Museum. Limited collections of natural history materials were first assembled in the main university building (now called Eddy Hall). These were later moved to Pillsbury Hall where the collections remained and grew until 1915 when they were moved again into the newly completed Zoology Building on Washington Avenue.

In that same year, 1915, Dr. Thomas S. Roberts, then a practicing physician, was appointed by the Board of Regents as Associate Curator of the Zoological Museum and Professor of Ornithology in the Animal Biology faculty. During his first year he was situated in one of the medical school buildings. The following year his office and collections were moved into the new Zoology Building. The first of the large habitat exhibits, the Woodland Caribou, was also moved at that time from Pillsbury Hall where it had been constructed back in 1911 by Jenness Richardson who had joined the staff as preparator. He then began work in the Zoology Building on the Deer, Beaver, and Dall's Mountain Sheep groups, which were completed in 1917.

Dr. Roberts reported in 1919 that the Museum received its first financial support from the University budget. Up to that time all activities of the Museum had been supported by private gifts. His report stated that the budget contained $2000 for Museum support in addition to the meager salaries of the staff. In 1919 William Kilgore, who had been an active volunteer, was appointed as Curator of the Museum. He was a tall, handsome, very capable, largely self taught bird student whose time was devoted to conducting Museum tours and the care and cataloging of the scientific bird collection that had even then grown to several thousand specimens.

The year 1921 saw the initiation of the Sunday public lecture series. These were held in the third floor lecture hall holding only about 100 persons. For a few seasons when attendance began to increase the lectures

Dr. Roberts & Will Kilgore explain the beaver group at the Museum

were given in the Music Building Auditorium. During the subsequent years, with the completion of numerous exhibits, the number of school groups requesting tours increased substantially and student assistants supplied additional help. Among these were several who have gone on to make their marks in biological fields. Dr. Gustav Swanson and Dr. Charles Evans were among them.

My Minnesota contacts began early in my senior year at the U. of Iowa when Professor Dill told me that he had been in touch with Dr. Thomas Roberts of the Minnesota Museum of Natural History about a preparator position. Records at the museum do not mention that although his preparator, Jenness Richardson, was an excellent craftsman, he was very secretive about his skills, not even allowing Dr. Roberts in his laboratory when certain operations were in progress. This irked Dr. Roberts greatly and he finally dismissed him early in 1926. He had heard that the University of Iowa had a course in Museum Preparation and asked if Prof. Dill had a graduating student who he would recommend for the position. Evidently Prof. Dill had sufficient confidence in me to suggest me for the position.

Being much interested, I of course went to Minneapolis for an interview with Dr. Roberts and to look over the Museum. At first I

was a bit awed by the size and quality of the exhibits but I had youthful confidence in my ability to handle the assignment of completing one of the big 10 by 20-foot panoramic displays and I was quick to accept the offer of the job. In this I attained one of my life's ambitions to get a position in an area like Minnesota where a great deal of undisturbed natural territory still had escaped the developers.

I found Dr. Roberts to be a very friendly and approachable person and I'm sure he was favorably impressed by the fact that my principal biological interest was in ornithology. He was in the midst of writing about Minnesota birds and planned to publish a book by that title. So we "hit it off" perfectly and there was no doubt but that I was to be his new preparator. I remained with Prof. Dill for the remainder of the second semester of my senior year for some additional training. After graduation I bought a second hand Model T Ford car; drove to Sioux City Iowa to attend my brother Harold's wedding; then went on to Minneapolis to what proved to be the beginning of my 43 years of service to the Minnesota Museum of Natural History.

During these years my admiration for Dr. Roberts continued to increase and I went to him for all kinds of advice. In fact I soon came to consider him as my second father. When the time came for the annual meeting of the American Ornithologists Union in Salem, Massachusetts he asked me to drive his car for him and to attend the sessions of the meeting. Later we attended several AOU meetings together. At these meetings I met a number of the outstanding ornithologists of the country as well as getting acquainted with the young Roger Tory Peterson. I also met Walter Weber, then on the staff of the Field Museum, who later painted a number of the illustrations for the Birds of Minnesota.

Dr. Roberts had graduated from the University of Pennsylvania in the 1870s and had become the family physician of several wealthy Minneapolis families. During his active practice he remained interested in birds and when retired from his active medical practice in 1916, he stayed on as consulting physician to these families while he took up teaching ornithology at the University of Minnesota. One of his clients was James Ford Bell who was then Chairman of the Board of General Mills. Mr. Bell was a staunch supporter of Dr. Roberts and helped him financially in his efforts to establish a museum at the University of Minnesota. Together they supported the building of several large habitat exhibits in the biology building including the Caribou, White-tailed Deer, Beaver, Black Bear and Heron Lake Bird groups.

Dr. Roberts was, of course, an enthusiastic supporter of natural history education and concern for environmental preservation. In addition to his teaching ornithology, he and his friend and assistant, William Kilgore, gave programs for school children including tours of the museum displays.

I stayed at Dr. Robert's home temporarily until I found suitable housing near the U. campus. I was frequently invited to dinner with him and for a game of cribbage. Then at my hurry-up marriage (see Chapter 6) he acted as my best man. After Dorothy and I got settled in our new home we had him to dinner on numerous occasions as well as being entertained at his home frequently. At meals I always remember he had a foot pedal he pressed to summon the housekeep-

er for food service. His first wife was quite stern and formal and asked me not to park my "fliver" in front of the house on Pleasant Street but by the garage in the back alley. This Mrs. Roberts died soon after I arrived in Minneapolis and after several years Dr. Roberts married a petite 70 year old sweetheart of his early years who was very friendly and considerate of my welfare.

I recall Dr. Roberts telling about the following experience. When Dr. Roberts and his friend, Dr. Dart, were collecting birds in the Red River Valley, they stopped to ask some directions from a farmer and found that his wife was very ill with what they diagnosed as a severe case of appendicitis. They immediately placed her on the kitchen table and performed a successful appendectomy with the tools they were using to prepare bird specimens.

Among my first assignments was making field observations and collecting birds from areas in Minnesota that Dr. Roberts had not investigated. By 1926, Dr. Roberts was well along with his book Birds of Minnesota. In this effort he had the efficient help of Miss Mabel Densmore whose significant contributions to this work I am glad to point out.

In addition to his writing skills, Dr. Roberts was a pioneer in the use of motion pictures in generating greater interest in birds. In fact, in 1918 he delivered the first motion picture illustrated paper ever shown at an American Ornithological Union's annual meeting. Soon after my arrival at the Museum I found myself helping Dr. Roberts with movie work with his ancient 35mm Erneman camera, which was a really primitive photographic instrument. The exposures depended on the rate of the hand cranking, no exposure meters were available and slow black and white film was used. After those first stumbling efforts, I continued to combine movie work and field collecting, the results being extensively used in our Sunday Programs. These were very successful with the 600-seat auditorium in the new building often being filled twice with some occasionally waiting for a third showing.

After taking over the motion picture work from Dr. Roberts, I made many field trips around the state and elsewhere collecting specimens for the Museum and materials for the construction of groups, as well as taking movies of any wildlife actions that might be appropriate for our Sunday afternoon programs and for use with other groups visiting the Museum. Some of these trips were highly successful while on the other hand, I often encountered conditions far from favorable for photography. The following is a quote from a letter I wrote to the family dated Wednesday July 12, 1950 from Delta, Manitoba where I was working with Al Hochbaum, Peter Ward and the staff at James Ford Bell's Waterfowl Research Center on Lake Manitoba:

"Here I am toasting my toes by the fireplace with a 40 mile wind driving the rain over the marshes in a day as far from a photographing day as I have yet seen. Early this morning I got up about 5:30 and drove through the mud a couple of miles to where I had put up my blind on Monday evening. I found the cattle had pushed it over and the wind had finished the job of completely wrecking it beyond recognition. I untangled it and brought it into the workshop where I straightened the tubes and repaired the broken ones until it is again in usable condition. So you see things are not going so well."

Conditions did improve and I ended up getting some very nice shots of blue-winged teal and baldpates to justify my stay at the Research Center.

MUSEUM PERSONNEL

Dr. Roberts continued as Director of the Museum past the usual retirement age by special action of the Board of Regents and remained active until shortly before his death in 1946 at the age of 86. I was then appointed to the Directorship of the Museum. With the resulting changes in my work I relinquished most of my preparation duties to John Jarosz who joined the staff soon after his return from duty in World War II.

John was a barber before the War with a hobby of taxidermy. Soon after being drafted for the War he found himself stationed for a long period in England. During his free time he collected and mounted several specimens of ducks, which he sent back home to his mother. The Customs Officer in St. Paul reported to her that it was illegal to import such specimens and they would have to be destroyed or given to an educational institution. She, of course, chose the latter and called the Bell Museum. I went to St. Paul to examine the specimens and found them to be some of the best mounted birds I had ever seen. Soon after John was discharged from the armed services I went to visit him and found more excellent mounts in his attic so we immediately interrupted his barbering career and added him to our staff. He proved to be a superb taxidermist and museum technician and contributed extensively to the building of the remaining habitat displays in this building.

The field of mammalogy in the Museum's program was strengthened with the appointment of Harvey Gunderson as Curator of Mammals in the early 1940s. After a service break in World War II, he continued building up the mammal collection, taught a course in mammalogy, and published a much-used book on the Mammals of Minnesota. Harvey died February 23, 1999.

Dr. Roberts, in his later years, gave up the teaching of ornithology, and Dr. Dwain Warner, a Cornell graduate, took over as instructor of Ornithology. He was a very capable and enthusiastic person who was instrumental in establishing the important Radio-tracking Project at the Cedar Creek Research Center and carried on extensive studies of bird behavior and migration in Mexico.

In the mid-60's Richard Barthelemy joined the Museum Staff as Public Education Supervisor. A very imaginative person with great energy and initiative, Dick made a definite contribution to the Museum's education efforts in the "Touch and See Room" where children handle the exhibit materials. The enthusiastic use made of these displays has been well worthwhile even though they require occasional replacement of specimens.

HABITAT GROUPS

The new Museum building was completed in 1940 with extensive financial backing of Mr. James Ford Bell. The Minnesota Museum was later renamed the Bell Museum in honor of him and the Bell Family.

One of my challenging assignments was moving the six major displays that had been previously constructed in the Zoology Building into their new settings in the new Museum: Caribou, Deer, Beaver, Bear, Dall's Sheep and Heron Lake. Actually these groups had been built in sections in anticipation of possible moving. Even so, the sections were so large that twisting and turning them down the stairs was a real acrobatic process. The elevators were too small to accommodate them. A real problem came when we realized that the backgrounds were painted on canvas and cemented onto the curved background walls. To avoid tearing them we started at one end with a heavy pole the length of the width of the painting and rolled them like rolling a rug. This required digging, prying and tearing them from the wall, often tearing considerable masses of plaster sticking to the rolled painting. Preparing to cement them onto their new background required many hours of scraping. Several were too short and wide strips of white canvas were needed to complete the tops of the paintings.

In moving the large groups we employed Mr. Edward Brewer, a local artist who had an uncanny ability to copy the tones in the original paintings. He did a remarkable job of completing the sky areas of the paintings where the new cases required wider sky areas. In the Heron Lake group some of the original sky was damaged beyond repair and on these areas the very famous wildlife artist, Louis Agassiz Fuertes, had painted some flying birds. These Brewer copied very successfully on the new canvas sky.

Once these groups were moved, our major effort was to complete the ten, large habitat displays needed to occupy the allotted spaces in the new building. As the prepara-

tor I spent most of my time for some years in this group building effort. Following is a list of these exhibits:

1) Pipestone Prairie (completed)
2) Lake Pepin Birds
3) Timber Wolves
4) Moose
5) Hardwood Forest
6) Cascade River
7) Sandhill Cranes
8) Elk or Wapiti
9) Migrating Geese
10) Tundra Swans.

Credit should be given to the artists who painted the original backgrounds of all of the large habitat exhibits. Mr. Harry Rubens, a local landscape artist, did the Heron Lake background. Mr. Bruce Corwin, a widely known artist who had done numerous similar large background paintings at other institutions, did the Deer, Black Bear, Beaver and Caribou backgrounds. All ten of the most recently completed ones were the work of Francis Lee Jaques, a permanent member of the staff of the American Museum of Natural History whom we borrowed whenever one of our groups was ready for background painting. Jaques not only painted the large backgrounds but also aided materially in

Francis Lee Jaques planned and painted many of the museum groups

Preliminary sketch of the timber wolf group

Model of the timber wolf group

Breck with mounted timber wolf

Completed timber wolf group

their planning and should be credited with the major design of most of these recent groups.

The work in the foregrounds of all ten of these recent groups was shared between John Jarosz, our very capable preparator and myself. Ruth Self, Dorothy Mierow, and Helen Chapman did much of the actual preparation of the wax plant reproductions in several of the major exhibits, especially the Hardwood Forest Display. A number of students were also employed temporarily to do a good deal of the actual work of casting and assembling the plants in the exhibits.

The Pipestone Prairie Bird group had been partially constructed when I arrived in 1926 and one of my first undertakings was to complete that exhibit. This work consisted mainly of reproducing the plants, most of which were made of a mixture of beeswax, carnuba wax and paraffin. They were cast in plaster of Paris molds made from the natural leaves with stems of copper wire tapered in nitric acid. I mounted most of the birds but I did have a challenging job of relaxing a poorly mounted whooping crane and re-mounting it in a much more lifelike attitude. Also in creating the prairie grass I made a double-edged, foot-powered cutter that cut blades from a specially made green cel-luloid. About 100,000 blades were cut and embedded in papier-mâché along with dried natural grass blades to obtain the effect of a natural prairie.

In later exhibits of the moose, elk or wapiti and wolves, such large mammals were far from being just "stuffed." First, of course, I skinned the freshly killed animals and roughed out the skulls and leg bones. These bones were then preserved and dried, ready for arranging in the lifelike pose for the exhibit. A small miniature model of the fin-ished group had been previously construct-ed and the bones were then supported with metal rods in the positions copied carefully from the model. The musculature was then molded over the skeleton with paper mâché following the measurements of the skinned carcass. The skin, which had been tanned

without disturbing the hair, was preserved and cemented onto the statue of the animal. Appropriate glass eyes were then set and the mounted specimen was ready for the fin-ished exhibit.

Soon after moving to the new Museum we planned to have a moose group occupy one of the large cases at the end of the dis-play corridors. This was first sketched out roughly as to its contents to be collected in the field. First among the required materials was, of course, a moose. We wanted a Min-nesota moose, which required getting a per-mit for its taking. This we had no problem in getting. The best habitat for moose we found to be the extensive black spruce bogs north of the Red Lakes along the Canadian border. Norris Camp was the Department of Natural Resources' headquarters for that area, so we arranged to center our search at that Camp. Several Museum staff members including Harvey Gunderson, our Curator of Mammals, and I, along with Pat Patterson of the DNR set up our center of activities there.

On our hunt a few days later, I recalled see-ing a possible moose for our use, but after examining it with my binoculars, I decided that its antlers were a bit too small, and I passed it up. The next day Pat Patterson shot what I believe was the same animal. It had an antler spread of only 44 inches. Since we had a permit for only one animal, we de-cided to accept it for the exhibit. It had fallen in the water in a swamp some distance from Norris Camp, not a very convenient place in which to work. Consequently, we got a cou-ple of logs and nailed cross boards on them to form a sled-like structure onto which we rolled the huge animal. Then with a tractor we dragged it up to the Camp for the prepa-ration work. First I photographed numer-ous angles of the carcass and made plaster negative molds of the eye and nose before I started to skin the body. After this was completed we removed the legs and head and roughly cut off the flesh for transporta-tion to the Museum. I carefully weighed each part and, after adding the weight of blood a veterinarian estimated it had lost, the weight of the live animal totaled 1069 pounds, just a bit over half a ton.

In the Moose group the animal was so tall that it presented a special problem since the glass was only six feet high. The setting for this group was the soft muddy margin of the lake shore, so I actually cut off three of the feet and a portion of the legs and sank them deep into the mud with one leg lifted to show the character of the foot with its split hoof. The water surface in this group is made of several plastic sheets joined under floating branches and water lily leaves. You may not have noticed small fishes swimming in the water.

As I recall, one of the wolves in the exhibit weighed 107 pounds, which was exceptional for a Minnesota wolf. For the construction of the Wolf group, Warren Nord and I went up on the north shore of Lake Superior and made large rubber negative molds of the rock surfaces. These were reinforced with plaster of Paris to hold the flexible rubber molds in place. These were brought back to the Museum where plaster casts were made from the molds and colored to match the natural rock surfaces. Several casts were made from each mold, and when they were fitted onto the frames at different angles, it was not obvious that they were identical. The gnarled white cedar tree had its twigs clipped off and marked with laundry tags. These were preserved, dried and colored and replaced on the identical branches from which they came.

Turning to the Lake Pepin Bird Group, the materials forming the beach line were collected at Sand Point near Frontenac and replaced in the water-deposited strips as they lay on the beach, which had been photographed for positioning. The lighting of this group presented a special problem. The group was lighted by a bank of lights distributed all along the top of the case so no shadows were cast by the birds and larger objects. To correct this to resemble sunlight, I scattered dark colored sand under each object to resemble natural shadows.

In the Goose and Swan group, Lee Jaques suggested using chromium plated copper sheets laid loose on the base. This allowed for warping and twisting, giving a realistic appearance of a slightly disturbed water surface. The reflections adjacent to the painted background presented the problem of two different reflections, the painted objects being incorrectly reflected in the shiny chromium surface. He corrected this by painting the water where the foreground and background joined an opaque, non-reflecting color, thus eliminating the incorrect reflections.

When building the new museum we decided to limit the subjects treated in the 16 large habitat groups to the Minnesota scene. This is composed of the three ecological environments, namely the southeast hardwoods, the northeast conifers and the western prairies. This rendered the Newfoundland Caribou

Bruce Heyward, John Jarosz, Ruth Self, Breck and Dorothy Mierow discuss the Hardwood Forest group

and the Alaska Dall's mountain sheep inappropriately out of place. The plan called for the eventual replacement of the Dall's Sheep with a Bison Group, which still has not been done. In the case of the Caribou, the decision was made to reconstruct the new foreground to represent the northern Minnesota black spruce and sphagnum moss area surrounding the Red Lakes while the background already in place depicted well the northern Minnesota habitat. The Newfoundland caribou is considered to be simply a regional subspecies of the woodland caribou and could be considered as representing our Minnesota animals.

Both the Heron Lake and the Pipestone Prairie Groups show bird species correctly found in these habitats but are much more crowded together than would be found in nature. All the bird groups built later in the new museum present only those concentrations normally found together in nature.

I am considering the early history of the Museum as ending with my full-time retirement in 1969. Since a new Director had not been appointed, I was asked to continue on a half time basis for another year, placing my actual retirement as 1970 with the appointment of Dr. Harrison Tordoff as Director.

I feel sure that the Minnesota Museum (now the Bell Museum) of Natural History over the years has worked effectively toward changing public opinion in Minnesota from a pioneer philosophy of "Conquer Nature and Rebuild it to Meet Human Needs" to "Respect For Nature For All of Its Gifts and Live and Let Live All the Wonderful Diversity of Life That Surrounds Us." However, we cannot succeed in bringing about this change of attitude unless we humans can adequately curb our explosive reproductive rate resulting in an over-population that is presently wreaking so much havoc throughout the world.

One of my early duties at the Minnesota Museum was the building of a series of small portable habitat exhibits about two feet square and ten inches in depth with photographic backgrounds. Color prints of that size were not available at that time and I took 5 by 7 inch black and white photographs, which were enlarged to 20 by 24 inches. These I colored with transparent watercolors. For the foregrounds I mounted the birds, mammals, reptiles, amphibians and insects and reproduced the plants in wax. These groups, 150 of them, were circulated through schools during the school years and to the state parks in summer. In recent years their circulation has been discontinued and many of them are on extended loans to various schools and parks.

Several dozen minor habitat displays are housed in the four narrow corridors of the Museum. These have backlighted transparent backgrounds. I photographed these in black and white in the field and colored them with transparent watercolors. The positioning of the lights illuminating these must be carefully adjusted in order to blend the backgrounds with the three-dimensional mounted specimens and wax plants in the foregrounds. Since my retirement these have been poorly attended, thus causing them to become almost complete failures as habitat displays.

STATE PARKS

Soon after World War II, Donald K. Lewis returned from service in the Navy to Red Wing, Minnesota where he had left with a fine record as a biology teacher. He had been known by many for his ability to generate interest in his students as well as in the public in the conservation of Nature. In an interview at the Museum his experience and enthusiasm in this field impressed both Dr. Roberts and me, and he was soon added to the Museum staff as public relations person. His primary duties were conducting tours both visiting school groups and the general public and the training of docents in this work.

About that time I had approached U. W. Hella, then Director of State Parks, about the parks' lack of any naturalist's services for park visitors. Since Mr. Lewis's duties slacked off with schools not in session, I felt that it would be appropriate for me to assign him to duties as Naturalist at Itasca State Park in summers while still a member of the Museum Staff. Mr. Lewis was well pleased with this arrangement and did a good job for several seasons with the State Parks Department, eventually assuming the salary for his services. From this meager start, arrangements were made for other naturalist services in other State Parks. Mr. Lewis and I cooperated in locating and hiring the additional naturalists. Then a further step was made when I, with extensive help from Donald Lewis and Harvey Gunderson Museum mammalogist, established self-guiding nature trails in still other State Parks. From this beginning the nature interpretation services in the State Parks has developed until now (1996) naturalists are serving in 19 parks and self-guiding nature trails are available in 27 parks.

LITTLE SPOTTED SKUNK (D.O.R.)

We often deplore the heavy toll that our highway traffic takes of our wildlife – and rightly so. In September 1939 in central western Minnesota I counted 93 prairie garter snakes killed on an eleven mile stretch of pavement. Just south of the Twin Cities I counted 142 tiger salamanders crushed on a quarter mile of highway; near my home I found leopard frogs being killed at a rate of 12,000 to the mile, and several thousand white-tailed deer are killed annually on Minnesota highways. Although this is a tragic loss to the wonderful diversity of life we are attempting to preserve, it is true that often I have benefited extensively from this loss.

A great deal of the data regarding the natural range of the reptiles and amphibians of Minnesota reported in my book by that title was secured by identifying road kills as I traveled all over the state, often with other missions in mind. In fact herpetologists now recognize widely in their literature the designation DOR as meaning "Dead on Road" Many not severely damaged DOR bird and mammal specimens have been picked up and preserved for the collections of the Bell Museum, including a swallow-tailed kite.

One such DOR specimen, I recall, led me to an especially interesting and embarrass-

ing experience. My family and I had been visiting my parents in Brooklyn, Iowa and were enroute home when I noticed a DOR little spotted skunk. Normally I wouldn't have considered retrieving such an odorous specimen but I needed one for a habitat group at the Museum and had been wondering how and where I would secure such a specimen. And here it was! It was in good condition for mounting and, since it was winter, it would be frozen and somewhat less odoriferous. So I decided to tie it on the rear bumper for the rest of the way home. It seems we needed some slight repairs for the car and had to drive into a garage. There my specimen began to thaw and give off considerable odor, much to the displeasure of the mechanic. However, I retained the carcass all the way home without further resentment on anyone's part.

On arriving at the Museum I immediately put my smelly specimen up on the roof of the Biology Building where it remained frozen over night. The next day I put on rubber gloves and a long lab coat and proceeded to skin the animal and dropped the skin into a container of gasoline hoping that this would at least partially remove the odorous oil. I then removed my gloves and long coat and returned to my laboratory.

My wife, Dorothy, was attending a small party at one of her friend's house and we had planned on my picking her up on my way home after work. This I did and fortunately she met me at the door. To my surprise, she began holding her nose and shoved me back from the door to avoid contaminating the house. A bit later she noticed my glasses were somewhat foggy and on cleaning them they thoroughly contaminated her handkerchief. Obviously my rubber gloves and long coat had failed to protect me adequately. I should have known that odorous oil particles had settled all over me beyond the protected parts. Later at home I bathed, washed my hair, hung all my clothes on the outdoor clothesline and I am not sure whether or not I had to send my suit to the dry cleaners. At least I had learned how thoroughly it is possible to be polluted by a skunk's all-encompassing fumes.

INJURED ROUGH-LEGGED HAWK

At the Bell Museum we often had people bring in bird specimens that had hit windows or were found dead on highways but in good condition. One of these proved to be a beautiful but somewhat emaciated American rough-legged hawk. (line drawing is chapter heading, page 20) The person finding it told of locating the bird perched on a fence post and that it acted surprisingly tame. It soon became obvious that it had a broken wing and could not fly, although it was quite active otherwise. Just why he chose to lambaste it on the head was not explained. This happened before the days of the Raptor Center at the University's Veterinary Department. It was fortunate that it was brought to the Museum since it proved to have had a very unusual injury. The heavy humerus bone of the wing had been badly broken many days before and the bird had survived by catching grasshoppers or a mouse or two. The sharp-pointed tip of the humerus had penetrated the skin for an inch or more. Even though the broken ends had not lined up properly, the osteoblasts (bone buildings cells) had deposited new bone material as to connect the two ends fairly firmly but at an angle that would result in a crooked wing when completely healed. The unusual nature of the development was that the osteoclasts (bone destroying cells) had gone into action just beneath the skin and had cut a deep groove around the projecting point of the humerus. Had the bird survived longer, the groove would have deepened sufficiently to cause the jagged tip of the bone to drop off. While the bird would have been somewhat handicapped in its flight, it probably would have survived since this species of hawk lives primarily on large insects and small mammals. We were greatly disappointed that the bird was not brought in alive since this would have been a wonderful example of how Nature often heals very severe injuries in wildlife.

BOONE & CROCKETT HEADS

Sometime along in the mid-1940's I was approached by a representative of the Boone and Crockett Club about becoming an official measurer of game heads that might meet their standards for inclusion in their record books. This organization for many years had evaluated trophy head of big game so I felt pleased to accept the job from a Twin Cities' sportsman who was about to retire after having held the job for many years. This gave me the opportunity to see, photograph, or sketch some rather remarkable antlers whose owners considered their trophies to be candidates for the Boone and Crockett record books.

Submitted heads were classified as (1) typical or (2) atypical. The second class included antlers that had one or more (often many more) points that were obviously not shaped like any one of the points regarded as typical of the species. During my period as measurer I encountered a number of really massive typical sets of antlers which inspired the painting of a buck on the river bank (Plate 2); Many of these came from animals that had fed on food very rich in calcium while some developed their strange formations after having experienced serious injuries to their antlers while still in the early velvet stage of development.

In addition to the ungulates (hoofed animals), records were also kept simply of the size of the skulls of such species as bears, mountain lions, and jaguars and tusk length for walruses.

REASSEMBLING EGGS

Just a few days ago we were recalling little jingles from our childhood when Dorothy brought up:

Humpty Dumpty sat on a wall
Humpty Dumpty had a great fall
All the king's horses and all the king's men
Couldn't put Humpty together again.

I recalled that I had actually reassembled an egg while making a small museum display. I had located a woodcock nest out in the Fort Snelling area containing four eggs. Not wanting to take the mother woodcock's whole family even for a museum exhibit, I waited a few days for the eggs to hatch. I then took and mounted two of the chicks to show their camouflage pattern. Then I very carefully reassembled two of the hatched eggs to complete the four egg set normally laid by the bird for the museum display.

Spiny softshell

Chapter 4: Graduate Theses

In reviewing work relating to my graduate theses, I encounter some problems regarding the chronology of the work I did in the herpetology field. No such problems occurred with my Master's thesis on the marsh hawk or northern harrier. Nearly all of my work with this bird was done within the period 1930 to 1933, which led up to my promptly receiving the degree in 1934.

Immediately after completing that research I undertook my Ph.D. thesis problems, which continued through seven years until my degree was granted in 1941 and the popularized version of *Reptiles and Amphibians of Minnesota* was published by the University of Minnesota Press in 1944. This did not terminate my research in the field and two of my most important reports appeared after the publication of my book. My work on turtles was reported in 1955. The toad work resulted in four papers (jointly with John Tester) in 1959 and 1960. Here my reviews will appear in order, first my marsh hawk thesis, second the published book, third the toad work, and lastly the turtle report.

MASTER'S THESIS

While getting better acquainted with the natural environment of our new home in the north part of Minneapolis I naturally went on north of the city in search of natural areas. In Blaine Township of Anoka County I found fairly large tracts of partially wooded, slightly swampy, open terrain inviting inspection. During one of my field trips in this area I found myself hopping unsteadily from one grass-covered hummock to another, making my way across a mucky willow-dotted meadow when a "whoosh" over my head made me dodge instinctively to avoid I hardly knew what. Then, coming in just over my head, a big bird mounted rapidly in front of me and I recognized an angry female northern harrier. I changed my course somewhat to get to firmer ground as sharp little daggers scratched my scalp. Of course, the fact was that I had inadvertently stumbled too near the nest of a ground-nesting marsh hawk and naturally it resented the intrusion.

After getting permission to register in the graduate school for a course or two each year, I laid plans for a Master's Degree along with my full time employment. Several seasons' work would probably be required to complete a thesis study so as soon as I was assigned to Dr. Samuel Eddy as my advisor I suggested an extensive study of the northern harrier as an appropriate thesis subject. The value of this hawk was at that time a controversial subject. My suggestion was approved and I immediately set about learning more about this exciting raptor.

The northern harrier was at that time a common inhabitant in Minnesota, and in spring and early summer nearly every day's jaunt along the byways in the prairie parts of the state one would encounter the birds at some interesting stage of their life cycle. Here again we have an exciting member of the avifauna being rapidly pushed aside by Man's takeover of the land to provide for the ever-increasing flood of humanity that is surging over the face of the earth. Thus we also face the elimination of many wild species of plants as well as the animals, typified by the fate of the northern harrier, as our economy, teemed with technology, has replaced Nature's complex environment with what Man has deemed to be improvement in his situation. As a result, humans, at least for the present, are living a far more comfortable life than did their predecessors, but the question is pertinent, "Is comfort the 'summum bonum' of our lives?" An environment composed of many interrelated elements that Nature has evolved through millions of years of adjusting and readjusting to survive in our various habitats is much more interesting than an artificial world made by humans and for humans exclusively. Furthermore, an environment made up of elements is far more flexible and stable than the monocultural complex of inhabitants comprised of only those food plants and animals beneficial to humans.

Early in spring I watched a harrier fly over a meadow, dive down at a steep angle, then zoom up to its original level and make a barrel roll and, for a few wing beats, it actually flew upside down. Then rolling back it dived again. This performance was repeated several times as it circled about the meadow. These strange gyrations were actually the courtship flight of the male harrier. Undoubtedly a female was either flying or perching nearby as the object of this amorous performance.

In nesting the female usually selected a grassy opening in a marshy meadow among clumps of willow bushes and elevated enough to be above the water level of any but unusually prolonged rainstorms. Here the 4 to 6 eggs were laid and the young hatched after an incubation period of about

31 days. Being a ground nester it provided great opportunities for observation with a minimum of effort spent in constructing and placing a blind about 15 feet from the nest. After spending five entire days in such a blind from before sunrise until after sunset I found that during the incubation period and the early life of the young the smaller gray male did most of the hunting for the family. Contrary to what one might expect, he very rarely delivered the prey to the nest but flew over and called to the female announcing that he was "delivering the groceries." On hearing his call the female would fly up from the nest and position herself below and slightly back of the male. He then dropped his prey and she retrieved it in her talons and returned and fed it to the young at the nest. (Plate 3) In watching dozens of these spectacular aerial transfers of prey I very rarely saw her miss. But once I saw and photographed a case where the male dropped two items of prey simultaneously. This confused the female and she missed both but deftly executed a barrel roll, dived and caught one of the bits of prey before it hit the ground.

Since incubation begins with the laying of the first egg, the young hatch on successive days. This results in the young varying as much as six days in age. (Plate 4) As with most hawks, the females are larger than the males. If the oldest of the young happens to be a male and the youngest a female, there is a good possibility that all may survive. If the situation is reversed there is a good chance the youngest, a male, will not survive. This actually happened when the female arrived at the nest one day without food. Seeing the tiny male lying dead in the nest she calmly picked it up and fed it to the remaining young.

Harriers are often seen engaging in aerial play. This is especially frequent when the young are learning to fly. The adults pass prey to them, thus serving both as food and as practice in aerial acrobatics. On several occasions I saw the male picking up clumps of grass and dropping them. Later I realized that these grass clumps were suspected mouse nests from which the bird was hoping to shake out a mouse.

A few ruffed grouse were present and once I found where one had been killed. Many grouse feathers were strewn about and I particularly noted that no easily recognized tail feathers were among them. Later in the day I visited a great horned owl's nest and there were the missing tail feathers identifying beyond doubt the predator responsible for the kill. On examining the pellets cast by this owl near the nest I found an easily identified skull of a screech owl, the only record I had for this species in the area. This big owl is well known to prey on other owls.

I visited this area occasionally in winter when no harriers were present. Once while skiing I ran across the tracks of what I was reasonably sure were those of a prairie chicken in the fairly deep snow. I followed them for some distance and they suddenly came to an end with no wing marks indicating that the bird may have flown, but the disturbance in the snow suggested it must have plunged down into the soft snow. No marks revealing where it might have emerged from its snowy sleeping quarters were evident so I made a wide circle and cut back to about where I thought it might still be resting. As I suspected, it suddenly burst out striking the tip of my ski on its exit.

This report represents only a few interesting details gleaned from my study conducted mainly during 1932 and 1933. The total study resulted in a 122-page thesis carried out in partial fulfillment of the requirements for the Master of Arts Degree, which I received in 1934.

The following conclusions were derived from this study of the food habits of the marsh hawks in a sand plain community in eastern Minnesota.

1. The male marsh hawks, and probably the females to a lesser extent, engaged in aerial performances during courtship, one of the principal features of which was their turning upside down by a sidewise turn, which could hardly be described as a somersault.

2. Nests of these hawks were invariably placed on the ground in short willow brush which grew on low peat meadows. Six eggs composed the normal clutch of the marsh hawk in this region. The males did not aid the females in brooding the eggs.

3. Pairs of marsh hawks nested as close as two hundred yards apart and exhibited little evidence of resisting the presence of other marsh hawks.

4. These hawks showed a strong tendency to nest on successive years in the same clump of brush.

5. The period of incubation of the eggs was from thirty to thirty-two days.

6. The young hawks hatched on consecutive days and in several cases one or two of the youngest failed to survive due to food competition of their nest mates. Female nestlings soon became somewhat larger and heavier than the males. As a result it seems probable that the distribution of the sexes among the young is an important factor in determining whether or not the youngest ones will be able to survive.

7. The young marsh hawks required the protection of the adult female at night for two or three weeks only, after which period the female roosted on the ground away from the immediate vicinity of the nest. The female did not protect the young from the sun after the first two or three days. Even at that early age the young were able to move about and kept in the shade of the brush around the nest. The young hawks kept the nest clean by moving into the surrounding brush in voiding their waste.

8. The female marsh hawk spent nearly all of her time guarding the nest from a nearby perch or feeding the nestlings. The latter duty was performed exclusively by the female. She regularly picked up and carried away the pellets cast by the nestlings and the larger bones remaining from the prey.

9. The marsh hawks began hunting well after dawn and stopped at early dusk. Their average feeding activity at the nest began at about 5:30 a.m. and rose gradually until about 8:00 a.m. It remained high until about 5:00 p.m. when it gradually declined, stopping at about 8:00 p.m.

10. During the greater part of the nest life of the young, the male captured about 80% of the food consumed by the nestlings. The male transferred practically all of the prey he secured to the female in midair who then fed it to the nestlings. On rare occasions the male brought food to the nest but left immediately without apparently noticing the young.

11. Each pair of marsh hawks studied hunted over an area of about one square mile. These hunting ranges overlapped in places at which the birds showed no resentment over each other's presence.

12. The young began to fly at about five to six weeks of age. Their first prey consisted of grasshoppers and beetles while some fruit was taken at that time. The young were sufficiently agile when only seven to eight weeks old to, in midair, catch prey which had been dropped to them by the adults. The young remained in the vicinity of the nest for about three weeks after learning to fly.

13. Thirty-one different forms of food, including mammals, birds, reptiles, amphibians, insects, and plants, were recorded as taken by the marsh hawks. Mammals comprised about three-fourths of the food taken. Striped ground squirrels made up the largest single item in their diet while young cottontail rabbits were almost equally important. Small birds in numbers of individuals ranked high in their diet, but constituted only a very small portion of the bulk.

14. One of the three pairs of marsh hawks studied most closely showed a marked liking for domestic poultry. This same pair also took more young pheasants than did the other two.

15. One family of four young marsh hawks was calculated to have consumed sixty-three pounds of food up to the time of taking wing.

16. Specimens of mammals collected on Section 3, Blaine Twp. Anoka County & donated to the Museum:
Peromyris – 5
Red-backed mice – 6
Microties – 5
Blarina – 1
Sorex – 1

PH. D. THESIS

In choosing my Ph.D. subject I had little trouble in choosing the reptiles and amphibians of Minnesota. Dr. Gustav Swanson had made a small collection of these animals while on the staff of the Bell Museum. This was just getting under way when he accepted a position elsewhere and since then little had been done on the herpetology of the state. Thus the field appeared to be open

Breck PhD Graduation - 1941

for some serious attempts to expand our knowledge of the subject as an appropriate research field for the Bell Museum to undertake. Furthermore I was already traveling widely throughout the state while collecting material for the building of the large habitat exhibits which would give me good opportunities to collect specimens of reptiles and amphibians. (Plate 5A) Heavy traffic on our highways was destroying literally thousands of these animals. Herpetologists already recognized this and were using the designation "DOR" in published reports meaning "dead on road". This source of specimens produced for me a large percentage of the distribution data for my proposed work. I chose to put special attention on the life history of the black banded skink, Eumeces septentrionalis, a small lizard found widely throughout Minnesota and about which little was known.

After receiving my Master's Degree in 1934 I spent much of my spare time on this work and seven years later, in 1941, it resulted in my thesis approval for my Ph. D. degree. After being reedited somewhat for public use, it appeared in 1944 as the volume *Reptiles and Amphibians of Minnesota* published by the University of Minnesota Press. It went through three printings as the popular handbook on this subject for midwestern naturalists.

A condensed summary of the nature and content of this volume can best be presented by sharing the review the book received in the *Chicago Naturalist* written by H. K. Gloyd, a staff member of the Field Museum in Chicago.

Reptiles and Amphibians of Minnesota
by W. J. Breckenridge

"The study of amphibians and reptiles has received less attention in the north central United States than in many other parts of the country and the increasing number of students interested in these vertebrates will welcome Dr. Breckenridge's book. It results from a large amount of field work, a review of the published literature, and a study of

museum specimens including much new material collected by the author and his associates.

The introduction deals briefly with the history of herpetology in Minnesota, tales about reptiles and amphibians, the distribution of these animals in the state, field methods, care of reptiles and amphibians in captivity (by Milton Thompson), the bites by venomous snakes and their treatment, the preservation of specimens, and classification including keys for the identification of amphibians and reptiles in Minnesota. The keys include species from adjacent areas thought likely to be found eventually within the limits of the state. Records of certain species known, or thought to have been erroneously reported from the state and those to be expected but not yet actually recorded are discussed in a hypothetical list.

The body of the work treats the 45 species (5 salamanders, 13 frogs and toads, 3 lizards, 16 snakes and 8 turtles) known from Minnesota in systematic order using the common names and the Latin binomials in the headings even though only one subspecies occurs in the state. For the species in which subspecies are known and named the number of subspecies recognized is given in a separate paragraph and those found in Minnesota are indicated by their scientific trinomials. A map for each species shows individual known records for the state and a smaller map of North America is inserted to indicate the general range although in a scale too small to be thoroughly satisfactory. In the text the species are described with a minimal use of technical terms, the geographic ranges are stated (often quoted from the fifth edition of the Steineger and Barbour check list) and under habits brief general accounts of the natural history of the species are in many cases supplemented by original data from the observations of the author.

The 52 figures in the text are reproduction of photographs and drawing by the author. There is an adequate glossary, a bibliography of 163 titles, and an index.

This book will be useful to anyone interested in herpetology: to the beginner, especially if he resides in the region covered and to the more advanced worker because of the original observations recorded."

LATER HERPETOLOGY WORK

Toads

While working on my book *Reptiles and Amphibians of Minnesota* I became intrigued with what a really remarkable yet puzzling and inconspicuous little animal the toad was. I found that the Manitoba toad (*Bufo hemiophrys*) that inhabited the Red River Valley in northwestern Minnesota had many unsolved problems concerning its distribution and survival in the exposed and seemingly uninviting prairie habitat. Dr. John Tester, an ecologist at the University of Minnesota, agreed that this would make an appropriate subject for study and together we undertook some extensive research into the toad's habits and life history. An area in Mahnoman County proved to be an excellent area in which to undertake this work since it was owned by the Minnesota Department of Natural Resources and was designated as the Wabun Prairie Research area. This would guarantee our having undisturbed access to it over the several years (1957-64) we might wish to continue the research. The subject matter involved in the total series of projects was Population, Growth Rates, Local Movements, Hibernation and the toad's possible involvement in the formation of the Mima Mounds on the prairie.

The annual life cycle of this amphibian was, of course, well known. This involved laying its eggs in spring in temporary ponds, the eggs hatching into tadpoles which live in the water until they metamorphose later in the summer into terrestrial adults. At first we simply considered this toad to be quite common but we knew nothing about their actual populations per unit of prairie until our hibernation studies were completed.

Much data on the rate of growth of individuals was accumulated which indicated that sexual maturity was not reached until the end of their second summer. Thus they would not breed until the spring of their third year. Local movement studies required repeatedly recognizing individual toads. To do this we marked them by two different methods:

(1) Clipping one of the toes on the front feet indicated units (1 to 10), on the left hind foot indicated tens, and on the right hind foot indicated hundreds. Regeneration of the toes occurred but the regrown toes were recognizably different and their identities could be read up to at least 12 months.

(2) Radioactive tagging was done by injecting a tiny bit of radioactive tantalum which looked like a quarter inch piece of the lead in a lead pencil under the skin of the back. Animals so marked could be located with the use of a scintillation counter that could detect an animal up to about 20 feet. 84% of toads so marked had daily movements of less than 100 feet, 4% moved 200 feet or more.

The average summer's movement of the 18 most traveled animals was 565 feet. This suggests what might be considered as a home range. Only two individuals showed any tendency toward homing. Toad #225 was originally taken on the northeast shore of the pond on June 1, 1959 and placed in a control pen 300 feet to the north. After 20 days it disappeared from the control pen and was located 4 days later 1280 feet to the southeast across the pond. It was immediately returned to the control pen from which it again escaped 2 days later. After 7 days it was found 1120 feet to the southeast only 160 feet from its former location.

Toads hibernate by digging in a rotating motion with sharp projections on their hind feet moving the soil aside and allowing it to fall back over the animals as they penetrate more deeply into the ground. In other words they bury themselves without leaving any visible hole.

In choosing a site for hibernation, the toads chose small mounds on the prairie some distance back from the pond in which they breed and lay their eggs in spring. These mounds called "Mima Mounds" after similar mounds in a Mima Indian Reservation in Oregon, are from 10 to 50 feet in diameter, a few are larger. The origin of these is still somewhat in question, although pocket gophers, skunks, badgers red foxes and several species of mice and shrews burrow in them. It appears that toads effect their structure by their burrowing in them for hibernation. A surprising amount of soil is moved in this way. In 1961, a total of 253 adult toads and 3025 immatures burrowed in one mound having an area of about 800 square feet. If the average depth of burrowing was considered to be 3 feet, these toads would have moved a total of 85 cubic feet of soil in this mound in a single year. We believe that this volume of soil displaced annually for hundreds or even thousands of years may be a significant factor in the formation of the Mima type of mound in this area in Minnesota. A graduate student, G.A.Ross, working under Dr. John Tester made a detailed study of these mounds. He is credited with the senior authorship of the article on this subject.

When a toad carrying a bit of radioactive tantalum was found digging in for hibernation, a three inch hole was dug 5 to 6 feet deep with a soil auger at a point 12 inches laterally from the toad and capped with sod. This could be removed in winter to allow a scintillation counter to be dropped down the hole. The highest reading of radiation indicated the position of the animal. By weekly visits throughout the winter, we found that marked toads dug down to a depth of about 20 inches early in October. Then during February and March when the frost line approached the toads, they became active and burrowed deeper to avoid freezing, although some remained slightly within the freezing zone and still emerged in good condition in spring. The one found hibernating at the greatest depth was at 46 inches.

Until this study was made we had not realized that, at the time of their emergence from hibernation, the toads found the frost in the soil melting both from below from the heat in the earth and from above from the atmospheric heat. Thus the animals could not emerge in the spring until the shrinking frost layer was at about 18 inches from the surface.

At the beginning of our studies in 1959, 6 out of 7 marked toads burrowed in the Mima mounds leading us to wonder if most of the toads in the area were using the mounds for hibernation. Following this lead we constructed 18-inch metal fences around two of the mounds, each about 100 feet in circumference. These were placed on April 26, just after the surface soil was free from frost and before the toads had emerged. Another fence was placed on the open prairie nearby. When the toads began to emerge we were really amazed by the results as they came in. Not a single animal appeared in the pen on the open prairie while the astonishing total of 5711 toads emerged from the two pens surrounding the Mima mounds!! Our suspicions as to their choice of hibernating sites were verified and, with these data, our ideas with regard to the populations of toads in the area were actually multiplied several times.

This study resulted in four major scientific reports: three published in the journal Ecology in the United States and one in a similar journal in Finland. See the "Publications" chapter for details on these reports.

Soft-shelled Turtles

Much of the wildlife we have in our mini-wilderness home on the River we get personally acquainted with, such as the deer, squirrels, geese, wood ducks and chipmunks. But one we only see rarely in summer, and, believe it or not, it hides deep in the mud of the river banks for the entire late fall, winter, and early spring. This is the spiny soft-shelled turtle (*Apalone spinifera*) which is really quite abundant here in the Mississippi. (Plate 5B) This being a reptile that I would be including in my book *Reptiles and Amphibians of Minnesota* I felt I should learn more about it, especially since it was so abundant in the river right in front of my home.

While lunching on our little deck over looking the river, we would occasionally see one of these turtles pull itself up onto an exposed rock and simply lie there sunning itself for as much as an hour. They appeared in various sizes from a couple of inches to well over a foot across. A question often asked about these big turtles was "How old would this big one be?" This simple question was not answered in the books I found available so I decided to find the answer myself which turned out to be a really time consuming bit of research.

I tried several types of traps and settled on a barrel-shaped structure made of a number of wire loops covered with cord netting closed at one end with a slit-like opening at the other. Since turtles are largely scavengers, I baited my traps with meat placed in a punctured tin can in the back of the trap. The odor of the meat drifted down stream where the turtles would follow it up and into my traps. With the help of my teenage son, Tom, we set and tended several traps for short periods over seven summers (1948-55) and we succeeded in capturing 170 turtles. Once taken, we dropped them into a large sack and climbed the muddy riverbank to the house where we weighed each specimen and measured the width and length of its shell. We then marked each with a semi-circular notch cut in the rim of the flexible leathery shell with a leather punch. Two or three notches arranged like the hours on the face of a clock enabled us to recognize individually each turtle trapped. These were then released in the river where we hoped to recapture them later. Many of them reappeared in our traps several times. One of them we took seven years after it was originally marked.

With the mass of data secured, we were able to construct graphs indicating the rate of growth of many individuals over varying periods of time and these combined to answer the question "How old are some of these big turtles?" We were a bit surprised to find that these turtles never did grow up to an adult size but continued to grow throughout their lives but at a slower rate as they grow older.

Females grow to be much larger than males. The largest female reached a length of 17 1/2 inches, which proved to be, according to my calculations, a bit over fifty years old. In the case of males, the largest was only 7 3/4 inches in shell length. So few males were recaptured it did not seem feasible to attempt accurate age determinations for them. This study resulted in a five-page article in the herpetological magazine *Copeia* for February 18, 1955.

White Ladyslipper

Chapter 5: Family History

I really puzzled over how to include accounts of the family members when the career of each is deserving of a book in itself. I now think it best to record here only a few episodes of each that we would like to remember about their careers as they relate to our family history.

GRANDPARENTS

I was never fortunate enough to have seen my grandparents on my Dad's side of the family. They had lived just north of Bennington, Vermont, only a stone's throw down the road from the home of Ethan Allen of the historic Green Mountain Boys. One of the first skirmishes of the Revolutionary War took place at their homestead. British sympathizers approached some colonists barricaded in the Breckenridge home. When the British saw the guns of Ethan Allen's Green Mountain Boys pointed out of the windows they decided to retreat without firing a shot. A stone historic marker recognizing this incident stands at the home site. The building itself was burned a number of years ago. Mother had made a large charcoal drawing from a tiny print of the original Breckenridge homestead that hung in our parlor for years. The family visited the homestead while on an eastern trip back in about 1920.

Regarding my Morther's parents, I have recollections as a very small youngster of visiting them in their retirement home in Davenport, Iowa where Mother, Bessie Lang, lived as a young lady. Both of her parents were born and raised in Scotland. On deciding to leave there they were undecided as to whether to go to Australia or the United States. They, of course, chose the latter and on arrival here they finally settled on a farm a few miles north of Davenport, Iowa in about 1850. Mother's father must have been a hard working, efficient farmer since they won awards at the local county fair for having the best kept homestead in the community. Their ten children were all born there with Mother being about the middle one of the children. Two younger sisters died of diphtheria when still youngsters in 1874. At the outbreak of the Civil War her father was called up for army service and I recall Mother telling how happy the family was when he returned from the draft board meeting with the good news that he was rejected due to some defect in his vision.

PARENTS

Father (Robert James Breckenridge)

Dad was born on a farm just outside of Bennington, Vermont on March 31, 1869. There he spent his early years attending elementary and high school. He worked during his

Robert James and Bessie Lang Breckenridge in Brooklyn, Iowa

summer vacations and for a short time after high school at a furniture factory operated by a Mr. White. Soon after graduation he moved west to Davenport, Iowa where he lived with his older sister, Mary Azubah, whom we always called Aunt Matie, and his aunt. There he attended a business college. During this time he must have first met Bessie Lang, my mother, whom he later married.

After graduating from the business college he took passage up the Mississippi on a commercial steamboat to the Twin Cities of Minneapolis and St. Paul and then on north by rail to Duluth. During his brief stay there he worked with a construction company that was building the big aerial bridge across the mouth of the St. Louis River between Duluth and Superior, Wisconsin. Later he went on north to Grand Rapids on the Iron Range for employment with the T.B. Walker Lumber Company. Dad was well trained in bookkeeping and mathematics and was first assigned fieldwork to "Scale Trespass." This entailed following the survey lines of the Walker

Company property and identifying where neighboring lumber companies had cut trees belonging to Walker. He then calculated the number of board feet these trees represented for Walker to bill the trespassers for the stolen lumber.

Dad later spent time as paymaster in several lumber camps where he had numerous rather wild and exciting experiences, some of which he related to us boys, but he never took the time to write about them. After leaving the Walker Lumber Company, he operated a small grocery store in Grand Rapids where he had a good deal of contact with his Ojibwe Indian customers. One old chief named Drumbeater occasionally went on a binge when he would deposit some of his more valuable articles of beadwork with Dad for safekeeping. After evidently his last binge he never returned for his belongings, and Dad kept them as mementos of his Indian experiences. These I eventually inherited and later gave to the Archeology Department at the University. We still have preserved a small notebook Dad kept with a few business calculations, but of greater interest were the 300+ Ojibwe words and phrases with translations we found in the back of this little leather notebook. I often referred to these as a youngster when my neighbor chum, Ralph Dayton, and I played Indian as we often did. Dad must have had some social contact with pretty young Indian maidens since his lexicon contained these phrases:
"Ne-sog-e-ah" – I like you
"Ohgee-me-shin" – Kiss me or give me a kiss
"We-gee-wish-shin-nock" – Will you come with me this evening?

Years later I received a copy of the first issue of the Grand Rapids newspaper printed in about 1895 in which I found Dad's grocery store advertised. He was Chairman of the City Council, a position comparable to Mayor. He was still in his 20s at that time. I have no knowledge of just when or under what circumstances Dad returned to Davenport and married Bessie Lang, my mother, on December 27, 1893. In 1894, however, they moved to Minneapolis where they lived on Harriet Avenue. There he took a job in a grocery store for a year or so to accumulate funds with which to buy the small hardware store in Brooklyn, Iowa. I often wondered how he happened to buy this business so far from either Davenport or Minneapolis until I realized that Mother had several brothers and sisters who had taken up farming in Madison Township near Brooklyn. They no doubt had learned that the store was for sale and passed the word on to Dad and Mother.

Dad would occasionally return from work all tuckered out from the task of unloading a railroad carload of woven fence wire. Those were the days when woven wire fencing and barbed wire were taking the place of the live Osage orange hedges, split rail and wooden board fences, and stone walls for keeping livestock in their proper pastures. Dad's hardware store did a very profitable business in selling woven wire fencing that came in heavy rolls of 200 to 300 pounds each. Two or three men were hired to help Dad with the exhausting task of unloading the coiled fencing from the freight cars. First they went into sturdy dray wagons pulled by teams of draft horses for several blocks to the store, then down a steep alley to the back of the basement where the heavy rolls were stored. This work must have been very heavy, physical exertion for Dad. No wonder he arrived home completely exhausted after such a day's strenuous work.

I recall Dad's mentioning that he used to play ball on the field where the Millers professional baseball team later played. Mother kept busy with her painting and we still have an oil painting of Minnehaha Falls that she made while living in Minneapolis. Dad died of pneumonia following a stroke on April 20, 1943 at the age of 74.

Mother (Betsy Graham Lang)

Mother was born on the Lang family farm in Long Grove, Iowa, north of Davenport on August 12, 1861. I recall her mentioning that her brother, Guy, was sleeping in a bed with a metal frame when lightning stuck the house. It followed the metal of the bedstead, badly injuring Guy and leaving him with somewhat impaired vision throughout life. She had numerous tales to tell about their life on the farm. One that greatly interested me was how they had a huge Saint Bernard dog that they trained to work a treadmill, which turned a churn for making butter. She also told about a neighbor who made molasses that they stored in a large wooden barrel for the winter. When they neared the bottom of the much-used barrel they discovered, much to their amazement, the carcass of a cat. Their comment on the situation was "Well, at least it was our own cat."

Robert Breckenridge with sons Harold, Robert and Walter (1914)

Breck's brother Harold and family - John, wife Ona May (Wilkins), and Jodi

Breck's brother Robert and family – Esther, Eleanor, wife Mildred (McLain), Bruce and Harriet

The Lang family finally retired and moved to Davenport in the 1880s. While visiting them there they took me to a local museum where I recall I was frightened by a big black bear mounted standing high in the lobby. Little did I realize then that in later years I would be mounting animals that large for a museum in Minneapolis.

Mother did not have the exciting life that Dad had. But in addition to her regular rural school education, she had music training and often entertained us with organ music from our foot-pedaled organ. And her art training gave her a life-long hobby. She worked in several media – charcoal, pastels, watercolor and oil. Watching her at her artwork and seeing her art materials constantly at hand no doubt had much influence in steering my interest into the art field. After Dad's death Mother lived at home with help for a time. Then she stayed with us three boys for a

few months each, but she was at my brother Robert's home in Ames for a year or so and later for a period at a nursing home in Minneapolis under my and Dorothy's supervision until her death on July 16, 1947 at the age of 86.

SIBLINGS

Esther

My sister, Esther, was my parent's first child, born in 1895 soon after my parents moved to Brooklyn, Iowa. She was taken ill in 1903 and died of a brain tumor. This was the same year I was born, so naturally I have no recollections of Esther. From photographs, however, I can see that she was a very beautiful little eight-year-old girl and her death must have been a terrible loss for my parents.

Robert

It has always puzzled me that each of us three boys spontaneously developed differing interests that he followed throughout his life. Robert, the older of my two brothers, was always interested in mechanics with *Popular Mechanics* being his favorite magazine. He was usually considered as the family tinkerer whenever anything went wrong such as the kitchen sink pump or the lock on a door. This interest continued through his graduation with a Master's degree from Iowa State College in Ames, Iowa. He then joined Dad in handling the operation of the hardware business in Brooklyn. After ten years in that occupation, he returned to Ames for graduate work and soon was given an Associate Professorship on the faculty. He gained membership in several professional and honorary organizations and continued on the faculty until shortly before his death. Diabetes followed by cancer of the liver brought about his early retirement and his death on December 20, 1966 at the age of 68.

Harold

My second brother, Harold, early showed an interest in animals and in farming. Soon after we moved to the outskirts of Brooklyn, Dad built a large poultry house where Harold raised chickens for both egg production and meat for our table. He also had a small loft of white king pigeons for a time. While still a teenager he worked on our uncles' rural Madison Township farm. His cousin, Allan Lang, had a herd of prize-winning black Angus cattle, which Harold groomed and aided in exhibiting at County and State Fairs in the region. On June 10, 1926 he married Ona May Wilkins, a home economist as well as a member of the state champion basketball team.

After getting his agricultural degree at Ames, he advanced to become a County Agricultural Agent for a number of years before joining the staff of the DeKalb Hybrid Seed Corn Company. There he soon advanced to become one of their regional representatives. This position he occupied until his death on March 31, 1977 of a heart attack at the age of 77.

CHILDREN

Betsy

Betsy, our first child, was born on August 9, 1935, while we were living in Minneapolis at 2957 Pierce Street. At a very early age Betsy showed signs of having a remarkable memory and was very self-reliant. Not long after we moved to our new home on the Mississippi River, the Brackens, we built a small cabin playhouse out of the many logs left from clearing the woods for the house. Betsy often led the neighborhood kids in playing house there. She loved Laura Ingalls Wilder's Little House books and the kids under Betsy's direction would reenact some of the experiences described in the books. As a child she wrote to the author and received personal replies, and later as an adult she presented programs on Laura and her life throughout the state.

She attended the one-room school half a mile from our home, Riverview, through 8th grade, then Anoka High School. Always interested in food preparation and homemaking, she studied home economics and television at the University of Minnesota and Iowa State College in Ames, Iowa, and worked for several years in the Betty Crocker Camera Kitchen at General Mills. Later she freelanced and edited cookbooks for several organizations.

In 1960 she married architect Peter Norum and they adopted a daughter, Jennifer, and a son, Timothy. Jenni married Chris Bates in November 1993, and their sons, Cole and Sam, were our first great-grandsons. They now live in Des Moines, Iowa. Tim married Marci Reid, an elementary school teacher, in May 2000 and they live in Weatherford, Oklahoma.

In the very midst of her so successful career, we were deeply grieved when Betsy was taken from us by cancer on January 19, 1994 at only 58 years of age. Some time ago I noted a strange coincidence. Soon after moving to the Brackens I transplanted a small hard maple tree from a maple-bass-

Dorothy with Tom, Barbara, and Betsy, Mother's Day 1944

wood forest near Lake Minnetonka. This maple seed must have germinated soon after Betsy's birth. Both Betsy and the tree grew to healthy maturity during the following years here at the Brackens. In early 1993 when Betsy was taken seriously ill, I noticed that the maple tree had a few top branches without leaves. Betsy revived for a time but when cancer began sapping her energy seriously more branches of the maple died. And in the spring of 1994 after Betsy's passing the sap did not flow and no leaves appeared on the tree. A species, many of which grow to be 100-year-old monarchs of the forest, but this one, like Betsy, died at its vigorous middle age. Now (1996) the tree's leafless form still stands strong and tall as a memorial to our Betsy.

Tom

Our son, Thomas Robert, named after Dr. Roberts, was born prematurely on March 26, 1938. He was off to a slow start, but had grown to a husky two-year-old when we moved to our Mississippi River home in Brooklyn Park. He was lucky to survive the following experience with that river.

During our first few seasons in our new home on the Mississippi River we had many happy times exploring our little three-acre mini-wilderness and getting acquainted with our new neighbors. But one event that sticks in our memories almost ended in tragedy. The wooded riverbank at our home was quite steep and twenty or thirty feet above the river level depending on the season. We had intentionally avoided cutting steps down to the water so the youngsters would not be lured without supervision to go down to the river.

One early winter day, I believe in 1943, our son Tom, then four or five years old, and two of his slightly younger friends, Steve Swanson and Dougie Lang, much against our frequent warnings, climbed down the river bank and ventured out onto the river ice. According to Tom's recollections of the event many years later (1995), they noticed some oddly colored ice just ahead and well out from shore. Curious to know what it was, they went to investigate and were shocked to discover that it was ice too thin to support their weight. Sharp cracking sounds and Tom and Steve were plunged up to their necks in the icy water. It was too deep for them to touch bottom so they thrashed about trying to climb out onto the ice that repeatedly broke under their weight. Tom shouted to Dougie to run for help but he just stood and cried, not realizing the seriousness of the situation. Tom first succeeded in getting out but in trying to help Steve he broke through again but was lucky enough to crawl out onto the thicker ice. Still unable to rescue Steve, Tom chose to scramble up the riverbank and run for help at our house. Steve's mother, Irene, fortunately happened to be coming over to our house and got Tom's message and tumbled and slid down the bank hoping to rescue Steve. Her recollection was that she first saw the hole in the ice but no Steve and her heart skipped several beats before she caught sight of him safely on shore and heading for home. Fortunately he had been able to break his way through the thin ice and reach shore just before Irene arrived and a very thankful mother then hustled her shivering youngster

Family portrait - 1946 Dorothy, Betsy, Tom, Barbara, Breck

up the bank and into their warm home. In the meantime Dorothy had peeled off Tom's dripping snowsuit and wrapped him in a warm woolen blanket and neither youngster suffered any ill effects from his near tragic chilling plunge.

For some time Tom and I had planned a canoe trip down the Rum River from its source in Lake Mille Lacs. It was on August 29, 1952 when Tom was 14 years old that we actually took off. Dorothy, Betsy and Barbara drove us up and we loaded our gear in the canoe at the bridge near Vineland on the west side of the lake. They returned home expecting us to arrive there in two or three days. We fumbled a bit locating the actual channel that was the outlet of the lake. It was a bit choppy but we arrived okay. From there on we made occasional portages around dams, Lake Onamia and other small lakes until 6:20 in the afternoon when we pulled up at a nice beach for the night. Numerous wood ducks, hooded mergansers and a canvasback flushed ahead of us on the way down. We encountered a good many rapids and riffles where the canoe took a few scrapes. This bothered us since we had borrowed the Jaques' aluminum canoe for the trip. While we were cooking our supper it began to rain

but we tipped the canoe over for protection and hurriedly set up our tent, then finished our supper and finally rolled in about 9:00 p.m.

The next morning my diary read: "Rained nearly all night and at 6:00 A.M. it was still raining so we turned over and slept till 7:00. Still raining. We sat up and ate some doughnuts and Sugar Crisp cereal and pears. Read a while and practiced the Morse code. A young great horned owl kept giving a one-syllabled raspy squeak at regular intervals of about a minute nearly all night. Once I dreamed I was ready to give Tom a poke thinking I was sleeping against the tent wall and a bear was sniffing and snuffling around outside after our food. As I awoke, Tom was sniffing and grunting as he shifted position, which set off my dream. At 8:00 A.M. it appeared to be stopping raining so we rushed around and packed up everything. Launched the canoe and just as we were ready to push off it started raining again."

It rained steadily nearly all morning and we were continually navigating rapids and shallows that further damaged our borrowed canoe. About noon we landed at a store near Milaca, only 25 miles down river from Mille Lacs, and phoned home. We were very disappointed to have to terminate our long-planned trip. But with no prospect of the rain stopping and the low river causing damage to the Jaques' canoe, we thought it best to request a rescue from home so we could sleep that night in a warm, dry bed rather than in a dripping tent.

Along with Betsy, Tom attended Riverview School, with eight grades and twenty-six students, then on to Anoka High School. There he was only mildly interested in athletics but he was a member of the hockey squad and played in a few league games. He developed an interest in drag racing and together with his neighborhood chum, Warren Sjoberg, remodeled a second hand Model A Ford. During his senior year, Tom drove this car to a high school choir concert in which he was singing. He was wearing a new suit and did not want to wrinkle it, so he did not buckle his seat belt. At a 90-degree turn he was forced off the road by a speeder coming the other way. In the rollover he went out through the top and badly damaged his nose and upper lip, but suffered no other serious injury. After several sessions with plastic surgeons he made a really remarkable recovery.

Always interested in helping people, Tom went on from high school to get a degree in sociology at the University of Minnesota. He attended Hartford Seminary for a ministerial degree and while he was there he married Marilyn Saure, a promising young student from Fergus Falls, Minnesota. Their son, John, was born in Fergus Falls in the summer of 1963. While serving as a minister in Brattleboro, Vermont, and then in Minneapolis at Lynnhurst Congregational Church, they had two more children, Sarah & Mary. With three youngsters heading for college and Marilyn becoming an ordained Lutheran minister, Tom joined the Dain, Bosworth investment firm in 1978 before setting out on his own in 1989 as a financial consultant.

John married Lee Ann Jackson in October 1993. They moved to the Brackens, the house where Dorothy and I spent most of our married life, when we left for our retirement home in Golden Valley. They have two sons, Samuel and Christopher.

Mary married David Quello in December 1993 and Sarah married David Schwietz in October 2000 and they currently live in the Twin Cities.

Barbara

The stork came a bit early with our Christmas baby, Barbara, on December 14, 1943, in the third year in our new Mississippi River home. She spent her elementary school years attending Riverview, still a one-room school through third grade, and went on to Anoka High.

Barbara's love of theater began showing up while at Anoka and grew when she attended Grinnell College in Iowa. When she was cast in "Major Barbara" we surprised her by driving down for the performance without her knowledge, a really happy occasion. At Grinnell she completed her B.A. degree with a major in speech correction but returned to Minneapolis where she got an M.S. in Library Science at the University of Minnesota. She took a job with the Baltimore County Public Library in Maryland where she stayed until recently. There she also pursued her interest in community theater which she shared with a talented young actor and electrician, Bruce Franklin, whom she married in 1969. Bruce died in 1991.

Of our three children, Barby seems to have inherited more of my interest in Nature than the others have. She enjoys hiking and often mentions seeing especially attractive native flowers. Her most exciting hike, no doubt, was her 10-day trek in India with her cousin, Esther Blackburn. A party of 10 made the trip, which took them up to rather high elevations in the Himalayan Mountains, but they passed up tackling 29,000-foot Mount Everest. She now enjoys wildlife at the Brackens, which she purchased when John and Lee Ann moved to Australia in 2002.

Parasitic Jaeger - sketched during honeymoon

Chapter 6: Marriage and Honeymoon

DOROTHY

On arriving in Minnesota for my new museum job in 1926 I still was very busy paying off my college debts with my munificent $1800 annual salary to consider anything serious regarding marriage. But I did date a good many girls, none of whom suited me as a lifetime mate. With my consuming interest in the natural world, I did not develop an overwhelming interest in social contacts especially of the fair sex. With no sister then in the family, I always felt ill at ease with girls. I had few dates while in high school and only a limited number while in college. Parties at the Phi Gamma Delta Fraternity house, while I was a member during my junior and senior years, forced me to have a few dates, but I found I was too busy with my studies, athletics and fieldwork collecting specimens for my museum work to allow for much dating. A dance or movie on weekends seems to have filled my entertainment requirements.

However, in 1933 I finally met Dorothy Shogren, a capable and very beautiful Swedish home economist who quickly convinced me that she was "IT."

Dr. R. G. Green of the University of Minnesota Bacteriology Department had been studying tularemia for several years, a disease of humans contracted from grouse and rodents, with the view of finding an explanation of the cyclic nature of their populations. He instigated an expedition for the purpose of determining the limits of the range of this disease in more northern latitudes. I was to accompany him in the capacity of collector and also to make general collections of natural history materials from the regions we visited for the University of Minnesota Natural History Museum.

Dorothy as a home economist

Elaborate planning and gathering equipment had taken several weeks prior to our departure date of July 26, 1933. Dorothy Shogren and I were planning to get married when I returned from the Churchill expedition, but this part of our plan was interrupted, as Dorothy relates in her account of our brief courtship and marriage and so we made a honeymoon out of the trip. Things began to happen on Memorial Day, May 30, 1933.

"Not realizing what a memorable day this would be, I accepted an invitation to go on a picnic with my sister and her boyfriend on Memorial Day, May 30, 1933, since the fellow whose fraternity pin I was wearing had gone fishing. Breck was with another girl, but we were obviously attracted although Breck hesitated to interfere with that engagement. However, he did interfere. Two weeks later he called and a month later he gave me a diamond. We had planned to be married in the fall. Breck had been planning for months to go on a seven week expedition to Churchill, Manitoba on Hudson Bay with Dr. and Mrs. Robert Green, both bacteriologists at the University of Minnesota. They were to study tularemia, a disease of humans transmitted by ticks on rabbits and grouse. Breck and Dr. Green would collect the specimens in the field. The Greens would then pick off any ticks found and send them back to the University. Then Breck would skin the specimens for the Museum and some of the meat we would eat. You see we were genuine conservationists even in those early days.

"On the evening of July 25 my mother, my sister and I had a farewell dinner for Breck, who was leaving the next day, and also for Dr. and Mrs. George Conger who were leaving for India and a trip around the world. Dr. Conger was a philosophy professor at the University and had been an interim minister at First Congregational Church. At the dinner I made the casual remark that I had met Dr. and Mrs. Green the night before and they had said it was too bad they hadn't

known that Breck had a girlfriend and I could have gone on the trip too. Mrs. Conger immediately decided it was a great idea and it would make a wonderful honeymoon. It sounded like a pretty wild and impossible idea to me. I said I had a job and Breck was leaving in less than 24 hours.

"I was managing the Crossways Tea Room in the First National Bank in St. Paul. There was just no way it could be done. But Mrs. Conger was very persuasive and had an answer for every objection. Then I remembered that there was a five-day waiting law. Dr. Conger, who had also thought his wife's idea was really crazy suddenly said,'I think I can take care of that.' Then there was a trip to the Greens to see if they really meant what they said and a trip to Dr. Thomas Roberts, Breck's boss for his OK on my going. Late that night we decided if a license was available we would go through with the plan. Imagine! A chaperoned honeymoon!

"I went to work at seven the next morning and received the much awaited call from Breck in the late forenoon. I then quit my job during the noon rush; drew money at the bank, stopped at Montgomery Ward to buy long underwear, flannel pajamas and an air mattress. The Greens had an extra sleeping bag. Quitting my job was one of the hardest things I had ever had to do. How unprofessional! You can imagine Mrs. Ostrowski and Mrs. Peters' reactions. 'Miss Shogren, this isn't like you. Someone has talked you into this.' Weeks later, however, they had a shower for me.

"I met Breck and we bought a wedding ring. Meanwhile at our house my mother, my sister, Elizabeth, and Dr. Conger, packed my dufflebag complete with rice and confetti and a white ribbon around my new boots, a gift from Breck the week before. When my mother called my friend, Charlotte Jacobson, to invite her to the wedding, she suggested having it at her home since we were in the midst of moving. Mrs. Conger arranged

48

for flowers and refreshments. Elizabeth and Dr. Roberts were our attendants. Dr. Conger was the minister and there were a few guests. When my friend, Dorothy Good who worked for the Minneapolis Journal asked to get time off to go to the wedding, her boss thought it would be worth sending a reporter and a photographer. I heard Dorothy Good say, 'Now don't put this on the back page. See that it goes on the society page.' It actually appeared on the front page. We were married at 4:30 p.m. and left on the train at 5:30 p.m. July 26, 1933.

"After this rather unusual beginning we both have felt that we made a wonderful choice. During our sixty three years of married life (1996) we have borne and raised two daughters and one son, all of whom have developed highly successful careers for which we are very thankful and proud."

After that hectic wedding day, we finally scrambled onto the train at 5:30 p.m. and settled down to do a bit of relaxing. Then followed a not too romantic dinner in the dining car and a not much more romantic night in Pullman berths. Arriving next morning in Winnipeg we checked in at the Fort Gary Hotel and immediately, as guests of Mr. Cunningham, Conservation Commissioner of Manitoba, we were taken to Portage la Prairie on Lake Manitoba to visit James Ford Bell's Duck Hatchery and hunting lodge. On returning to Winnipeg we enjoyed being taken by the Greens to a fine dinner at the Fort Gary Hotel and what we call our real wedding night.

Then we spent a day on the train traveling to The Pas where we completed our supplies and toured that interesting city. I recall that many homes had their front yards fenced and planted with remarkably tall, handsome dahlias and lupines as they grow here in these high latitudes. We visited a small church on the outskirts of the town, where we were told that a ship's carpenter, wintering in The Pas in 1856-57 had constructed the pews.

On leaving The Pas, we found the train to Churchill was made up of freight, passenger, dining and Pullman cars and was strictly local in its service. Dr. Green had made previous arrangements for us to stop at Cormorant Lake, Mile 42, to collect a few grouse and rabbits for ticks to check for tularemia's possible occurrence here, at a point part way to Churchill. Here we occupied a cabin under the auspices of the Forestry Department. We collected locally for a couple days, then went by canoe with Mr. Cowan to his cabin at the north end of Cormorant Lake to add a few specimens from that area to our research. Later we contacted an Indian, Bill McKenzie who took us south to Moose Lake to add spruce grouse to our collections. I recall getting several grouse and we roasted one over the campfire. I took my portion in my fingers while McKenzie handled his with his knife and fork. I took several mice in my traps there and made this comment in my notes, "One mouse appeared to be something unusual, having characteristics of both Microtus and Peromyscus." Later this specimen proved very puzzling and we considered the possibility of its being a new species for this area. In fact we decided to stop enroute back from Churchill to see if we could get additional specimens with these characters.

That evening the weather turned against us and, "a black cloud threatened rain and we set up a tent and rolled in. The wind blew hard all night and nearly blew the tent over." And on the start of our way back my notes commented, "strong winds came up and strong misgivings came up in yours truly's breast as to whether we could get across Little Cormorant Lake. But Bill was very confident and we struck out and arrived at camp at 11:00 a.m. with no greater mishaps other than shipping spray in large quantities."

Elizabeth Shogren, Dorothy, Breck, Dr. Thomas Roberts - July 26, 1935

After returning from the Moose Lake trip we did more local collecting for a couple of days before packing up for the 400-mile train ride to Churchill. Dr. Allan, a parasitologist from the Department of Conservation of Manitoba, who joined us in Winnipeg, decided to return to Winnipeg. He had been a rather uncooperative member of our party and we were relieved to have him go back. We had collected 44 birds and mammals while on our stay in Cormorant Lake. A very congenial black porter who was also conductor, cook and waiter, served our meals enroute to Churchill. The food was well prepared and we remember particularly that he would get off and pick blueberries and prepare wonderful deep-dish blueberry pie. Numerous stops along the way gave us chances to get off and look over the tiny communities that had grown up along the railway. The residents were Chippewayan Indians and whites. No Eskimos had come this far south.

We finally arrived at Churchill at 6:00 p.m. and with no hotels or motels and too late to set up tents, we checked in at the Hudson Bay office. There they agreed to take several others and us across the river and four miles up to the Hudson Bay headquarters for the night. While waiting we overheard staff people debating whether or not it would be safe to take canoes or the big 36-foot scow since it was windy and the river a bit rough. We were pleased to hear they decided on the scow. Dorothy and Mrs. Green, seated on packs, were given a blanket and a little Indian girl crept under the foot of it to keep out of the wind. We felt that we were actually in the wilderness on this crossing. On arriving we were transferred to canoes to make the landing in pitch darkness. After chatting with Mr. Wynn, the Post Factor, and having cup of tea, we rolled in at 2:30 a.m. for some much-needed rest.

We arrived back in Churchill the next morning, August 14, and went about setting up our tents a mile and a half east of the elevators, not far from the Hudson Bay Transport Office. Next we contracted with Charlie, a Belgian resident, as cook and handy man to relieve us of some of the camp duties. I began exploring locally as to where I could take a few ptarmigan or snowshoe rabbits. I also set out a trap line of 25-30 mousetraps for mice or possibly collared lemmings. Our stay in our tents became something of a battle with the weather, although they served us quite well for several days.

One morning I was getting breakfast in the cook tent when in walked an Indian without any word of invitation. I greeted him and kept on with my breakfast preparations while he stood in a corner of the tent, apparently simply curious as to who we were and what we were doing. He obviously was not drunk nor at all belligerent but just curious. He stayed only a short time and walked out without saying a word but evidently satisfied with what he had learned about us.

The elevators were the largest commercial development that had originally promoted the recent development of Churchill and the building of the railroad. In studying a globe, one can see that in shipping wheat from the Canadian Prairies to Europe the way through Churchill was on a direct route that was considerably shorter than by way of Duluth, the Great Lakes, and the Saint Lawrence River. Strangely enough, a vessel going east out of Hudson Bay, passing south of Greenland and Iceland, would go in an almost straight line to England. We found that at the Churchill loading docks, where it was fresh water, the vessels could load a foot or more below the danger line since in entering the oceans they were buoyed up to the proper depth by the heavier salt water.

In the Churchill River we often saw considerable numbers of belugas or white whales where they were conspicuously playing and jumping out of the water. Fisherman were shooting some of them and dragging them to a rendering plant where they were prepared for various commercial uses.

One evening the sky blackened and the wind and rain kept increasing until we began

wondering if our tent was going to stand the strains. I finally slipped on my raincoat over my pajamas and faced the storm just long enough to pound the tent stakes a little firmer and put on an additional rope and stake. We weathered the blow O.K. but didn't get much sleep that night. We later learned that a canoe had been blown up over a house nearby, so I guess we were lucky to have weathered it as well as we did. As a result of this experience we rented a tarpaper shack in the area where we stayed for the remainder of our Churchill visit.

The Greens were anxious to get evidence of tularemia from still farther north, so we chartered a small, 25-foot yacht, the Odnay, equipped with motor and sails, from an Icelander, Palmer Sigurdson, and his son, Oscar, to take Charlie and me to Nonala 95 miles north of Churchill. The Bay was so shallow along this shore that we had to travel a number of miles from shore to be sure of avoiding rocks. We found that the Post Factor at Nonala was Mr. Winter who had been on South Hampton Island and had met ornithologist George Sutton, who happened to be there at that time. Winter took us in his canoe three miles north to where a small group of three families of Eskimos were living. I recall hearing music coming from one of the shacks and we thought we were going to hear some Eskimo music but it turned out to be music from a small phonograph. Back at the Post Winter

Dorothy posing with moose antlers

asked if we would like to see an arctic fox den and, of course, we said we would. "Well, go west about a mile and the den is right there near the bush. You can't miss."
Yes, here we were definitely north of the tree line. Unfortunately we did not see any arctic hares. We did not blame ourselves after we heard an Eskimo say he had not seen any either for some time. I was sorry I had not read a comment from the writings of Preble of the U.S Department of the Interior. He stated that the way to find hares was to fire your gun into the air and if they were within hearing they would make a spy hop high into the air out of curiosity. I did succeed in collecting a few mice, birds and plants.

I recall that enroute home, I stood on a box in the hold of the yacht and used the deck as a table on which to skin the birds I had collected. A fly buzzing about my head pestered me and, in swatting at it, I knocked my glasses off. They went flying far into the darkness of the ship's hold. I crawled back over many boxes and packsacks wondering whether I would ever find my glasses and if I did would they be broken. But I did find them, hanging by their bows on the top edge of a cardboard box, unbroken!

Enroute back, a storm blew up and we were tossed about considerably by the rough waves. Later the folks at home told us they were really worried about our safety. But our good luck held out and we arrived undamaged.

Mrs. Green was taken ill soon after we arrived in Churchill and she was admitted to the hospital for several days with what the doctors thought might be tularemia. Dorothy recalled that they thought it could have resulted from a spider bite, but there was a very good chance it was from a tick bite, which would confirm the doctor's diagnosis.

On one occasion while hunting I caught a young collared lemming in my hands. It was such a cutie I brought him home for the others to see. We made a little cage filled with grass in which it could hide. Scientifically speaking he was of the genus "*Dicrostonyx*", but not wanting to burden him with such a long title, we shortened it to simply "Dicky." We thought it would be less disturbed by all the action in the tent if we placed his cage just outside, which we did. Later we were startled by a loud rattling sound near the tent and on investigating, we saw a big black Eskimo sledge dog trotting off unconcernedly. He had spotted Dicky in his cage and had pounded the cage on the rocks as to liberate Dicky. But he was no sooner free than he was grabbed and swallowed up by the husky sledge dog.

Soon after the tents were put up, Charlie called attention to a small bird seen hopping into our tent. It proved to be a water pipit, an insect eating, tail bobbing bird like the spotted sandpiper, palm warbler and several wagtails, a habit important in their field identification. Evidently it had flown into some obstacle but appeared normal except that it could not fly. Mosquitoes and flies that got into our tent usually gathered in the upper, warmer parts of the tent. We found that the little pipit would perch on one's finger and would pick off the insects from the canvas when carried within pecking distance. This was an easy way to feed the little visitor, which we did several times during the day. When it was no longer hungry we put it in a small box with some soft grasses and it snuggled down comfortably, we thought. However we were disappointed when later we found it had gone to the Pipit's Happy Hunting Grounds. But it still lives as a scientific specimen representing its species in the Museum's bird collection.

We concluded our work at Churchill on August 28 and started the long train ride back toward The Pas. However, Dr. Green and I decided to stop over at Cormorant Lake for a couple of days to make an effort to collect another specimen of the dark mouse that we thought could be a rare or even a new species of these rodents. Dorothy and Mrs. Green continued on to The Pas for a restful couple of days awaiting our arrival later.

Dr. Green and I contacted Bill McKenzie and Harold Erlendsen and we made the 30-mile trip to Moose Lake. There I set out a line of traps in the same area where I had taken the unusual specimen. I got a number of mice but none resembling the one we were after. Enroute back, a storm developed and high waves began building up. The last lake before reaching Cormorant Lake was especially rough and Dr. Green and I decided to walk around the lake. But Bill McKenzie insisted they could make it in the canoe even though the waves were so high that he and his canoe disappeared every time he ran between the waves.

The two of us sloshed through the rain and wind along deer and moose trails through the tall grass near the shore for two miles where we encountered an old muddy wagon road for another mile to the railroad at mile 39. This left us three miles on the railroad tracks to Cormorant Lake (mile 42). We were really tuckered out on arrival. McKenzie and Harold had the roughest going they had ever had keeping the motor going, keeping the tarp over the packs from blowing away and bailing the rain and spray constantly to keep them afloat. They made it to Cormorant Lake all right but they, like us, were a really exhausted pair on arrival.

The next morning we boarded the train and met Dorothy and Mrs. Green in The Pas where they had had a pleasant and restful time, very much in contrast to our rough and unsuccessful experience at Cormorant Lake.

Later, back at the Museum, we examined the unusual specimen and decided that it was not a new or rare species but simply a melanistic individual of the local race of the red-backed mouse.

We never did see any scientific report of the results of our trip regarding the presence of tularemia. But an article in the *Minneapolis Star Tribune* quoting Dr. Green stated that, "The ticks are the most common carriers of tularemia and other similar wild animal diseases continue to (occur) to and beyond Cormorant... They disappear, however, about 100 miles this side of Hudson Bay. None were found around Churchill."

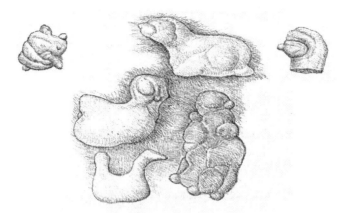

Limestone concretions that wash out of the riverbank are nature's sculptures

Chapter 7: The Brackens

On returning from Hudson Bay in September 1933, we rented the north half of a duplex house on 22nd Street NE in Minneapolis. And in 1934 we rented a house at 2957 Pierce Street in northeast Minneapolis. There I struggled with a coal-burning furnace where one room in the basement housed our winter's supply of coal. This found me getting up at 4:30 in the morning to dig out the clinkers from the furnace, tossing in some kindling and a shovelful of coal and waiting to be sure the fire was properly started to heat the house by breakfast time.

When we began looking for an out-of-the-city place to live, a 2¾ acre tract that happened to be available attracted our attention, largely due to the presence of a 20-acre island opposite it in the Mississippi River. A long time resident of the area, Al Mattson, assured us that although the logging operations of the Rum River Boom Company scarred up the island somewhat 100 years ago, it had been virtually undisturbed for nearly a century. We were assured by the Northern States Power Company, who had bought the island from the Boom Company, that they had no plans to sell the island and that no bridge or buildings were to be built on it. So we felt that we could look forward to at least a few years of wilderness status for the island, which could serve as a productive reservoir of wildlife. With this in mind we bought the property.

We immediately began wondering about the history of the island. I looked up some old maps in the library of the Minnesota Historical Society and found one dated 1887 that showed it as Casey's Island. We never learned who Casey was, but shortly after moving to Baltimore, our daughter, Barbara, met a fellow, Tom Casey, whose family had owned river property directly opposite The Brackens for many years. He still made yearly trips there to check up on it. It's a small world! Further investigation turned up the name Banfill Island in the records of the Northern States Power Company.

In more recent maps the west bank of the Mississippi is indicated as in Hennepin County and the east bank in Anoka County. The question came up as to which county the island was in. The strange fact came out that at the time of the original survey there were actually two islands with an angling channel of the river separating the two. The county line followed the channel between the islands. Probably during logging operations of 1860 to 1900 the channel was gradually filled in and the two islands became one. After a period of uncertainty, the legal determination was made that the county line should follow the main channel, that was the east channel, and the island became assigned to Hennepin County.

The Brackens – 8840 West River Road

Three tiny rocky islets in the channel near the lower end of the island, locally known as "The Piers," aroused our curiosity since they appeared to be man made. Again our local source, Al Mattson, revealed that lumberjacks built these. They first built log cribbings which were later filled with rocks to serve as anchorages for the log booms or chains of logs. These booms could be set in place across the channel in the fall before the river froze over. Logs were then allowed to fill the west channel in what the loggers called a "mill pocket." Here the logs were stored, frozen in the ice, throughout the winter. In early spring the booms were removed and the logs allowed to float down stream to the mills in Camden so operations could start before the big drives could bring logs from farther up river.

BACKGROUND INFORMATION CONCERNING BANFILL ISLAND

The following information was prepared by Wade Larkins of Northern States Power Company.

"An original patent was given by the Government Land Office to one John Banfield in June of 1851, who is the original owner of record. We next find that this particular island was owned by Alexander Ramsey, an early day Governor of the state of Minnesota. Following Mr. Ramsey's ownership we find that the land was transferred to John Nininger in 1856. The Nininger family has a historical significance from the fact that they erected a large showplace on the Mississippi River below Hastings, which was the talk of society in the early Minnesota days. This showplace, in the form of a hotel, was a fashionable vacation spot for people taking scenic steamboat trips up the Mississippi, originating principally in the St. Louis area. It is mere presumption on our part, but there is a possibility that Mr. Niniger had some similar thought in mind when he acquired this particular tract of land. The difficulty of transportation to this area possibly precluded any development in the manner we have surmised. The next land transfer of note finds this island to be owned by the Fridley family for whom the town site of Fridley was later named. We have no information as to what use they intended to make of this property. In 1868 this land was deeded to the St. Anthony Falls Water Power Company, who in turn deeded the property to the Mississippi and Rum River Boom Company in 1870. The directors of these companies contained the illustrious names of Samuel H. Chute, John S. Pillsbury and others. The Mississippi River Commission map, prepared in 1890, indicates that this island was developed for use in logging operations. The island was literally cut in two by a channel excavated diagonally across its midsection, quite possibly for sorting the logs of various owners, preparatory to sawing at Minneapolis. The two islands then existing were called Big Casey and Little Casey Island. We have no information as to how Casey got into the act. The maps prepared at these dates show the location of a number of log booms, indicating the possibility that a sawmill once occupied this site. This is a presumption on our part, but if considerable quantities of sawdust remain on this island to date, the presence of a one-time sawmill here could probably be confirmed. Logging operations in this section of the river presumably came to an end in the early 1900's and this island was then taken over by the Mississippi River Electric Power Company as necessary to flowage rights for hydroelectric operations along the river. The Mississippi River Electric Power Company deeded this property to the Northern States Power Company in 1916. The title has rested with N.S.P. and its subsidiaries since that date. The Northern States Power Company acquired rights on this island for its hydroelectric properties along the Mississippi River."

On first moving into our new home on the Mississippi River, there were a good many logs lying around from clearing the space for the house. Also, we first planned to make a circle drive leading to our front door, which called for cutting a few more trees. Then it looked reasonable to clear the space within the circle drive for a garden. All these operations added to the number of logs piled about. The question then came up as to what

Tom & Betsy at the log cabin playhouse

to do with the logs. Someone came up with the suggestion of a log cabin, which sounded logical, so up went the log playhouse cabin. Unfortunately most of the logs were basswood, which decays rapidly, so we realized that it would be a temporary undertaking, but youngsters stay in the kid stage rather temporarily too, so that was no drawback. After several seasons the cabin deteriorated and some mischievous boys broke a window and vandalized it somewhat. The cabin's brief history came to an end as we transformed it into firewood for our fireplace.

One might assume that on arriving at our new home on the River we would immediately cut stairs down to the river. But since we had two small children we felt that such easy access to the dangerous waters did not seem reasonable, so we passed up the construction of steps. We did occasionally scramble down the steep bank to use our canoe or to gather concretions.

IZAAK WALTON & BRECK'S ISLAND

Prior to our moving to the area I learned that the North Minneapolis Chapter of the Izaak Walton League of America had been organized in 1932 and, in 1936, built a substantial clubhouse four doors south of us. At the urging of George Laing, who lived next door to it, and others, I joined the organization and have remained an active member for the 56 years that have elapsed to the present 1997. The Waltonians own about four acres of the wooded banks of the Mississippi and originally preserved it wild, except for a small parking lot near the road, expecting that no cars would use the walking path to the clubhouse. But as the years passed and members grew older, a road and a larger parking area were cleared. Also, as taxes increased, the building was enlarged with toilets and kitchen equipment installed for member dinners and to enable them to rent the building for income needed to cover taxes.

Neighbors Carl and Irene Swanson, Becky Knopp and her parents, Floyd and Betty Anderson, Louie and Lavonne Dinzl, Vera and

Dick Brown among others were very active members. George Richert and George Laing were among the very early members. I took an active part in programs with my series of Audubon lecture films and travel pictures. For a few seasons I laid out a short self-guiding nature trail and initiated the highway cleanup of a couple of miles of Highway 252.

I served as president for a couple of years soon after World War II. Our actual conservation accomplishments were mainly the educational programs arranged for members. The programs dealt with natural history, environmental preservation and supporting legal action in those fields. Numerous travel programs were scattered in. For several years the Chapter provided gift subscriptions to the conservation magazine World Watch for several area schools. As the years passed, taxes increased still more and in recent years we have served pancake breakfasts and held annual garage sales to keep up with expenses. I contributed a couple of series of drawings for notepaper sales and a colored print of a kestrel (Plate 16, also in Chapter 9) to add a small trickle to our income over the years. The movies that I produced for the Bell Museum's use and National Audubon's lecture programs were occasionally shown at meetings.

When I retired from the Bell Museum in 1970, the Northern States Power Company donated the river island opposite the clubhouse to the University of Minnesota with the suggestion that it be renamed from "Banfill Island" to "Breck's Island." Legal efforts were made to change the name, but long-standing historic regulations did not permit such changes in spite of considerable support for the move, and the island remains Banfill Island. Later, in about 1980, the Chapter bought the island from the University for $100. I must have helped the League's progress significantly, since in 1996 they renamed the organization the Walter J. Breckenridge Chapter of the Izaak Walton League.

BIRDS

When we moved to The Brackens in 1939, we immediately put out bird feeders of various types to bring in as many birds as we could. Over the course of the 56 years that we spent there, we recorded about 180 species. Some were very special; I have devoted a separate chapter to wood ducks and have discussed my contacts with great horned owls in the chapter on birds of prey. Only a few were all year-around visitors to our seed feeders and suet. These were: chickadees, white and red-breasted nuthatches, downy, hairy, red-bellied, and pileated woodpeckers (Plate 6A), cardinals (Plate 6B), blue jays, goldfinches and, in recent years, house finches. Rose-breasted grosbeaks (Plate 7A) and Baltimore orioles (Plate 7B) brightened the feeders in summer and in winter pine siskins, purple finches and redpolls were present. Some rarities have visited our woods over the years. Late one fall a Carolina wren appeared and survived through the winter until February. We felt that we helped it some by placing a cloth covered electrically heated trivet that kept some bits of hamburger unfrozen on the steps near the feeders. One spring found a broad-winged hawk starting to build a nest near the road, but it finally gave up due to too much traffic, no doubt. Briefly, a worm-eating warbler (the first record for the state on April 30, 1962) was found singing in the woods and a few years later, a hooded warbler put in its appearance, a real rarity in Minnesota. A yellow-billed cuckoo once raised a family in a low gooseberry bush in the woods. One fall Dorothy spotted a varied thrush, a rare western species, which stayed well into the winter with us. Late one evening we noticed what we thought was a chipmunk among the dead leaves that turned out to be a woodcock.

From limestone left over from the house construction, I built a birdbath resembling a section of limestone wall with two levels of depressions containing water supplied as a drip from a small underground plastic tube leading from our outdoor faucet. This has attracted a good many exciting avian guests and is kept under almost constant observation in hopes of spotting any new arrivals that may be stopping off on migration or seeking territories for nesting. In addition to the many species of birds that have visited the bath, others ranged in size from honeybees to white-tailed deer. Squirrels of four species: red, gray, fox, and flying have been seen.

Although dozens of species of birds are attracted by our birdbath during spring, summer and fall, the warblers come in conspicuous numbers and afford many hours of exciting concentrated observation. These birds regularly migrate in flocks made up of several different species in both spring and fall. I recall photographing 4 or 5 species in a single exposure during one of these warbler waves. At these times they often come in repeatedly to drink or bathe, which gives one opportunities to study their varying identification marks. This is most appreciated during the fall migration when most species have assumed their non-breeding plumages that are far less distinctive than their bright spring plumages.

Once in the late afternoon of July 24, 1988, Dorothy looked up from her work and was amazed to see three Cooper's hawks perched on the birdbath. She called for me and I rushed for my camera and was fumbling with the adjustments when all three left. One immature bird was considerate enough to return a few minutes later and casually took a real bath. It accommodated me by posing several times for pictures, one of which came out quite well.

I do not prevent our birdbath from freezing in winter. Birds can always use snow to slake their thirst. Some will bathe in the water during sub-freezing weather and can suffer or even die when their feathers freeze.

My urge to paint a picture of the American goldeneyes came one winter while watching a group of these hardy ducks swimming, diving and feeding in an unfrozen patch of water in the River near my home. (Plate 7C) The river stayed clear of ice at that point because rapids prevented it from freezing except during extremely cold weather. These birds are in the diving duck group that normally spend their winters here. Their remarkable diving ability enables them to feed on crayfish, caddisfly larvae and other bottom fauna in open places such as this. Even extremely cold weather seems not to inconvenience this species since the water's temperature being above freezing actually keeps the bird warm. I noticed that this particular little flock would alight at the upper end of the open area and would gradually drift down stream with the current, diving and feeding enroute to the end of the open water. Then they would take wing and alight upstream to repeat their diving and feeding.

While working on this painting I recall puzzling over just how the light struck the ice and water surfaces and the colors of the various parts of the scene. This being the case, I would put on my parka and hike along the shore some distance to study my problem subjects, then return to my studio to make the corrections.

Toward spring these birds would engage in their strange courtship performances. The handsome males would approach the females and suddenly kick back their feet, throwing out a spray of water behind. Then, stretching their necks forward and puffing out their head feathers, they would bow, almost touching their heads to the water. Occasionally one would lay its head back on its back, then, throwing its head forward, it would utter a queer, high pitched quacking call. Again one would lay its head forward on the water and scoot threateningly toward its prospective mate or at a competing male.

Later in the spring when the ice broke up, these birds would migrate farther north to nest in hollows in trees, as do the wood ducks.

FLYING SQUIRRELS

One evening I turned on the light to see what might be visiting the birdbath, and out of the corner of my eye I spotted something sailing in to the tree near the light. At first I thought it must be a leaf being blown by the wind, but there was no wind blowing. Immediately the idea struck me that it might be a flying squirrel. Hoping that it was, I put up a small platform scattered with sunflower seeds. Sure enough the next night a pair of flying squirrels accepted my invitation and this event initiated a several year-long series of fascinating sessions with these captivating little chipmunk-sized squirrels. They were strictly nocturnal and always appeared on a regular schedule a little after dusk. The feeder was on the trunk of an oak tree, only six feet from the windows of the glass-enclosed porch where we frequently entertained dinner guests. (Plate 8A)

Dorothy often mentioned that our "floor show" would start at a certain time and the little actors would invariably come scurrying down the tree trunk at about the appointed time. Not just two, but occasionally as many as six, would put in their appearance. Lots of action ensued as they dashed up and down and around the tree trunk. I often commented that they appeared to defy the law of gravity as they ran up just as fast as down. They would often get sunflower seeds, run up a few feet, turn about and, clinging by their hind feet, manipulate the seeds with their front feet while hanging up side down. Their huge black eyes stood out prominently against the smooth, brownish gray pelage of their backs and contrasting with their backs, a black line bordered their white under parts. Folds in the white area revealed the presence of the very flexible "wings" expandable skin that stretched out "spread eagle" for their gliding flight. We only rarely saw the flying flight since they evidently came into our oak tree high up among the upper branches above the field of our spotlight. They well deserve the term "arboreal" since only rarely would they run down to the ground. They stayed high up to avoid the stray cats that occasionally tried to sneak up on them. On at least one occasion a cat succeeded; one morning I found a flat little furry tail at the base of the tree after one of our floor shows the previous evening.

After four or five years of enjoying these little actors they suddenly abandoned our feeder and now it has been several years since we have been visited by these charming miniature squirrels. Whether some predator such as a great horned owl, a fox or stray cat may have eliminated entirely our local population, or they had simply relocated their territories, we have never been able to determine.

BEAVER

With binoculars in hand, I was strolling along the riverbank when I encountered my neighbor, Billy Manning, peering intently across the river at what I thought at first glance was a muskrat cutting a V-ripple along the shore of the island. These little furbearers usually favor the marshes where they can build houses of the abundant cattails. But this little eccentric would have been a bank muskrat that burrows in the bank for its home. However, a quick look with my binoculars told me it was too big, so it must be a beaver as Manning had already determined. These big rodents were present but not commonly seen in the river since they were mostly nocturnal. But this one, in broad daylight, steered for the shore, landed and started up the bank toward a big, 27-inch cottonwood tree whose trunk was deeply girdled. He appeared to be intent on cutting a few more chips from where he had worked for at least a couple of seasons past in his attempts to fell this huge tree. But this time he had no such idea in mind. He waddled only a few feet up the bank to a clump of sandbar willow switches three or four feet high. Cutting one, he dragged it back into the water. Then sitting calmly in the shallow water he set about peeling his dinner of tender, juicy willow bark. His technique was to cut around and around the wand, rotating it with his front paws while the white, peeled stick progressively projected from the other side of his jaws. Both hands were on the unpeeled end of the wand as he nimbly manipulated it through the mill of his huge yellow incisors that perfectly removed the bark exactly like a flute player running through a difficult musical passage. What an amusing shot for one of my films of the ecology of the island. But as is so often the case, I had no camera in hand, was too distant for a close up and the late afternoon light was too dim for a good exposure. But the scene has stuck with me for years along with many other wildlife experiences I have had but have not been able to record for others to enjoy.

Returning to the cottonwood mentioned above, I later found where the beavers had felled several only slightly smaller trees and cut and carried away many of the limbs in the water. I wondered where they had taken them and examined the bank for some distance for the food pile I thought must be nearby. Several years before I had found such a pile of tangled branches 6'-8' wide and perhaps 30' or 40' long. It appeared to be a disorganized assemblage, but it obviously was sufficiently well put together that it remained anchored to the bank and showed no signs of drifting away. This would soon have frozen into the ice where the branches below the ice would remain available as the beaver's winter food supply. In larger rivers such as this, the beavers make no efforts to dam the waters but burrow in the bank from below the water level. Then they excavate a chamber above the water level as their winter home. From the burrow entrance they can swim under the ice to retrieve the branches from the food pile. One might think it a rather terrifying experience for the beavers to be forced to swim long distances with only a lung-full of air, but they have the remarkable ability to breathe out the lung-full of oxygen-depleted air into a large bubble that rises and spreads out against the ice. Here the bubble absorbs a new supply of oxygen from the water and is then breathed in again by the beaver. It thus is capable of traveling indefinitely under the ice.

Early one spring a family of beavers took up residence on the island and undertook to dig a bank burrow and home chamber. But in this case their calculations were erroneous as to the height of the bank. They cut away the ceiling too near to the surface and it began to cave in. Not daunted by their developing problem they climbed the bank and pushed up a considerable amount of soil onto the cave-in. On discovering the dirt-moving job, I wondered what miniature bulldozer had been at work on our island. On another occasion a beaver family had the same problem and they dragged up branches and built what resembled a normal beaver house. I climbed up onto it and sat quietly for some time and finally they began chippering and chuckling inside. Probably they were discussing whether or not the roof of their house was going to hold up under this unanticipated strain.

WHITE-TAILED DEER

I awoke early one spring morning to find a beautiful doe white-tailed deer and two yearling fawns quietly nibbling away in my raspberry patch. My thoughts were, "How wonderful to be able to watch such friendly wildlife right here on our premises." However, later that spring when the same trio very effectively mowed down to stubs the entire row of healthy broccoli plants, we were not so happy. These experiences typify the century long debate that is still brewing over just how the deer population should be managed. (Plate 8B)

Here in the Minneapolis-St. Paul area 150 years ago, deer were common and widespread. Pioneers and settlers at that time struggled to survive and hunting deer provided a good share of their food supply. But when the deer population began to drop, the gardens of the pioneer housewives were still being decimated by the scattered remnants of the herd. Then the cry was to eliminate completely the destructive pests. I recall Dr. Roberts telling about a hunter with his dogs in the early 1900s chasing down and shooting the small herd of deer living just south of Lake Harriet. These were the very last deer known to remain in the Twin City area. For years afterwards deer were extremely scarce, if not actually absent from the surrounding Hennepin County. Then the tables turned and conservationists began to encourage the remaining stragglers. Gradually deer have, as many would say, saturated the countryside. And much debate is still going on about how many, if any, should be permitted in the Twin City area. We can only hope that the Department of Natural Resources can maintain an adequate number of these wonderful game animals both to satisfy hunters' hopes of getting a trophy buck and to keep within appropriate limits the damage they do to our orchards and gardens so that we may enjoy them.

While remembering our Halloween snowstorm of 1991, I recall a strange happening in our little mini-wilderness. The morning after our 10" snowfall I decided to get a bit of exercise with my snowshoes following only slightly cleared trails and enjoying the beauty of the snow covered trees. I had gone just a short way when I encountered a freshly fallen tree trunk lying across my path. After getting over the barrier, I found myself looking directly into the face of a yearling buck deer, 30 feet away, with one foot raised suggesting he was about ready to take off. I stood motionless and began talking to him in a low nonabrasive tone to assure him I was not a threat. The deer continued to stand like a statue so I began to retreat slowly. Still my friend did not move and I continued on through the woods to my driveway and back to the house. I knew that other deer had spent the day in our woods and I felt that this one would lie down for the day.

A couple of days later I went out of my back door to get some wood for my fireplace. As I rounded the house I glanced at the front door and there on the stone approach to the door was my friend, the yearling deer, lying comfortably only 20 feet away and staring directly at me, but making no move to leave. Again I spoke to him in low reassuring tones and quietly backed away until I was concealed by the corner of the house. Then, hurrying to my studio, I got my camera and returned to find my friend still there. Each of us was puzzled over what to expect of the other. Very slowly I approached still closer and succeeded in getting several photographs. Still no move on his part, so I retreated again and got an ear of corn. But I was puzzled as to just how to present it to

him. I couldn't throw it to him slowly in the face of the law of gravity and I felt sure he would never allow me to reach out and feed it to him from my hand. So I finally tossed the corn into the snow a few feet from his head where he could reach it if and when he chose. As I anticipated he did not choose to take the corn but got to his feet rather unsteadily and only then did I realize that the uplifted front foot I had seen the day before was attached to a very severely broken front leg. The poor animal, never looking back, hobbled slowly along the riverbank leaving me to wonder if the unfortunate creature was actually giving up the hope that I might have been able to help it out of its difficulties. Why would it otherwise have chosen to come and lie down at my doorstep? I couldn't help but think of the ancient Roman story of "Androcles and the Lion." When I told the story of the event to my wife, Dorothy, she commented, "I'm sure if it ever goes down over the steep river bank it would never be able to climb back up." And, sure enough, I found that my story ended in tragedy. When a few days later I looked down from my riverbank deck I saw the unfortunate yearling lying dead in the shallow water of the river below. It no doubt had been a traffic victim and suffered from much more than a broken leg.

RUFFED GROUSE

Although we found no moose, bear or timber wolves browsing, hibernating, or hunting on the Island, we do find some of the lesser animals taking advantage of our little private sanctuary. In fact we might say we actually witnessed the demise of at least one species from the fauna of this area. The ruffed grouse was no doubt originally one of the regular residents of the Island and the forested strip along the river, but it was on its last legs, so to speak, when we arrived on the scene. One early spring morning at breakfast we suddenly opened wide our sleepy eyes when a ruffed grouse alighted on an ironwood tree near the riverbank and began feeding on the still tightly closed catkins. We enjoyed watching it climbing a bit unsteadily along the limb, turning this way and that, to reach far out for a particularly fat catkin.

Several months later we were looking out over our garden when a grouse burst out from the border of the woods. It shot across the garden and appeared heading squarely for our screen porch. We held our breath momentarily thinking it was going to crash headlong into the porch screen, but at the very last moment it zoomed up and over the porch and across the river toward the island.

Another grouse, or possibly the same bird, was not so lucky. Our breakfast was suddenly interrupted by a crash of splintering glass and, rushing out the front door, we found a ruffed grouse squeezed in between the storm window and the window itself. It had evidently mistaken the reflections in the glass for an opening in the trees. Carefully avoiding the jagged glass, I reached in and lifted it out to find it stunned but not seriously injured. Laying it carefully on the ground where it was partially concealed in a flowerbed, we watched it for nearly a half-hour when it finally stood up, fluffed out its feathers and took off for the Island.

A couple years later, while hiking on the island, I stepped over a fallen log and, from almost underfoot, a bright rusty-tailed ruffed grouse flushed and hurtled away, finally fading into the distant brush. With that

disappearing bird, the species also faded out as a member of the fauna of our wilderness sanctuary. Many times in recent years I have searched in vain, wondering why such a favorable little forest with numerous moss-covered drumming logs couldn't continue to attract this wonderful "King of Game Birds."

DECK

As I look back over our 56 years of living on the banks of the Mississippi River, I am puzzled over why I waited so long before putting into action my plan for a deck projecting out from the crest of our high bank. What a wonderful lunching place to take greater advantage of our riverside view!

Soon after my retirement in 1970, with our family grown and "out of the nest," I had more time to undertake this rather extensive building project. I must admit I have always had a strong tendency to be self-reliant. I loved to accomplish things on my own rather than organizing and relying on the efforts of others.

I first laid out my plans for the construction on paper. I realized that it would take some pretty heavy lifting, but my always-helpful son-in-law, Barbara's husband Bruce, had

Breck (shown here in 1995 at 92 years of age) on the deck over the Mississippi. For many years, family and friends enjoyed watching wildlife from the deck that Breck built entirely by hand after his retirement in 1970. It collapsed in 1996 when the bur oak around which it was built plunged down the bank.

already foreseen I might need some sort of energy multiplier, so he had given me a fine mechanical "block and tackle" device. With this at my disposal, it may have helped to finally get me into action on this project. I had all the timber required growing right in my little forest, and with my own muscle and my five-foot crosscut saw (before I acquired a chain saw), I cut several 20-foot oak logs eight to ten inches in diameter. These were too heavy to carry so I rolled them on short pieces of log from the woods to my building site. Then digging holes for supporting timbers, I began the construction with the help of my block and tackle suspended from a large limb of the big bur oak, and the deck gradually took shape. A ten-foot wooden walkway led along side of the big oak out to the 7 by 10-foot platform. This was adequate for several guests to enjoy the inviting view of the river and the cottonwood-bordered island beyond.

We enjoyed this form of the deck for some 15 years before we realized that decay was weakening some of the construction. Just last year (1994) I demolished the outer extension and reduced the size of the platform to about 5 by 7 feet, just enough to seat two or three persons for lunch or a quiet period of watching for whatever wildlife might be passing along the river. In view of my own aging physique, I accepted the generous offer of my neighbor, Louis Dinzl, to help me construct the somewhat shortened deck. He was an experienced carpenter and actually supervised this phase of the deck's construction. Over the years we have seen many little happenings enacted on the stage in front of this little rustic deck, no one of which deserves a lengthy report, but each at the time has afforded us considerable interest if not actual excitement.

I have only rarely made identifications of really rare birds from my deck perch. But two such sightings stick in my memory. One of these was when I pricked up my ears on seeing a strange newcomer pop into view from upstream. I quickly tried to distinguish certain field marks that would support my suspicions as to its identity – size of a ring-billed gull, a narrow dark band across its otherwise white under parts, a tail with elongated, sharply pointed central tail feathers and a dark back becoming darker on the head. I had only a quick look at the bird as it flew low over the water, downstream and out of my sight, but I had become acquainted with the species while on several arctic trips so I felt sure of my identification of the bird as a parasitic jaeger, a gull-like predator for which we had only a very few Minnesota records except on Lake Superior.

Quite a different rarity appeared during the drought period when the river water level was very low, exposing large areas of dry gravel. The snow bunting was fairly common in the fall and winter in the open prairie areas of the state, but its appearance in the wooded regions along the Mississippi River was quite unexpected. I had seen the bird frequently in the dry prairies of arctic Canada and Alaska, but when this unexpected snow bunting dropped in on the gravel area in front of my deck, it was lured by the similarity of this to its arctic habitat. Furthermore a single bird was unusual since this species almost invariably comes in large flocks, often numbering into the hundreds. To find this bird in these conditions is unusual; I left the deck and climbed down the bank to verify my identification.

Deer are almost constantly active on the island opposite the deck but only rarely do we catch fleeting glimpses of them since they are most active in the early morning and at dusk, while our lunches usually take us out to the deck at the noon hour.   But on one rare occasion we noticed activity among the bushes just back from the shore of the island and out stepped a slender, graceful white-tailed doe in its bright reddish summer pelage. Then a tiny spotted fawn appeared, took a long healthy drink from the river and then, much to our surprise, another fawn followed its twin for a drink. Then the doe slaked her thirst before the family retreated into the safety of the willows along the shore. Another wildlife actor, a beautiful dark brown mink, broke the monotony of one of our noonday lunches by appearing on the bank of the island. It proceeded to investigate carefully in, under and back of each fallen log or patch of driftwood where it presumably hoped to disturb a mouse or chipmunk from its hiding place for a chase and a possible meal. It continued probing for a hundred more yards along the shore before disappearing from my field of vision.

AN ATTIC MINK

Dorothy and I were sitting at our breakfast table one morning when we heard a scratching sound coming from the attic. "Well, I guess we must have another ambitious red squirrel invading our premises," we both thought. We occasionally had one of these active little rodents enlarge some small crack at a corner of our shingled roof, allowing it to squeeze in to prowl about in what must have been a chance for some exciting exploring. I usually live-trapped such intruders and released them a few miles up the River Road in a wooded patch away from any residents. In this case, I set my trap baited with sunflower seeds. The next morning as I climbed the stairs, I detected an odor that I thought must be some neighbor's tame ferret. However, on investigating my captive, I couldn't believe my eyes when I saw not a ferret, but one of its wild cousins, a beautiful, rich brown mink! I had never heard of a house being invaded by an animal considered to be wild and distinctly unfriendly toward humans. It had probably gained access to our house while in pursuit of mice, although we thought we had blocked all openings that would prevent even mice from entering. I, of course, was quite pleased to have the opportunity to examine a live, uninjured mink almost in hand. It is a well-known fact that mink are serious predators on wood ducks, birds we cherished as occupants of houses we had built especially for them. One might think, "Why not eliminate such a killer when I had the chance?" Actually nearly all creatures have enemies that prevent them from becoming too abundant. I felt that I should not interfere with Nature's functions, so I took my mink, trap and all, to my deck by the river for release. I had hoped to get a picture of the animal as it searched

the deck for access to the riverbank below. But it outwitted me by dashing from the trap, instantly recognizing its escape route, and scurrying down one of the deck support poles. I was disappointed not to get the picture but was much pleased to see the beautiful mink disappear so quickly back into its wooded habitat along the river.

BRACKENS BOTANY

Regarding the wildlife we have observed in our "mini-wilderness" I am including the Island as part of our little wildlife sanctuary, since it has no human occupants and still today (1995) is little disturbed by the bustling activities of advancing suburbia. Here we have identified 180 species of birds, 40 species of mammals, 20 of reptiles and 2 of amphibians. This involved some 56 years of hiking, paddling, photographing, studying, and snowshoeing to encounter this diversity of wildlife.

During the first few seasons when we were just beginning to get acquainted with our wild surroundings, I collected, identified and preserved specimens of about 125 species of the plants of our area. Among the plants, the trees, of course, were the dominant forms. The abundant species on the higher ground were the white elm, red or slippery elm, basswood, hackberry, green ash and black cherry while the soft maple, willows, cottonwood and black ash dominated the low riverbank areas. The understory on the upper levels found ironwood, alternate-leafed and gray dogwood, prickly ash and red-berried elder. Before our arrival our lots had been moderately grazed by goats and cattle resulting in the open nature of the woods as we found it. This admitted a few species of prairie plants such as turks-cap lily and goldenglow. We have carefully avoided any disturbance of the plant life and the thickening of the undergrowth. With the reduced light, these prairie plants have disappeared. We had one choice plant, the little purple showy orchis together with the strange ghostly white Indian pipe, that have also disappeared.
Actually it was the field of botany that gave

us the name for our mini-estate "The Brackens." Our family name, Breckenridge, began with the spelling Brackenridge, having its origin from the bracken ferns found in the hilly ridges of the Scotland-England border country. We were a bit disappointed not to find this fern on our lot, so we introduced a few plants that survived for a few years, but have all but died out recently. This species prefers sandy soil, that we do not have, which explains its disappearance.

RAISING HONEY BEES

As soon as we became the owners of our small mini-wilderness estate on the banks of the Mississippi we began planning to produce our own honey. This proved to be a major project and I'm not sure that we would have undertaken it if we had actually realized what a strenuous operation it turned out to be. But we were young and ambitious at the time and we pitched in vigorously and have really enjoyed the undertaking. My record book shows that I got my apiary equipment in the spring of 1942 and we harvested our first 65 pounds of honey from a single hive that fall. I was surprised to find in this book that I continued raising bees for 38 years.

My equipment to get started included two wooden hive bodies about two feet square. My single colony was housed in one of these hive bodies equipped with 10 or 12 frames. A frame consisted of four 1" wide strips of ¼ inch wood fastened in an open square that supported a thin sheet of beeswax. Both sides were covered by hundreds of circular impressions that the bees would build up into tubular cells for rearing of young and later to contain honey. These were placed vertically, side-by-side, to fill the hive body. A single frame will weigh several pounds when filled with honey.

Only one queen is active in such a colony. Her sole purpose is to lay eggs, one in each of the thousands of cells. The larvae then hatch and are fed until full grown. Then their cells are capped with wax and left until the grub-like larvae metamorphose into adult bees when they eat their way out of the cells to take up their lives as workers, drones (males) or queens. Reproduction takes place mainly during spring and summer. Then in late summer and fall all fifty to eighty thousand workers in the colony toil hard storing honey in the wax cells to provide food for the colony to survive over the winter. In a strong, healthy colony, the amount of honey stored is considerably more than required to feed the wintering adult bees. Bees do not hibernate but remain active in the hive throughout the winter. In the fall we could harvest this extra honey, leaving what we consider to be an adequate supply to provide food for the wintering colony. When the hive body becomes filled with honey, an additional hive body full of frames, called a "super," is placed on top of the hive. Sometimes as many as six supers might be added to a very strong colony in addition to the original hive body.

Harvesting honey was an all day operation in late summer or fall. Honey is very heavy and a full hive body can weigh as much as 80 pounds. So obviously the harvesting work can be a pretty strenuous task.

First, actually taking the honey from the hive is a tricky, somewhat hazardous job. Here my heavy, white coveralls with the wrists and ankles tied shut, bee proof canvas gloves and, of course, a hat and headnet complete my harvesting uniform for protection from the aggressive bees that resent being robbed of their hard earned supply of honey. In my wheelbarrow I have an empty hive body covered by a bee-proof lid to receive the honey filled frames. Removing the hive cover disturbs the working bees. A smoker puffing smoke over the mass of bees causes most of them to move down into the hive and forget to attack the intruder. Each frame, heavy with honey and covered with bees, is lifted out of the hive and the bees brushed off with a wide bee brush. The frame is then dropped into the empty hive body in the wheelbarrow and the top quickly placed over it. When this hive body is filled with honey-laden frames I wheel it into the garage and close the door to keep out any bees attracted by the odor of the honey. The honey is removed from the frames with a barrel-shaped tank equipped with a cage-like carrier revolved by a hand crank. Each cell of the frame, when filled with honey, is capped with wax. These caps have to be removed by slicing them off with a heated, long-bladed knife and the frames placed in the cage-like holder in the extractor. When filled, the holder is whirled rapidly by the crank and the honey thrown by centrifugal force against the side of the extractor where it trickles down and is removed through a valve into containers.

The whole harvesting process becomes a family affair with the youngsters watching and occasionally dipping a finger into the luscious honey and licking it off for a tasty sampling of the product. Dorothy's role was to gather and meticulously clean the various containers for collecting the honey as it comes from the extractor. One of my strongest colonies once produced 260 pounds of honey – enough for all our family's needs for the year plus gifts for many friends. As the kids grew older, they took more productive roles in the honey harvest, but it continued for some years to be a family affair. When they all grew up and left home Dorothy and I were left alone with the whole undertaking. We carried on for a few years while finding it more and more strenuous as the years passed. In 1980, after 38 years of beekeeping, we gave up the project and sold all of our equipment to another active apiarist.

FOXES

Although we occasionally see red foxes trotting along the riverbank or even snoozing at midday on top of our woodpile, our major source of evidence of their nocturnal presence at our river home was their tracks in the winter snows. Fox tracks around a huge elm near the riverbank once led me to leave some food scraps for the visitors. For several nights the morsels disappeared with tracks tentatively identified as those of a red fox. Wondering if my guess was correct, I set up my camera with a flash in the shelter of the birdbath a few yards from the big elm. A fine thread attached to the camera led to a juicy bone for bait. In the morning the bone was gone and the camera set off. I had the camera loaded with a 12-exposure film pack so I reset the apparatus for several consecutive nights with good results. Of course, we were anxious to learn what the camera had recorded when the film was processed. The recognizably good pictures contained a small menagerie of our night visitors. Among them was our neighbor's big black retriever, a stray cat, two raccoons and even a rabbit that accidentally tripped the thread. All these in addition to, not a red fox, but a gray fox, a species we had not known was living in our vicinity. So for a number of succeeding nights we supplied our choice visitor with table scrap tidbits and my apparatus took several more pictures.

While hiking on our island one day, I stumbled upon a fresh looking burrow near a large fallen log. I could not find recognizable tracks for me to make sure of the burrow's occupant but I assumed it was a woodchuck. A few days later I was picking my way carefully toward the burrow, hoping to spot its owner, when suddenly a sharp, little terrier-like bark attracted my attention off at right angles to my line of approach to the burrow. There, standing conspicuously in plain view, was a beautiful red fox. After it assured itself that I had seen it, the wily animal trotted off in a direction away from the burrow obviously trying to lead me away from his family's home base.

With this identification made, I placed a blind some 30 yards from the burrow and invited my 8-year old grandson to join me hoping to get some movies of the foxes. One cub finally appeared and played briefly with a strange-looking tapered object I could not identify. The cub soon retreated into the burrow and refused to come out, so we went over to examine the plaything, which surprisingly proved to be the backbone of a large fish. The explanation for its presence here was that there was a backwater of the river nearby where spawning carp could be seen with their backs showing above the water. Here the fox could have gotten a good meal without more than getting its feet wet.

CONCRETIONS

During the drought years in the 1930s the Mississippi River channel by our home all but disappeared. In fact it stopped flowing entirely and all that remained was a disconnected chain of puddles. We found lots of entertainment in walking the streambeds searching for oddities such as boom chains from the logging days. Many clams showed up that were not visible when the water was at normal levels. Undoubtedly one of the oddities that aroused the most lasting interest was the concretions. These were noticed at first simply as strangely shaped stones that our youngsters picked up and commented on what they looked like – odd faces, mammals and birds or just abstract forms. They had no idea where they came from or what caused their strange shapes until they noticed that many were only partly exposed in the eroding soil along the shore. They began asking me questions about them and the only answer I could give them was that they were called concretions and that chemical deposits in the soil formed them. I had some sketchy knowledge of them, but their abundance here stirred my curiosity and I contacted several geologists at the University, finally inviting Dr. Herbert Wright, a specialist in the study of glacial soils, to look over our deposits. We had been digging in the bank while installing our septic tank and this gave him the opportunity to examine the various deposits and his explanations were very revealing. Three principal glacial deposits formed our bank. At the bottom of the river was a red soil of an acid character that had been deposited by the glacial advance from the Lake Superior area. Many thousands of years ago, after that ice melted, the area must have been a quiet lake for many years, laying down from 10 to 15 feet of fine clay. Then the last glacial advance, the Mankato, covered this area. Having come from the northwest, it brought in another 10 to 15 feet of calcareous soil. During recent centuries, rain falling on the surface dissolved calcium from the upper layer. In percolating down, the water passed through the clay layer and, on encountering the red acid soil, began depositing the calcium. Cer-

tain organic materials such as bud scales or rootlets attracted the calcium particles and very slowly (how many years is unknown) the calcium accumulated in layer after layer on the growing concretions. Where several of these happened to be lying close together, the calcium cemented two or more concretions together to form odd shapes. And as the flowing river washed away the surrounding red soil, the limestone-like concretions slid down into the riverbed waiting for us to pick them up for our collections.

We now have them resembling a woodchuck, a little chicken, a mother and children, a Volkswagen and an elephant with an enormously long trunk. (Illustration is chapter heading) Strangely enough, a half-mile down stream these formed around horizontal roots which produced concretions several feet long and only an inch or so in diameter. A neighbor boy first showed me one of these about five feet long. On investigating the area I uncovered another over 12 feet long. A Smithsonian Institution staff geologist happened to be visiting the Bell Museum several years ago and we got to discussing concretions. I asked him if he had ever encountered such long, snake-like concretions and his answer was, "No, I don't recall ever seeing any." And when I asked him if they would like this particular 12-foot specimen for their collections, his enthuslastic answer was, "Very definitely, yes. I'm sure the Museum would be delighted to have the specimen."

Soon after this conversation I was scheduled to speak on an Audubon Screen Tour in Washington D.C. so I packed up the specimen in three or four-foot sections and delivered it personally to the Museum for their permanent collection. The following is the data that accompanied the 12-foot concretion given to the U.S. National Museum in March 1970:

"This specimen of concretion when assembled is slightly over 12 feet long. It was formed in laminated clay layers 15 to 20 feet below the surface in a layer of 6 to 8 feet of gray glacial drift laid down by the most recent glacial invasion into this region which

receded about 10,000 to 12,000 years ago.
The exact location of the find was in the west
bank of the Mississippi River approximately
two and one half miles above the Belt Line
bridge (Highway #694) over the river. Pro-
ceed north on the West River Road (Highway
#169) to 85th Avenue North, turn right,
east, to its dead end a couple hundred yards,
continue on east over private property and
down over the bank to the water's edge.
This is about nine and a half miles upstream
from the power dam, which represents the
original St. Anthony Falls. I'm sorry I did not
check the range and township designation of
this find.

This may be considered as a gift from the
Bell Museum of Natural History, Univ. of Minnesota."

Dr. W. J. Breckenridge
Director, Bell Museum

Wood Ducks

Chapter 8: Wood Ducks

Our first excitement over wood ducks came the very first spring while we were still settling in our new riverside home. At breakfast one morning we were really excited when a female wood duck alighted on a limb of the big oak tree on the riverbank to be followed closely by a beautiful male. "Do you suppose that we will be lucky enough to have wood ducks actually nesting in the hollow trees in our woods?" was the question going through our heads at that moment. We had no idea what an important role these colorful, unpredictable tree ducks were to play for us in the years following. (Plate 9)

Although wood ducks originally nested exclusively in hollow trees, they have become accustomed to substituting man-made houses for the cavities. (Plate 10) So we soon made several houses available for them. To many neophyte birders, to see a duck perching high up in a tree is a real surprise. Actually there are a number of northern waterfowl besides wood ducks that do just that. Buffleheads, American and Barrow's goldeneyes, and American and hooded mergansers all may be found searching for cavities in trees for nesting. Wood ducks prefer surprisingly small openings for nesting cavities – as small as three and a half inches across. Wood ducks provide no nesting materials but depend on the pulverized rotten wood to form the depression for the eggs. Normally about 9 to 15 eggs compose a clutch

and no incubating is done until the clutch is complete. This is to make sure that all the eggs will hatch at about the same time. The female lays one egg early in the morning and visits the nest only once a day for the few minutes needed to lay the egg. This allowed us to count the eggs at about midday without disturbing the female. Since the female visits the nest only once a day, many people fail to realize that ducks are nesting in their houses. If one is not alert and doesn't see the bird enter or leave the house, he will assume that no eggs have been laid. The first two or three eggs laid will be buried in the nest material, but as more eggs are laid the duck plucks down from her breast to cover the eggs. By the time the clutch is nearing completion, a double handful may be found. During egg laying the female is usually accompanied by the male. He will sit nearby and await the female's leaving the nest and accompany her down to the river for the day. (Plate 11) Regarding the birds' entering the nest cavity, some observers have stated that a duck will fly directly into the cavity at full speed. I have watched birds enter nests scores of times and I have never seen this happen. (Ed. Note: Or as WJB once reluctantly agreed, "It is possible, but only once.") Severe physical injury could hardly be avoided if they did this. As I have seen, the ducks will fly in slightly below the level of the entrance, then swoop up and grasp the edge of the entrance, tip up and enter the cavity.

A second or even a third female we found will enter and examine the same cavity with no animosity being displayed by the birds. To us as observers, these searching flights were very time consuming and at times became very annoying, particularly when I felt I should be leaving for work after breakfast. When two or three pairs crisscrossed in the trees, the confusion made it practically impossible to keep track of mates and which duck was inspecting which cavity. This might last for only a few minutes to an hour or more. Occasionally our calculations as to the date of the onset of incubation was confused by the appearance of two eggs in a day, indicating that more than one duck was laying in the nest. This may continue and develop into a serious competition as to which female will incubate the set of eggs. In some nests the number of eggs goes far beyond the ability of a little female wood duck to cover. In 52 nestings on which I have kept data, 14 have had 20 or more eggs. In 1966, one of our houses contained 30 eggs, which were laid by two or possibly three females. A couple of possibilities for action on my part were considered. First, I could do nothing and see how many eggs would hatch. Second, I could remove 10 or 12 eggs and feel quite confident that she could bring 18 or 20 eggs through to hatching. In this case I chose the first alternative while realizing that in turning the 30 eggs some would most certainly be rolled out beyond the reach of her body heat and the embryos would die. I found that this did happen with 20 of the eggs and she emerged with a brood of only 10 young.

The most surprising dump nest in our experience was in a very choice hollow basswood tree leaning out over the river. I made an egg count every 3 or 4 days and on several occasions 6 or 8 eggs appeared in that period. Finally an enormous clutch of 35 eggs was deposited. Evidently the task of incubating such a mass of eggs was too much for either of the two or perhaps three laying ducks and the nest was deserted. I then removed the entire clutch and to my amazement more eggs began to appear and 12 more were laid before the nest was finally abandoned and

Watching for trouble

no young ever produced in that nest that year. I thought that 47 eggs in one nest in one year was something of a record for even a tolerant wood duck.

The same basswood tree where the ducks carried on their 47-egg competition was again occupied the following year. I had shinnied up the leaning tree on various occasions to check the progress of the nest and I had noticed an inch wide crack extending for some distance up from the base of the tree. On this particular occasion I had halted my climb momentarily to catch my breath and, peering into the crack, I saw the black beady eyes of another climber, but he was inside the hollow trunk while I was wrapped around the outside. Adjusting my eyes to the dark interior, I finally recognized, with something of a start, a little spotted skunk staring at me only inches from my nose. Realizing that he could not possibly turn around in such close quarters and train his vital artillery on me, I completed my check of the duck's nest and returned to the house to get my bee smoker, hoping to dislodge the intruder – but he refused to be dislodged. The crack in the tree trunk allowed too much smoke to seep out, rendering my efforts completely ineffective and I had to give up my effort. I was quite sure that the tree trunk was not hollow all the way up to the duck's nest, and I did not think that a spotted skunk was a sufficiently skillful arborealist to climb to the nest on the outside of the tree, so I simply surrendered the field to my adversary.

A day or two later I found that the duck eggs were hatching so I established a photographic blind for action early the next morning. Up at daybreak, I spent an hour waiting for some action on the part of the ducklings or their mother, but nothing happened. I was there for another hour and began to get concerned that something had happened to the brood. I recalled my spotted friend in the hollow trunk but did not think that he could have played havoc at the nest. Finally a strange, unexpected thing happened. A female wood duck flew in, not into the entrance as I had expected, but on the leaning trunk on the side opposite the doorway. Then clinging to the bark, the bird inched its way around the trunk and looked suspiciously into the nest. What a puzzle! Was this the mother of the newly hatched brood that had left the nest without my seeing it? I thought this was impossible. Had she been frightened and left the nest before I entered my blind? I was completely confused as to an explanation. After a few quick looks, the bird flew away. This did not clarify matters at all. So I immediately climbed up to the nest to find only a few fragments of duckling down and the shattered skull of a female wood duck. Obviously the little spotted predator had eliminated the family, but my questions as to the identity of the concerned female were unanswered. Could this have been simply an inquisitive neighbor that had known of the tragedy or is it possible that both females had been brooding the newly hatched family and she had been lucky enough to escape, not knowing what subsequently had happened? There is a case reported in the literature of two ducks incubating side by side in the same nest. I had no evidence that two birds might have been involved in this incubation. So still to this day, the mystery of the murdered mother remains unsolved. I do have reason to suspect the spotted skunk, but I have no real evidence to pin the killing on it.

Sometimes these birds choose strange cavities for nesting. Several springs ago my neighbor, Carl Swanson, heard a scratching sound coming from his fireplace. He thought it probably was a squirrel and it could easily crawl back up the chimney if and when it saw fit to do so. However, the following day he heard the sound again and, putting on a leather glove just in case it was a squirrel or a raccoon, he opened the draft and reached cautiously up over the damper in the chimney. He soon realized that the glove was not necessary since he felt not fur but feathers, and he retrieved a female wood duck. The poor sooty victim was seriously dehydrated as well as dirty and hungry so he dusted it off and gave it a long satisfying drink. He was a bit apprehensive about its ability to fly after being weakened by an unknown period of fasting. However, hoping for the best he took it out to the edge of the high riverbank and tossed it out over the water. To his great satisfaction the definitely below par little duck glided successfully down river a short way and alighted on the water apparently not too much the worse for its hazardous experience.

We have had a flicker and a flying squirrel make the mistake of entering our chimney, but never a wood duck. Since open chimneys do pose a threat to these forms of wildlife, it is a good idea to cap your chimney with a coarse screen of some type to prevent such accidents to the wildlife seeking homes on your premises.

Another strange nesting was found when a female wood duck chose to nest in a small cavity in a brick wall facing the alley back of a hotel in the middle of the business district of Minneapolis. Her brood hatched and when she tried to assemble her family, some of the ducklings wandered into the hotel lobby. An employee called the Department of Natural Resources and a Conservation Officer came and was amazed to find the female allowed him to pick her up and collect her brood into a small box. The story ended very successfully when he liberated them in a ducky looking marsh just outside the city.

71

One of our wood duck pairs were privileged to live for one season in a very special apartment designed to give us more data about their life habits and they produced some surprising results. I wanted to know how much time the female spent away from the nest during the long incubation period. To get this information I constructed a house with a movable floor set on four springs that would lift the floor when the bird left and drop back when it returned. The recording drum was a cake pan fastened to the hour hand of a Big Ben alarm clock. A recording tape was wrapped around the cake pan, which recorded the movements of a pointer attached to the moving floor. This gave me a complete record of the comings and goings of the bird for a twelve-hour period. Nesting material once jammed the complicated mechanism and I had to remove the house for the repairs. When I climbed to the house to take it down the female was on her eggs and gave no indication of leaving. I had to remove the big lag screw supporting the house with a large monkey wrench and with every turn of the wrench it almost touched her back, but this action did not disturb her. Finally I tied a rope around the house and slowly lowered the house to the ground with its incubating occupant still undisturbed. The repairs had to be done indoors so I carried the house into my shop and I actually reached in and lifted her from her eggs and released her out of the shop door. After the repairs were completed I replaced the house in the tree and within a couple of hours the duck returned to her incubation. On several occasions I thought it was remarkable that an incubating duck had allowed me to reach under her and place a band on her leg, but this case was certainly a good example of the extreme attentiveness these birds will exhibit when threatened with disturbance.

At this same special house, earlier in the season during the egg laying period, another most unusual event occurred. As noted above, the recording tapes had to be replaced twice a day. When I was away for a few days, my teenage daughter Betsy offered to change the tapes for me. One morning when changing them, she lifted the roof to glance at the eggs and was surprised, and not a little alarmed, to see the house nearly full of a mass of black and white feathers.

Probing more deeply into the mass of feathers, she found a number of small dead birds. With help from her brother, Tom, she got a bucket and removed about a dozen badly bruised carcasses of what proved to be tree swallows. The reason for this tragedy appeared to be that it had been an early spring and a light snow was falling the evening before. Early migrating tree swallows had noticed the opening in the wood duck house and, being accustomed to entering cavities for shelter and nesting, they had found the duck house to be a wonderfully cozy place for the night. The partially completed clutch of eggs covered with down undoubtedly made it even cozier. There they had spent the night and, since it was still chilly the next morning, they were in no hurry to leave the warm quarters. About sunrise the female wood duck arrived on schedule to lay another egg. Her body blocked the only exit for the unfortunate swallows and the duck, resenting the intrusion, proceeded to dispatch the trapped birds. After such a disturbance she left the house but did not actually desert the nest. She returned after the avian victims had been removed and, finding the eggs still intact, she laid the egg due to be laid that day. From then on the nesting process continued normally.

On one occasion I saw a female wood duck alight at a cavity 30 feet up in a basswood tree. The male accompanying her flew on beyond the tree to a perch where he could not see the female. Normally he would wait until his mate had completed her investigation of the cavity and they would leave together. In this case the female had not gone completely into the hole but remained with her tail projecting visibly. I was watching while shaving and was puzzled over why she did not either enter the cavity or leave within a few minutes. After eating breakfast I checked again and neither bird had moved. When I left for work I asked my wife, Dorothy, to watch and see what might happen. Her surprising answer later was that no change had occurred throughout the entire morning. After lunch we went to a memorial service for a friend and on returning about four in the afternoon the birds were still in the same positions. This situation seemed to demand an investigation so I borrowed a neighbor's long extension ladder and, as I put the ladder in place, the female appeared to pull herself free and both birds left. On examining the cavity I could find no V-shaped formation where her head might have been wedged near the mouth of the cavity. This being the case, I am still at a loss for a satisfactory explanation for this unusual performance of these birds. At least it did provide an excellent example of the almost unbelievable attentiveness on the part of the male duck.

There is no doubt that the most exciting activity of our wood ducks was when the female would bring her brood out of the house to begin their precarious growing up existence. This happens as soon as the eggs have all hatched and the ducklings have dried off and are anxious to get going, usually on the very next day after hatching.

Our friend, Gustav Swanson, described this action admirably in an article "A Passion for Wood Ducks" that appeared in *Watchers Digest* March-April 1987 as follows:

"On the selected day the first clue to the timing of the emergence will be the appearance of the mother wood duck in the nest opening. She will come up from the nest cavity where she has been brooding the young and will survey the surroundings for signs for any disturbances or enemies. If she sees anything that might suggest danger she returns back into the nest cavity for a while before returning to the nest entrance to survey the surroundings again. In the case of the nest we were watching the hen conducted three such surveys over 30 minutes before she was satisfied. Then she dropped to the ground and began to call the young to come out. The ducklings only a day or less from hatching are remarkably strong and able to clamber a foot or more up from the nest to the entrance. Their claws are so sharp that they have no trouble in a natural cavity where the wood is rough or rotted,

but in nesting boxes made of smooth planed lumber Breck adds a strip of window screen as a ladder from the bottom of the box to the entrance hole, and the ducklings climb up this very quickly. In only a few minutes after the female we were watching dropped to the ground and began calling we had counted 15 ducklings appearing at the entrance and dropping out. Breck had counted 16 eggs in the nest so we assumed that one egg did not hatch.

"We were surprised at the vigor the ducklings displayed in bursting forth. Twice two ducklings reached the entrance at the same time and leaped out and once three left at the same time and the others, though coming singly, came in quick succession. They didn't simply drop down. They took off with a vigorous leap so that some landed five or six feet from the post on which their nesting was supported. The mother waited until all 15 had come out and then quickly began with calling the brood to the edge of the steep riverbank where they scrambled and tumbled to the water's edge. On reaching the water the little ones plunged in as expert swimmers right from the start and after heading upstream along the shore for some distance, they usually strike off across the fifty yards of swift current to reach the island where the female will feel relatively safe to raise her family.

"One of the Breckenridge's chief rewards for their wood duck efforts is being able to share with friends and larger audiences what they have observed and learned. As a bird artist, Breck has done wood ducks in pen and ink drawings for illustrations, in etchings and in paintings. As a skilled wildlife photographer he has made a fine comprehensive film of the life of the wood duck that has been shown widely around the country. But the very best way of sharing wood duck pleasures is to be able to invite close friends to one of the "Coming Out Parties" and with long experience the Breckenridges have developed this event to perfection despite the uncertainties and suspense. Breck's checking on the incubation stage has been so careful that he can nearly always predict the morning when the ducklings will come out, but the watchers must be patient because the exact time the birds appear varies so much.

"Dorothy prepares a distinctive breakfast for her guests. Sudden activity at the wood duck house may occur for an unpredictable period so she has developed an egg dish that can wait two or three hours on warm in the electric frying pan and still be delectable. Dorothy's "Slow Poke Eggs" is especially appropriate for bird watchers' breakfasts or any time when schedules may be uncertain. Here is her recipe:

SLOW-POKE EGGS

7 eggs
pepper
3 cups whole milk
2 teaspoons snipped chives
1 teaspoon salt
2 tablespoons butter

Beat eggs about 1 minute. Add milk, heated to lukewarm. Add seasonings. Melt butter in large electric skillet at 300°. Pour in egg mixture and lower heat to 200°; cover. Do not let eggs boil or bubble. Very low temperature is essential or eggs will be tough and watery. Cook 1 hour. Can be kept on warm setting until served.
8 servings. Bon Appétit!"

It will be of interest to wood duck watchers to know just how I determine the possible date for the coming out event. After I am reasonably sure that eggs are being laid, I will check the nest and carefully count the eggs. Say, on April 10 I find three eggs. I will not bother checking again until about April 20 when I may count 13 eggs. This could be a complete set but if I did not flush the female when I made my noon inspection, I can conclude that incubation has not started. On April 29 I find 14 eggs and the duck flushes from the nest when I make my midday inspection. This makes it obvious that the 14th egg was undoubtedly laid on April 21 and incubation was undertaken on that day. The incubation period for wood ducks is usually 29-31 days. Thirty days from April 21 would be May 21 and this would probably be the

day on which the young would be hatching. I probably would check the nest for hatching a day earlier to make sure my calculations were correct. Thus with a minimum of only three inspections of the nest, I would know when the young would be coming out.

A five-page report on the results of our several-year study of the wood ducks appeared in the January issue of the *Journal of Wildlife Management.* This was illustrated by a drawing of the recording apparatus used in the study, three bar graphs and three line graphs explaining the relation of temperature to the incubation period of the ducks. The condensed summary of the findings in the publication follows:

"An automatic apparatus recorded nest activity from a floating floor in a wood duck house. Laying of eight eggs in 1949 occurred between 5:00 and 8:00 in the mornings. Time female spent on the nest during egg-laying varied from 8 minutes to 3 hours and 11 minutes average one hour and 48 minutes. Nest attentiveness was recorded for 1948, 1949 and 1950. A definite tendency for the bird to sit closer on cool days was recorded. Normal time off the nest per 24 hours varied from 13 minutes to 4 hours and 40 minutes. The effectiveness of the down blanket was checked by thermocouple terminals cast in a plaster of Paris egg, which was screwed in position in the nest. In one period when the female was off the nest for 1 hour and 22 minutes with outside temperatures of 63F-61F, the nest temperature dropped 13.5F. A study of chilling due to disturbances driving the incubating hen off the nest indicated that the shortest incubation period (25 days) was recorded during the season when no major disturbances occurred. Incubation periods of 29-30 and 31 days were recorded on years when serious chilling of the eggs occurred. It is suggested that the shortest incubation period for any species approaches most nearly the period characteristic of the species since no disturbances will shorten the period but severe chilling greatly increases the incubation period."

Red-tailed hawk

Chapter 9: Birds of Prey

HAWKS

Ospreys

Once while lunching on the deck I heard a piercing whistle from downstream and watched for the osprey to fly by, perhaps carrying a fish. The bird did appear with a foot-long carp in its talons. I have keen memories of how well fitted its talons were for taking fish since years ago I had made a drawing for Dr. Roberts' *Birds of Minnesota* of the almost semicircular claws and the rough, rasp-like under surfaces of its feet that assured its holding securely any fish it might pluck from the water. This bird appeared to be eyeing an appropriate dead tree limb only 20 yards from my deck and it surprised me by alighting there. Although obviously aware of my presence, it was not alarmed and did not take off, but calmly began tearing its prey apart and swallowing it bit by bit. I began to move slowly and eventually went on eating my lunch while the friendly osprey did the same. I wonder if many ornithologists have ever had lunch with an osprey at such close range. (Plate 12A)

Again one of my "red letter" days on my deck involved an osprey. I was sitting on a rock by the water's edge just below the deck, Pentax camera in hand, photographing concretions, I believe, when an equally friendly osprey came along and alighted in the same dead tree but without a fish. It stared intently at the water below awaiting its chance to plunge for its prey. The bird actually allowed me to bring my camera slowly up and focus on the bird without disturbing it. My arm muscles began tiring before the bird finally plunged. I followed it down with my camera and pushed the button just as it hit the water. "What a striking shot this will turn out to be!" was my thought as the bird flew off with its fish. After waiting impatiently for the few days for the film to be developed, I was sadly disappointed to find I had a perfectly good picture of a huge splash of water, but no osprey. Obviously I had pushed the button a few thousands of a second too late.

Swallow-tailed Kites

I have never seen one of these striking birds in Minnesota, but I have seen them frequently in Costa Rica, Central America. Dr. Roberts reported seeing swallow-tailed kites every day while serving on a survey crew west of Anoka back in the 1870s. Today (1997) the bird is seen very rarely, perhaps once in 5 or 10 years. One specimen was picked up as a road kill in Marine-on-the-St. Croix on April 27, 1966. (Plate 12B) It was turned in to the Bell Museum and is now in the Museum's scientific bird skin collections. This is a tragic loss to Minnesota's wildlife fauna. A fairly approachable species, its disappearance can probably be credited to careless shooters unconcerned about losses to our wonderfully diverse wildlife.

Goshawk

The hawk depicted here is eyeing a pheasant. This is the largest of the three hawk species know as bird hawks, the accipiters. (Plate 13A) The smallest of the group is the sharp-shinned hawk, and the intermediate one is the Cooper's hawk. The word "accipiter" is derived from the Latin word, "accipere," meaning "to take or seize." All of these hawks have similar characteristics – long tail and short rounded wings - which make them difficult to distinguish, particularly in their immature plumage when all three have breast stripes running parallel to the body. As an adult, the goshawk is the most easily identified by its all-gray color and finely cross-barred breast. All hawks are easily misidentified. John B. May in his *Hawks of North America* reported that years ago when the Pennsylvania Game Commission gave bounties on goshawks, only 76 of the 503 birds submitted for payment were actually goshawks. In the field one cannot help but admire this bird's dashing, powerful flight ability as it hurtles through the woods in pursuit of one of its favorite prey species, the ruffed grouse, no mean flier itself in a short burst of speed. The short wings and long tail make it especially well adapted to twisting and turning to avoid twigs and branches in hunting. It is often appropriately compared to a fighter plane in aviation terms. This raptor, as with all predators, is often condemned for killing what Man classes as highly desirable birds. However, in recent years we have come to reassess this bird's value and are extending protection to all hawks as balancing factors in maintaining sustainable populations of all species, in other words, preserving our wonderful diversity of life.

Peregrine Falcons

One of my favorite birds is the peregrine falcon. (Plate 13B) Several Minnesota raptors have fluctuated greatly in abundance during the past century due directly and indirectly to human disturbance. The spectacular peregrine falcon has experienced contact with Man dating back into prehistoric times. Its hunting abilities attracted the attention of primitive humans who first realized the bird had possibilities for aiding his food gathering efforts. This resulted in its being subjected to semi-domestication in the activity of falconry. This at first was regarded as a practical means of securing food but it also became a sport engaged in mainly by royalty with the use of different species of falcons being limited to the various social levels of the ruling classes. Still today, falconry is the sport of a very limited group who are willing to engage in the burdensome care and training of the birds. Of the numerous species of falcons, the peregrine was the most widely sought after. The bird was found throughout the subarctic parts of both hemispheres, although it never was abundant or even common.

As with most raptors, peregrines are very aggressive and defend large territories. The presence of suitable precipitous cliffs on which to nest limits their populations. In Minnesota such favorable cliffs were to be found only along the Mississippi River, the North Shore of Lake Superior and a few in the Iron Range in the northeastern part of the state. My experience with the species began when I first arrived in the state in 1926. At that time hawks were regarded as destructive predators that should be eliminated as protection for the birds of value to Man. Hawk shooting was widely practiced by most sportsmen. During the early years of studying and evaluating birds, ornithologists often classified the various species as "beneficial" or "detrimental" with only the human point of view considered. The more we study the ecology of all the diverse forms of wildlife, the more we tend to view the entire fauna and flora as a complex organization with many checks and balances resulting in a somewhat fluctuating balance being maintained throughout our natural environment. Thus predators such as the peregrine are no longer seen as bloodthirsty, undesirable killers, but simply as controlling factors in maintaining the balance of the populations of the various species that the falcons prey upon. (Plate 14A)

Illustrating this change of attitude, we find that back in the 1930s bird watchers in Detroit, Michigan were much disturbed by the pair of peregrines nesting on one of their tall buildings and living on pigeons. They appealed to the police and induced them to shoot the offending falcons. In fact, one of Dr. Roberts' best reporting ornithologists who lived in southwestern Minnesota, Alfred Peterson, had a hobby of hawk shooting. He would occasionally send large boxes of hawk specimens to the Museum, many of which I prepared as scientific skins for the Museum's collections. This shooting of hawks was the major enemy limiting their populations until the discovery in the 1930s that the widely used pesticide, DDT was found to be causing these birds to lay thin-shelled eggs that failed to survive incubation. This subtle enemy caused peregrines to disappear almost completely from North America east of the Rockies including Minnesota.

Now we are reestablishing the peregrines and encouraging them to nest in the cities as checks on the pigeon populations. For years peregrines have nested on skyscrapers even in the largest cities, accepting them as suitable substitutes for rocky cliffs, with city-dwelling pigeons providing an excellent food supply. By careful protection of these birds and by restoring captive-reared birds to previously occupied cliffs, the peregrines are well on their way to recovering their original normal populations.

I recall hearing Dr. Roberts comment about encountering peregrines along the North Shore of Lake Superior back in 1879. On August 29 he saw a much-agitated pair of birds, indicating nesting on Carleton's Peak near Tofte. He asked me, when I made a trip along the Shore in the spring of 1927, to check Carleton's Peak to see if they still nested there. To make this reconnaissance, I drove my little Model T Ford along bumpy logging roads leading up back of the Peak. No trail existed up the mountain so I hoofed it up to the summit, watching and listening for the sharp "cac-cac" calls of the peregrine that could have indicated nesting, but without success. I recall distinctly that

during my climb, a dense fog engulfed all the surroundings of the Peak. On reaching the top I burst out of the fog into bright, sunny blue weather and, looking down on all sides, I saw nothing but fog. I had the odd feeling that I was on top of the world that consisted only of the treeless rocks on which I stood that were floating on a sea of fog. I believe this was the only time in my life when I had that strange feeling of isolation from the rest of the world – all due to my unsuccessful search for nesting peregrines on Carleton's Peak.

I had better luck on numerous occasions along Superior's North Shore. One spring I stayed briefly with an old fisherman, Hans Engelson and his family. He was attending his nets in the Lake and agreed to my going along to observe and possibly to photograph the flocks of old squaw ducks that were wintering on Superior. He and his helper had a fine catch of herring, and on returning close along the shore, I heard the characteristic calls of peregrine falcons. They appeared to be staking out their territory in a rocky cove that Hans told me they called the "Finn Church." We saw no signs of a nest but I kept in mind the location of the cove. On returning to his fishhouse I drove my car along the shore to where I estimated I was opposite the Finn Church. Pushing my way through the brushy cover to the brink of the cliff, I located a sturdy-looking aspen very near the edge. Grasping its trunk I leaned far out for a good view of the cove – and was I surprised and excited to find myself peering directly down on the back of an incubating peregrine! My close approach alarmed the bird that immediately flew from the nest and was joined by its smaller mate. They flew about, greatly agitated but made no threatening dives at me. The aerie was inaccessible without ropes, but I was greatly disappointed that my schedule did not permit me to spend more time at this exciting situation.

Later I discovered another peregrine nest near Little Marais. On this trip I often stopped along the highway where I could scan the shore listening and watching for peregrines. Near Kennedy Creek I noted that the outline of the ledges across the cove formed the profile of an Indian face and to my satisfaction, a circling peregrine soon appeared. I settled down for some careful study of its actions and sure enough, it alighted several times in the eye of the Indian face – undoubtedly a nest site. I found that I could approach the nesting ledge by climbing down and around the point of the cliff. Then, through the twisted branches of a gnarled spruce tree, I could see four downy white, half-grown peregrine chicks. The cedar tree afforded excellent cover for a photographic blind, so I loaded up gear and a small roll of burlap for this particular purpose and settled down in concealment for the return of a parent bird. After a long tedious but tense wait, the young birds began to stir and in came one of the adult birds carrying a black mass which turned out to be a large portion of a crow. After glaring belligerently at the strange new object in the cedar branches it proceeded to tear off bits of the carcass and fed them to the chicks. When my movie camera began to buzz, all actions halted temporarily, but they soon became accustomed to the strange sound and completed their meal. An enlargement from the resulting film appeared in volume one of Dr. Roberts' *Birds of Minnesota*, page 355.

All during my years with the Bell Museum, I justified my shooting a good many birds (with special Minnesota and U.S. scientific collecting permits) to aid Dr. Roberts in his writing the book *Birds of Minnesota*. Many species required series of several specimens to enable descriptions to cover plumage variations such as summer and winter plumages, first and second year plumages and simple variations in adult birds. Further collecting of specimens was required for building the habitat groups for educational purposes. Rare and endangered birds were never taken, but old specimens originally poorly mounted by taxidermists were relaxed and remounted for the groups.

In my early years at the Museum peregrine falcons were not common, but we knew that several pairs were present on the North Shore, and the taking of specimens was legal and justified, although I always hated to be asked to take them. We were anxious to have a small group showing this spectacular bird at a nest. In this case we decided that a nest with two young along the Superior North Shore would be sacrificed for this display. After shooting one adult bird I was lowered by rope to the precariously perched nest. There I made copious notes and took many photographs on the nature of the nesting situation and took the downy young. I made careful color notes of these live birds. They were then dispatched, skinned carefully and salted, for return to the Museum for mounting. Here a most unfortunate thing happened. We had no deep-freeze unit in the Museum but we knew that the Anatomy Department of the Medical School had one just across the street, so we got permission to store these specimens in their freezer until I had time to mount them. When I went to get them they were gone!! The Medical Department's explanation was that an inexperienced assistant had been told to "clean out the freezer" and this he did with a vengeance, without any consideration for our name plainly written on the package. Thus the preparation of our group was interrupted. The adult bird was mounted, the photographic background was completed, and the foreground constructed. We definitely did not want to take any more peregrines, young or eggs from the wild. What to do? After some thought, I carefully measured some of the Museum's egg collections and found that the white eggs of the marsh hawk were exactly the size of the peregrine's. So I carefully colored a set of marsh hawk eggs, a much commoner species of hawk, and the group was completed, not as spectacularly as it might have been with two cute, fuzzy young falcons but with a set of beautiful rich brown eggs in their place. No one has ever questioned the real identity of the eggs although the Museum staff was informed.

Several more nests of Minnesota peregrines were found with a couple that stand out in my memory as decidedly abnormal. The local conservation officer (then known as game warden) told me of a nest on the top of a cliff at the mouth of Crow Creek just above Encampment Forest. This one could be approached by simply walking 100 yards from the road to the edge of the cliff. There the nest was perched on a bare rocky surface on a level with the surrounding wooded terrain – a most unexpected location for a peregrine aerie. The other oddly situated nest was near the top of a limestone ledge along the Saint Croix River above Stillwater. Here I found where a portion of the cliff had cracked away from the main body of the cliff and had shifted out several feet, but appeared to be still firmly supported from below. I could climb out onto this disconnected segment of the rock and look down only a few yards onto the ledge supporting the nest. The warden told me that the nest had been occupied by peregrines the previous year and I checked it later that spring but no eggs appeared. So I was frustrated in not being able to photograph such an inviting situation.

The really satisfying project of restoring the populations of peregrines in Minnesota is a long story of its own. I had only occasional contacts with Dr. Harrison Tordoff, Director of the Bell Museum following me, and veterinarian Dr. Pat Redig, Director of the Gabbert Raptor Rehabilitation Center of the University. The Veterinarian Department did much of the field work and record keeping of the project. I kept in touch with their various successes as a member of the advisory Board of the Raptor Center for several years until my loss of hearing forced me to retire in 1994.

Red-tailed Hawk

In the painting of the red-tailed hawk at the nest, the flying bird coming in shows a pale reddish color on the underside of the tail. (Plate 14B) This is not partial albinism but is the normal color of the under side of the tails of all red-tailed hawks. This accounts for the fact that in field observations, one must study a soaring bird until it turns showing the rich reddish of the upper surface of the tail, which is the so-called red tail of the species.

The beautiful, pale-colored, red-tail is not a partial albino but a very light colored phase called the Krider's hawk. One evening a staff person from the Gabbert Raptor Center on the University's Saint Paul Campus spoke to the members of the Breckenridge Chapter of the Izaak Walton League about the work of the Center. She demonstrated with a rehabilitated Krider's hawk that was the palest I had ever seen. I later visited the Center and studied and sketched the bird in order to depict it correctly.

Prairie Falcon

On August 14, 1931, while on our way across the Wyoming prairies enroute to Allan Brooks' home in Okanagan Landing, Canada, Northrop Beech and I were constantly on the lookout for unusual prairie birds. One I was particularly anxious to see was the prairie falcon. A short distance east of the town of Sundance, we finally spotted one perched on a roadside fence post just ahead of our car. (Plate 15A) As we approached, it flew but alighted again farther along the fence-row. Since I was prepared to collect some bird specimens in Canada I had my 16-gauge shotgun in my luggage. Even though I did not have a Wyoming collecting permit, I decided to disobey the law and loaded my gun with a charge of heavy shot.

Stopping well away from the bird, I walked slowly toward it hoping it would allow me to get within range, but I was disappointed when it took off – but alighted again on a farther post. This time, taking no chance of getting close, I fired a shot just as it took wing, hoping that at least one pellet might bring it down. But off it went out over a thicket of low trees nearby. It appeared to fly reasonably well, but I thought it showed signs of unsteadiness, so I climbed the fence and circled the thicket. To my happy surprise, there lay my long sought prairie falcon, with its wings out-spread. My single shot had obviously penetrated its lungs, causing its delayed death. I actually hated to shoot such a beautiful, big raptor, but I felt justified since it would be used by Dr. Roberts in his description of the species in his book *Birds of Minnesota*.

We found that we were just approaching the town of Sundance, so we decided to put up for the night early to give me time to make drawings of this fine bird before removing and salting the skin for Museum preservation. It was a very hot day and I recall that our upstairs room in the hotel, which was the only accommodation available, was steaming hot. But in spite of the discomfort, I spent several hours recording numerous details of the specimen before completing its preservation, details I knew would be very helpful later in making the accompanying painting of this spectacular falcon.

Gyrfalcon

My memory connects the sighting of a gray gyrfalcon with a raven's nest I had located on a cliff near Wales, Alaska while on a collecting trip back in 1964. I had climbed the cliff high enough to photograph the nest with its two well-grown young. A few days later the nest was empty and I assumed the young had taken wing. But while scanning the cliff face, I spotted a cruising gyrfalcon that swooped up and alighted momentarily at the raven nest ledge before continuing its flight. It is just possible that this bird had been responsible for the disappearance of the young ravens and was making a final check to make sure no young remained in the nest. This, however, was pure conjecture on my part.

I have never seen the white phase of the gyrfalcon in the field but I got the details for this painting from a specimen in the Bell Museum's collections. (Plate 15B)

Kestrel or Sparrow Hawk

We often refer to the kestrel as a sparrow hawk, not because of its dining habits, but because it is the smallest hawk in North America. But it is no doubt the most colorful of all our hawks with its various patterns and shades of bright brown and black. It nests in cavities in dead trees, and I recall while I was teaching a class of bird students, I had located a nest hole in a very accessible box elder tree. On several occasions I gave

the students good looks at the bird, which was incubating eggs. We would approach the tree slowly and quietly, there tapping gently on the tree. Out would fly the kestrel in excellent range for the students to get acquainted with this attractive little raptor. Large insects are the primary food of the kestrel, but I recall once seeing a kestrel fly into a hold carrying a skink – a small lizard – to feed to its young. (Plate 16)

OWLS

Barred Owl

One winter morning at breakfast, while casually glancing out the window for any unusual bird visitors at our feeders, we suddenly realized that an inconspicuous object in a tree just beyond the feeders was not a mass of dead leaves, but a rather unusual visitor. A barred owl sat quietly staring at the small birds at the feeders. (Plate 17A) It remained there, motionless except for turning its head, for the greater part of the morning. At first we were a bit apprehensive about our new visitor being a threat to our siskins, chickadees, nuthatches and others, but after it sat for an hour or more without making any moves toward molesting them, we began to realize that the short-tailed shrews that occasionally dashed out from their tunnels under the snow to pick up a sunflower seed must be the object of the owl's steady gaze. This proved to be true since it did succeed in taking an unwary shrew later in the morning.

The following day the owl was again perched motionless in the tree by the feeders, but this time it appeared to be fastening its gaze on the undisturbed ten-inch deep snow several feet away from the feeders. There were no burrows showing where a shrew or a mouse might be expected to appear. But still its attention remained fastened on the clear, white, undisturbed patch of snow. Then suddenly it dived confidently into the deep snow and came up with another shrew. We then realized that we had just witnessed an excellent demonstration of the bi-aural hearing that owls possess. The facts are that all owls' two ear openings differ anatomically and send slightly differing messages to their brains. This ability is similar to the binocular vision that enables us humans to judge distance. Obviously the shrew in this case was making chewing or squeaking sounds enabling the owl to pinpoint its exact location under the snow.

Many carnivorous animals refuse to eat shrews due to the presence of poison glands about the jaws, but obviously this owl does not object to this poison. Neither does the screech owl since I recently examined some of their pellets to find them containing several shrew skulls. Later this barred owl accomplished another unexpected feat when it tackled an adult gray squirrel that was feeding beneath the bird feeders. A spirited struggle followed in which the squirrel escaped momentarily but was immediately recaptured. The owl took a firm hold on the squirrel and simply held on for several minutes while the victim slowly stopped squirming. When the owl finally realized that it had dispatched the animal it flew off several yards, dragging its prey, and again alighted in the snow. But eventually it actually flew to a perch ten or twelve feet up in a tree, carrying the squirrel. Its surprising ability to carry such a weight prompted me to check on the weights of these two animals and they proved to be approximately the same – a truly remarkable feat for this capable little raptor.

Snowy Owl

The spectacular, arctic-nesting snowy owl often visits Minnesota during years when the lemmings are scarce in the north. (Plate 17B) Many are shot since they are quite tame. One year we had a slightly injured one brought in to the Bell Museum. Dr. Warner decided to place it in a large cage along with an also slightly injured great horned owl. Both were large and appeared to tolerate each other very amicably for several weeks. Then one morning when we went up to feed and water them, the cage was a mass of white feathers. We realized that the great gorned owl was a bit larger and more powerful than the snowy, but we hadn't expected to have it kill and eat the smaller bird.

Screech Owls

Screech owls will often occupy wood duck houses either for nesting or for winter retreats for daytime resting. Once I was checking my wood duck houses for occupancy and on lifting the roof on one, I looked down on two screech owls crouching motionless in opposite corners of the house. I assumed they would nest in these comfortable quarters but they did not. Did the disturbance of simply looking at them cause them to vacate what could have been an excellent situation for nesting? I never found them nesting in any of my nearby duck houses, so my question was never answered.

Just this last winter of 1995, a single gray phase screech owl spent a number of days in a metal wood duck house. Pellets from the house told me that it had been living primarily on white-footed mice. They will often take small birds, but no feathers told me that this one was not taking my birds. I would often see the bird perching in the entrance during the daytime, presumably watching for mouse activity in the surrounding woods or in my garden.

This, of course, presented me with a fine opportunity to band the bird. I had secured some bands for wood ducks from our friend, Jane Olyphant, an experienced bander, who told me that screech owls could carry the same sized bands. Another friend, Louis Dinzl, brought his ladder to help me capture the owl. The house was constructed with a square, cup-like structure forming the bottom of the house. First we plugged the entrance with a cloth to prevent the bird's escape. Then we slipped down the cup-like bottom with the owl in it and slipped cardboard over it, entrapping the bird. We then took it into my shop to prevent its escape while being banded. I wore leather gloves since owls have very sharp claws. After banding it, we replaced the bird in the duck house but the disturbance was too much for it and it deserted the house as a resting retreat.

Great Horned Owls

Over the years at the Brackens, I have frequently encountered a pair of great horned owls on the Island, although I have little factual knowledge about them. This is *Bubo virginiana* to the scientist; hence I have given it the nickname of "Old Bubo." Flushing this big raptor on one of my first evaluating trips was one factor that convinced me that this area had at least some elements of a pseudo-wilderness. Down through the half century of my acquaintance with the Island's life, it is the exception when I prowl about for any length of time that I fail to spot one or both of these owls. I like to think that this is the same pair, but I have never captured and marked them and, having no characters by which to identify them individually, I can't be sure that these birds have survived this half century, although birds of this species have been known to live this long.

My contacts with Old Bubo have been so regular that it has become almost routine for me to make a tour of the north end of the island and have the big owl glide down from one of the big cottonwoods. It would fly silently directly away from me among the tree trunks toward mid-island where it would swoop up to alight among the larger limbs. (Plate 18) There its large size would blend surprisingly well with the limbs. As I made my round of the island, it might repeat this getaway flight on to the south end of the island or it would circle to the west and return to its original perch. Frequently both birds would follow the same routine. Only once did I discover the nest in the crotch of a large elm, thirty to forty feet up above the ground. That year I was gone from home during the nesting period and I made no visits to the nest. However, I felt that this would be one species whose nest I would have little trouble finding in subsequent years for further study. In fact I assumed that it probably would occupy the same nest repeatedly, as many large predatory birds will often do. Not so in this case. In recent years I have been much baffled by my failure to get any hint as to where the nest might be. My latest effort was to play a tape-recorded series of

owl calls in the evening when I was virtually certain the birds would respond with some efforts to locate and drive away the bird that was intruding into its territory, but I have gotten no responses whatsoever.

In later years many of the large elms have died of the Dutch elm disease and crashed down into huge tangles. No doubt their secret nesting site has had to be moved almost yearly. My knowledge of their presence today involves an occasional track story in the snow where a cottontail supplied a meal for Old Bubo, and at least on one occasion where a pheasant ran literally to the end of its trail and huge wing marks in the snow made almost certain of the identity of the winged predator.

Another great horned owl family gave me much more information on its habits and life style than did Old Bubo. This family also gave me more personal adventures while I acquired this information. This nest was high up in an old oak tree, one of several that made up a small grove three or four miles north from my home. After studying the situation, I decided that one of the neighboring oaks was perfectly located to provide a site for a photographic blind about fifteen feet from the nest, which I found contained four eggs. Knowing that great horned owls lay their eggs as early as late February, I calculated that, with an incubation period of 28 days, the eggs probably were well along toward hatching since I found the nest in April. At this late stage of incubation there would be little chance of the bird deserting the nest should I disturb it during my photographic preparations. With this in mind, a friend and I first fastened a trio of heavy poles as a base for my blind at about the level of the nest in the other tree. After a day or two I added more poles. Then, still later, I bent over some slender poles to form a dome-shaped frame. Over this I draped a burlap cover with observation holes. Still the bird had not deserted the nest, but the eggs had hatched during all these preparations.

I was hopeful and reasonably confident that the parent birds would not desert a nest that already had hungry young demanding to be fed, and in this I was not disappointed. The ambitious project was aimed at getting motion pictures of the feeding behavior of the birds. I knew that owls were largely nocturnal and that most of the feeding would occur when the light would be too weak for photography, but I hoped that as the growing young demanded more and more food, at least some feeding would take place when suitable daylight was available.

After another few days I visited the area for a final check before actually occupying the blind only to find a downy, young owlet on the ground below the nest. I naturally was anxious to see if it had suffered any injuries from its fall and stooped to pick it up when, WHAM! I was struck between my shoulders by a boxing glove full of needles. The female owl had hit me with her talons spread, penetrating my heavy woolen mackinaw, leaving several bloody scratches on my back. I had intended to replace the owlet in the nest but wondered "Dare I climb the tree with the aggressive mother owl perched nearby, ready to strike again?" I certainly would need both hands to climb among the almost thorn-like branches of the pin oak tree but I did have my packsack. So emptying it I dropped the fluffy youngster inside and started the climb. I soon discovered that as long as I looked directly at the bird perching in a nearby tree it would not swoop in at me, but the moment I turned my head it would try for another attempt at scalping me. So I found myself well occupied with my locating placements for my two feet and hand holds for my two hands, frequently untangling my pack sack and keeping an almost continual watch on the belligerent owl. Arriving finally at the nest, I found two other somewhat larger owlets in possession. After some strenuous contortions, I retrieved the fallen nestling from the depths of my packsack and confidently attempted to replace it in the nest. But no! the other occupants would have none of an intruder, as they seemed to consider their former nest mate and fought vigorously to prevent its acceptance in the nest. This unexpected complication kept me still busier with watching the adult bird, hanging on to my thirty foot high precarious perch and trying to settle the domestic hassle going on in the nest.

Finally (and fortunately for me) the older nestlings seemed to recognize the newcomer as having squatter's right to space in the nest and they all snuggled down together to keep warm. Reassured that owlet number three would not again be shoved out for a long tumble to the ground, I squirmed my way back down, keeping a continuous watch on the parent owl perched in the oak next door, and keeping in mind reports of other climbers to great horned owl nests who had received serious cuts or even lost an eye from just this sort of intrusion into an owl's home territory.

Soon after this I made several unsuccessful "sits" in my blind. One of my early morning vigils was interrupted by the weather. A strong breeze developed and soon clouds of dust began appearing in the air. This was in the 1930s during the Dust Bowl days of the drought. Anticipating a still stronger wind from the west, and finding my tree perch beginning to sway dangerously, I beat a hasty descent before my tree, with my added weight, might snap or be uprooted. However, this did not happen and I was able to continue my observations on several subsequent mornings.

After several unsuccessful morning watches in my cramped little blind, I finally determined that my disturbing the family routine in the early mornings by climbing to the blind was preventing any feeding of the young until several hours had passed for the normal quiet to be reestablished. With this in mind I determined to take really drastic steps to assure my success. I stuffed my packsack not only with my photographic gear but also with a warm woolen blanket, and ascended to my "flagpole sitting perch" at midnight. I curled up to at least try to sleep through the rest of the night in order to be on hand when morning light brightened enough for photography. I felt confident that if I really did doze off and began shifting about in my sleep, my safety belt would prevent my rolling out of my lofty bedstead. It worked OK and the crack of dawn found me still safely curled up in my tree top hideaway. In the gradually increasing morning light I set up my tripod and camera and awaited the coming of my actors on their precarious stage. The big question was: Would my actors wait with their acting until the light was bright enough for photography? In those early days of wildlife photography, only black and white film was available and it was by no means fast film. True, I had only recently acquired a light meter and I no longer would have to guess at my exposures. A check on the light? No, not yet, although I could see perfectly any action that might occur in the nest only fifteen feet away. Still more waiting - and no chance for pictures. Then suddenly a low "HOOT" and a faint rustle, and there, in perfect view, the big owl alighted – and with a pheasant's head in one powerful but deceivingly soft and furry looking talon. Now I would finally get the answer to the question I had often asked myself. "How would this huge clumsy bird go about feeding this tiny young?" It would seem appropriate that tiny bits of food should be presented to these little nestlings at the tip of some delicate forceps – not in the big curved beak of this clumsy appearing parent (and still too dark for pictures). But as usual I found that Nature has ways of solving many of its problems in unexpected ways. To my complete surprise, the big bird, holding the pheasant head in its talons, reached over and gripped its skull in its powerful beak just above the eye and wrenched off a tiny bit of the hard bone. (I could have done this only with the aid of a pair of pliers). Then instead of returning its head to its normal upright position, it continued moving it underneath its body as though it were going to stand on its head. But then moved it over toward the nestling, and, with its head upside down, held the little morsel of bone delicately in its inverted beak ready for the youngster to pick it off without the slightest difficulty. What an interesting movie this would make, but the light was still far too weak to record on film.

I had several opportunities later, but I never did get a single foot of movies of that action. Always when my meter told me to go ahead and shoot, the owl would fly over to a nearby tree and settle down to roost for the day. However, all the arduous blind building and tedious sitting was by no means lost effort. I still enjoy recalling the whole episode and years later I gave a talk to a local Audubon Society entitled "Movies I Failed to Get."

Hawk Owl

I was traveling one winter day along a lesser highway just west of Red Lake in northwestern Minnesota when I spotted a hawk owl perched on a dead snag about a hundred yards from the highway. I knew they were usually quite tame and approachable so I assembled my movie camera and tripod, donned my snowshoes and set off for the still quietly perched owl. As I expected, it allowed me to approach within quite close camera range. The bird eyed me curiously as I set up my tripod and focused for some wonderful screen-sized camera shots. I removed my mitten in order to get an accurate focus, but CURSES! My telephoto lens was frozen tight and would not budge from its long distance point of focus. I held it in both bare hands as long as I could stand the chill, but I ended up completely frustrated by my inability to focus on that remarkably cooperative bird. That was the only lens I had brought from my car, so all I could do was warm my hands and try again. But during my struggles the owl decided to take off, leaving me with nothing for all my efforts.

Great Gray Owl

I have never encountered this big northern owl in its nesting habitat in northern Minnesota. But some years ago (perhaps 1965-68) there was an invasion of great grays probably caused by deep snows in the north. There were 12 or 15 observations reported in the Twin City area. I followed up on one of these reports from north of St. Paul and got some excellent close-up still shots that gave me the inspiration and the details for this painting. (Plate 19)

EAGLES

Bald Eagle

Working in the kitchen one day, Dorothy glanced out the window frequently for any unusual visitors at the feeders, in the bird-bath or in the trees along the river. Some big wing movements in the trees caught her eye and, to her astonishment, two adult bald eagles alighted in the big bur oak directly above the deck. Knowing that I would be more than excited to see such a thrilling pair of visitors, she shouted for me all through the house, in the basement, in my studio and garage, but no answer. I was not in the garden or about the yard so she returned to her solitary enjoyment of watching the rare visitors until they finally took off along the river. A few minutes later I turned up at the back door, completely unaware of what had been happening. Actually I had been doing what any good conservationist should be doing – cleaning up trash from along our segment of the highway about a block from the house.

One of the highlights of my trips along the North Shore Highway bordering Lake Superior was my circling the Silver Creek Cliff just above Two Harbors where the road was literally carved out of the perpendicular face of the cliff. Originally there was a slight widening of the road part way around the cliff. This allowed one to park briefly for a chance to appreciate the view of the wide sweep of Lake Superior and on up the shore along the rugged rocky cliff itself. Stopping here once, I was marveling at the endless mass of blue water stretching all the way to the horizon when, in the distance, I spotted a large, dark bird hugging the shore low over the water. It stood out from the white gulls that ordinarily dominated the shore scene. I fastened my gaze on the oncoming speck that soon grew to exhibit a white head and tail – a bald eagle no doubt. The prospect of its passing below me, allowing me the unusual chance to look down on this majestic bird excited me. I was still more excited when it suddenly changed course and appeared to anticipate landing on a scraggly cedar tree clinging to the cliff directly below me. What a wonderful view I got as it swooped up toward the perch! But at the last moment it spotted me and plunged down again and continued on its course along the shore. Many times I have enjoyed recalling that exciting view of the eagle that I finally put on paper here.

The background in this painting is not of Lake Superior but a view of some islands in the Mississippi in southeastern Minnesota The gnarled, dead perch on which the bird is intending to land is from a carefully detailed drawing of the dead snag high above the river. At the time I had been laying out a self-guiding nature trail for the Minnesota State Park's Nature Interpretation Program. This picturesque snag attracted my attention and I took a sketching break to preserve it for my files. Here I have combined the bald eagle, the Mississippi River islands, and this snag into one composition. (Plate 20)

Sandhill Cranes

Chapter 10: Minnesota Work

BEARS

Back in the CCC days in the 1930s, I received an invitation from the Department of Natural Resources to investigate some hibernating bears still in their dens up in northeast Minnesota that the CCC boys had stumbled upon during their routine work in the woods. I, of course, jumped at the chance to see for myself just how black bears holed up for their hibernation. Did they actually dig holes in the ground and did they really sleep long and soundly through their winter sleep? During March there was still a considerable depth of snow on the ground in that area so I packed my snowshoes and parka along with my still and movie cameras. At least a part of the smaller back roads in the camp area had been kept plowed free of snow so we were able to drive to within reasonably easy hiking distance of the dens.

One might assume that big clumsy snowshoes would get badly tangled in brush while you were traveling off the beaten trails. But on previous trips I had found that, when the snow was deep enough to require snowshoes, the smaller brush I encountered readily bent aside under the pressure of the snowshoes and immediately popped back up as one passed along. Our relatively short hikes to the dens were easily accomplished.

Den number one would hardly have been recognized as a bear den when our guide pointed out a small hole in the snow about 3 or 4 inches across in fairly level ground. But there was evidence of occupation in that long ice crystals lined the hole. These had been formed from the breath of the occupant. However, with only a poke of a pole near the crystal-lined hole, a small area of snow caved in to reveal a much larger hole a foot or more in diameter. We found that all was well with the bear in this den and we had no reason to disturb her so we continued on to den number two.

On approaching this den we could see that this was at the base of a fairly large tree. A slight poke at the breathing hole exposed quite a large opening, about 18 inches across. As we peered into the cavity, a slight rustling sound indicated that the occupant was not sleeping. Hoping she would not make any belligerent moves, we crouched down and looked in more closely, but visibility was far from good. However, we could discern the light skin around the bear's nose at first. Then "What are those two other light spots that appeared beside her?" As we might have suspected at this early spring date, they were from the twin cubs that we guessed were about the size of small kittens. They could be as much as five to six weeks old since they were probably born in late January or early February while the mother was hibernating. Photography was out of the question since a black animal in a black hole isn't a very good subject without flashlights being available. But a long exposure with my still camera did reveal three white spots around the noses of the mother and the two cubs. After my eyes became adjusted to the dim light, I could make out the motion of the mother's arm as she reached around and pulled the cubs back out of sight. Not wanting to cause any further disturbance of the family, we retreated from the second den and its occupants.

On the second day of our visit we snowshoed some distance to den number three. This was quite different. A large tree had been uprooted by the wind and a large spread of roots had been pulled up, forming a reasonable shelter several feet across. Here a mother bear had chosen to snuggle down to take advantage of this protection. With a couple feet of snow partially closing the open side of the den, she was fairly well sheltered. We approached on our snowshoes to within a few yards where we could see a large mass of bear fur. Just what part of the bear we were looking at was a puzzle. No motion was visible so we got a long slender pole and began very gently prodding the mass of fur. Then, quite unexpectedly, two year-old cubs put in their appearance, obviously not as sleepy as the mother. They climbed over and beside the still sleeping mother, but made no move to leave the den, so we continued to prod until she finally uncovered her head, rested her chin on the snow bank and gazed very sleepily at us. This action revealed to us that she had been sleeping with her head between her hind feet and literally sitting on top of her head with her front legs curled about the whole mass. What a strange position to assume for a long winter's sleep. But her face, feet and ears were well protected by the fur coat of her back exposed to the elements. A healthy hibernating bear is known to have nearly six inches of fat over its back, which provides still more protection from the winter temperatures. We were not sure how quickly the mother bear might become active so, with our own safety in mind, we retreated leaving the happy (?) family with no further disturbance, free to go back to sleep, which they undoubtedly did.

Thus my observations at these three dens appeared to answer my two questions. Yes, they will dig holes for hibernation, although they will take advantage of natural protection whenever they can find it. And no, black bears do not always sleep soundly while hibernating, although some do and some do not.

Bruce's Bear

Since early childhood I have had a deep-seated urge to be self-reliant. My interest in Native Americans has no doubt been due in part to my recognition of their ability to live close to Nature in finding food and shelter in natural materials. I always enjoyed delving into the identification of all plants, trees and animals to learn how I could make use of them to live a life independent of all the complex technical materials humans have devised to further their comfort and convenience in their present civilized life style. This urge for self-reliance no doubt fostered my urge to visit far away places where few, if any, humans had ever been. This, of course, is all but impossible today where people have penetrated deep into the seas, climbed

Bruce Breckenridge with his bear

the highest mountain peaks and visited both poles of our planet. Yet I still like little-disturbed places where I can observe Nature in as near as possible to its primitive state. A few decades ago the Border Waters Canoe Country offered the least altered natural areas one could find in Minnesota. In fact, the presence of this canoe country was one of the important reasons for my being so excited about getting museum employment back in 1926 in one of the least disturbed states in the Union.

After getting well established at the Minnesota Museum of Natural History, I discovered that my brother's teenaged son, Bruce, had much the same conservation philosophy that I had and that he was anxious to take a trip in the BWCA. So we began arranging for such an experience. At that time the Museum secretary was Ruth Self who told me that her brother, Ed Wolverton, was a forest ranger on the Kawishiwi River in the heart of the BWCA. So we got in touch with him and planned to stop at his cabin for a visit on our trip. Required reservations for canoeing there were unheard of at that time, of course, so we simply rented a canoe from an outfitter in Ely and took off with a satisfied feeling that we were going to be, to some extent at least, self reliant for a couple of weeks. I did not bring along my 16-gauge collecting gun that I usually carried to collect bird specimens for the museum since this was to be simply a fun trip, not officially Museum sponsored travel.

As I recall, we arrived at Ed Wolverton's cabin on our second day. Since he was situated at a fairly rough rapids in the river, we pulled up to portage our gear. We found Ed at home with his coffee pot on, so we had not only help in portaging our packs and canoe but the opportunity for a very informative chat about conditions there and what was occurring in his work – where the portages were and what we might expect in the way of animal life along the way.

We left his cabin early in the afternoon and drifted quietly, watching for deer or moose until late in the day. We checked our maps and found we would soon encounter a portage over into another lake. Rounding a bend we expected to spot the portage but, on scanning the shore ahead with our binoculars, we saw motion and were a bit annoyed that we were to find another party taking off ahead of us along the portage. However, as we neared the landing, we were really thrilled to find that the motion was not another party but a black bear. We had hoped for some contact with bears possibly nosing about our food packs, but not at portage landings. We dug deep with our paddles, but before we could get within good viewing range, the bear took off up the portage trail. We almost dumped our canoe in our haste to land and take off after the retreating bear but soon lost sight of it as it turned off into the woods. But even more exciting was the sight of a bear lying dead right at the landing. It was obviously freshly killed, undoubtedly by the other bear. Why had they fought to the death? What would have prompted such a lethal encounter? Most territorial conflicts among animals do not result in death. The best possibility would seem to be that it was a battle over possible mates. We felt sure that we would not be accused of illegally killing the animal, so we took out our knives and skinned the bear with plans to have it tanned for a rug for Bruce. We salted it lightly with our limited supply of salt and added it to our packs. I can't imagine why we did not rough out the skull and take a few steaks.

The remainder of the trip over several lakes and portages gave us chances to get better acquainted with the gray or Canada jays that actually took food from our hands and to enjoy the reverberating yodels of the loons, a pair of which apparently nested in each of the lakes we visited. We had another special recollection when we revisited Ed Wolverton on our return trip. As we would expect, he pitched in with portaging our packs, but his eyes opened wide in surprise and puzzlement when we tossed off the bearskin.

"How on earth did you get this when you had no gun?" We chose to keep him in the dark for a while with some tales of stabbing it with our knives when the bear attempted to steal our food packs. He took our stories with a "few grains of salt" until we finally came out with the facts. He, of course, registered no objection to our taking it along as a memento of our really memorable canoe trip. Bruce later had the bearskin tanned and still has it as a memento of our much-enjoyed expedition.

SANDHILL CRANES

Pine County

Dr. Roberts was a pioneer in the use of motion pictures in teaching and promoting research in ornithology. I soon found myself assisting him in motion picture photography. Eventually he turned over all the motion picture work to me, which I accepted enthusiastically. In those early years we used a 35mm camera that was hand-cranked. The exposures on black and white film depended on the rate at which the crank was turned. Much editing was needed and a good many feet of film ended up in the wastebasket. Big modern telescopic lenses were not available which forced us to approach our subjects much closer to get the screen-filling shots we had always hoped for. This restriction was not all bad however. We used blinds a great deal, which was an advantage for us in that we were watching our subjects from much closer range than later when we used telescopic lenses. We got to know our subjects better and often heard low chuckling or cooing sounds from our bird subjects, many of which we would have missed had we been operating from a greater distance. After discarding our 35mm hand-cranked camera we got a more portable, spring-propelled 35mm Eymo camera. Still later we got one of the first Eastman Cine Special 16mm at about the time that color film became available.

During the period 1926-32, Dr. Roberts was very busy completing his two-volume work on the Birds of Minnesota. A few Minnesota areas were lacking information and one of my very choice assignments was to visit some of these areas and report on the bird life I encountered there. One of these assignments was to visit eastern Pine County where Dr. Roberts had had only limited contacts with Game Warden Sheridan Greig, who had reported occasional bird observations. I arrived at Warden Greig's home in mid-April 1930 and found I could headquarter at his home for my extended stay of a couple of weeks.

Early in my visit I received word from a Pine County farmer via Sheridan Greig that a pair of sandhill cranes was feeding regularly in his cornfield. This would present a fine opportunity for photography. On contacting him I found that corn shocks were scattered about over the field where the birds fed. One of these shocks could readily be rebuilt over my blind for ideal concealment. On arriving at the location, the farmer informed me that the birds had been coming in the late afternoons and early mornings to wander about, feeding for about an hour or more. It was about noon when I arrived so I lost no time in removing a suitably situated shock, placing my blind, and replacing the cornstalks as to appear like the many other shocks that were present.

I decided to enter the blind in mid-afternoon with a good chance for pictures that same day. I was very comfortably settled with my campstool. I even had an old carpet on the damp ground if it became necessary to kneel or sit down in manipulating my camera. The light was good for photography and I waited somewhat impatiently for the arrival of my subjects. Time passed and no subjects appeared. The light began to fade toward evening and I took repeated light meter readings to tell when I might have to abandon my vigil. When it became hopeless, I gave up for the day. I realized that the cranes might miss their hoped for schedule for one day, so I ate the meager rations I had brought and retired to my camp for the night.

At just about sunrise the next morning I reentered my cozy blind and waited hopefully for the birds' arrival. Several hours passed with no action in the field, and soon after mid-morning I left the blind and met with the farmer who was quite chagrined at the failure of the cranes to come to feed as he insisted they had been doing for the past several days. Still expecting success I reentered my blind early in the afternoon to be sure of being ready for them whenever they might decide to make their much delayed appearance. But still no success and another night passed with morning finding me again hoping for some fine crane movies from this really perfect setting. All morning I impatiently scanned the cornfield for cranes that did not appear. I had schedules to meet the next day and I could not keep up my watch indefinitely. After eating my lunch in the blind I decided to put in the entire day awaiting my uncooperative subjects. Then about mid-afternoon, to my great delight, in came the cranes! They alighted about a hundred yards from my blind and began picking casually at the ground and slowly began coming directly toward me. With the assurance that I was finally going to have my long-awaited success, I decided to take a few distant shots as an introduction to the close-ups that were surely coming. But as I sharpened my focus and pushed the control button of my camera, I got no action. HORRORS! Was my camera jammed at this vital moment? Yes, it appeared to require some sort of adjustment. So I hurriedly slipped it into a darkened changing bag for repairs. In the meantime I glanced out at the birds occasionally, only to find them calmly striding past my blind at ideal close-up photography range and with me fumbling to reactivate my camera. I never did get that blankety-blank camera functioning while the now cooperating cranes stepped carefully among the tangled corn stalks past my blind and off beyond photographing range, leaving me with no results after all my patient waiting and high hopes. This was without doubt the most frustrating experience I had in all my years of wildlife photography.

Nesting

That same month I also investigated the possible nesting of sandhill cranes along the Saint Croix River that formed the boundary between Minnesota and Wisconsin and had good crane habitat of marshy meadows on both sides. On my first day in the field I located a disturbed pair of cranes on the Wisconsin side, but found no nest. The next day I sloshed around all morning in the area and was getting tired, mosquito bitten and very sweaty when about noon I noticed a fallen log a short distance ahead. Picking my way toward it, I was not thinking especially about cranes but about a dry place to eat my lunch. I was suddenly shocked and actually frightened for a moment by a loud, hair-raising call before I realized that it was coming from a sandhill crane bursting up off its nest only a few yards ahead of me. I had heard their rolling, almost musical calls from a distance, but never from so close at hand. The bird alighted not far away and stalked about in alarm for a few moments before flying away farther into the marsh. I, of course, forgot entirely about my lunch. I slipped my Graflex Camera from my pack for a few quick shots of the nest and its two huge eggs before hurriedly retreating well away from the nest, hoping I had not disturbed the object of my search so seriously as to have it desert the nest. I felt sure that it wouldn't if the bird had been incubating for two to three weeks. With this in mind I waited before visiting the nest again and, as I had hoped, the bird was still incubating. So I set up my blind about 25 feet from the nest and spent quite a number of hours patiently waiting for the birds to perform adequately for the many feet of movies and still pictures I finally secured. Dr. Roberts was much pleased with the results and used a number of the shots illustrating this account of the sandhill crane in his book. The background in this painting is not of the St. Croix Valley, but the black spruce country near the Canadian border where I searched in vain for nesting cranes which I felt sure were nesting in the area. (Plate 21).

Capturing Cranes

On another of these trips I was reporting on the fall flight of the lesser sandhill cranes in the Red River Valley in northwestern Minnesota. By driving along side roads, I was able to approach within easy binocular range to count flocks of feeding cranes. When I spotted only two cranes stalking about by themselves, I became suspicious and studied their actions carefully to find that both had injured wings and were unable to fly. Probably some unsportsmanlike shooters had taken long-range shots that injured these birds, which prevented them from taking off with their migrating flocks. Again it was possible that they had flown into power wires. Whatever was the cause of their plight, the fact remained that, if I left them alone in their condition, they probably sooner or later would provide food for coyotes that were common in the area.

Another alternative I considered was to capture them and place them in the Como Zoo where veterinarians might set their wings and later release them back into the wild. This I decided to do, not realizing that the doing was more of a task than I had anticipated. The cranes' wings were not functioning well, but this was far from the fact with regard to their legs. My technique was to walk slowly, not directly toward one of the birds but in a broad spiral, getting gradually closer, hopefully without the bird detecting just how close I might be getting. I was sure, of course, that it would eventually take off at a run, and I would simply have to outrun it. I was in top shape physically and I had been a 100-yard dash man in college, but I must admit that the birds also were in tiptop shape as far as their legs were concerned. Fortunately the level prairie was reasonably smooth but not exactly a groomed cinder track. I was really puffing by the time I caught up to within grabbing distance, and only then did I run into trouble. First I tackled the pair of wings; they could still flap vigorously and a wing that size could strike really painful blows. But while I was subduing the wings, the legs came into action with their long, strong claws scratching at my arms, face and neck. And the bird didn't hesitate taking a few telling jabs with its long neck and powerful beak. Here I could have used a helper to manage such an aggressive adversary, but I did finally succeed in wrapping it all up in my arms. Then, "What do I do with my bundle?" My car did not have a strong screen between the front and back

seats as do the police cars, so the only secure place I had was the trunk of the car. Then the unlocking and opening of the trunk required another pair of hands. I can't remember just how I succeeded, other than that the struggling bird almost escaped a couple of times before I finally closed the trunk and took a huge sigh of relief.

Then there was the other injured bird to be considered. After taking a slight breather I set out to repeat the act, which, when completed, left me almost totally tuckered out. Somehow I was successful in subduing the second bird and squeezing it into the trunk without loosing the first bird. Then I laid down flat on my back for a much-needed extensive rest. This was probably one of the most physically strenuous day's work I had ever put in, but it gave me a tremendous feeling of success in my accomplishment. Further good feeling came from my having done a good turn for the cranes since I was then hoping that they could eventually be rehabilitated and released back into the wild.

This, however, was not to be. I felt much concerned about the well being of my captives, so on the long 100 mile trip home I opened the trunk partially several times to give them a bit of fresh air but I dared not allow them any exercise to loosen up their cramped muscles. But on arrival back home, I liberated them in my garage for the night before taking them to the Como Zoo. The birds survived, but their wings healed a bit crooked and they had to remain at the zoo as educational birds where they lived for several years on public display.

SPRAGUE'S PIPIT

One of my first extensive field trips with Dr. Roberts and William "Bill" Kilgore was in June 1928 when we made a careful check of birds from Pipestone, near the Iowa line, north along the western edge of Minnesota, up to the Canadian Border. The principal species we were investigating was to determine the Minnesota range of Sprague's pipit. We found it to be common all the way to Canada. In those years, quite extensive patches of virgin prairie still existed. The following year Kilgore and I covered the same route but did not encounter the species until we reached Wilkin County, about half way to the Canadian border. We discovered that we could very quickly determine the bird's presence by stopping at short intervals and listening for its bright, tinkling courting song coming from high up in the sky. The following excerpt from my field notes (that Dr. Roberts chose to include in his *Birds of Minnesota*) gives a good record of the aerial song of this inconspicuous but very interesting little lark, quite similar to the much-written-about European skylark.

"At first it could be heard giving three or four sharp 'chips' with very decided intervals, followed by a musical repetition of blended, very high-pitched notes sounding like the jingling of a set of tiny sleigh bells. The accented notes came in regular beats or throbs and gradually diminished in volume until lost to the ear, resembling a very high, fine veery song but lacking the inflection and given a little slower. The birds, being at such a high elevation while singing, made it difficult to determine the coordination of the song and flight. It seemed, however, to begin during a short sail on set wings followed by an ascent in short flights, like the horned lark, during which came the throbbing part of the song. During the sail the tail was spread and the wings up-curved like those of a singing bobolink. The song was repeated at short intervals for a period of fifteen to twenty-five minutes as the bird drifted around in wide circles. At the end it descended like a plummet, spreading its wings only when almost to the ground like a horned lark."

We were anxious to determine, if possible, just how high the bird really was while continuing its long series of veery-like songs. So we constructed a fairly large right triangle of small straight poles and, with Kilgore waving his hands when he felt he was directly beneath the bird, I would sight over the sloping side of my triangle and aim at the singing bird. The distance between the two of us then gave us the height of the bird. We later chuckled over what the people driving by on

a not-too-distant road might have been wondering what the purpose could be for such crazy antics of a couple of (normal?) adults. Our average of numerous observations was that the birds were about 300 feet above ground while giving their courting songs.

MINNESOTA RIVER VALLEY

My concern over the Minnesota Valley dates back to 1926 when I first took up my job as Exhibit Preparator at the then Minnesota Museum of Natural History. My first assignment was the production of a series of small portable habitat displays. I did most of my collecting of field materials along the Minnesota River in the Gun Club area just upstream from Fort Snelling, which later became a state park. Dr. Roberts was a member of the Gun Club. This contact permitted me to headquarter at the Gun Club while collecting, studying and photographing the wildlife of the Valley. I poled a small duck boat for miles in the shallow marsh in search of coot, gallinule and pied-billed grebe nests and occasionally one of Virginia or sora rail.

I did most of my collecting after the spring waterfowl migration, leaving only the resident ducks, blue-winged teal, mallard, a few ringnecks, ruddies and rarely a baldpate for study and photography. The young of some mammals, including woodchuck and skunk, were becoming active and became available as subjects for my exhibits. I recall clearly setting a small steel trap at a burrow expecting to get a young woodchuck but to my surprise a quite small stripped skunk appeared in my trap. I was not prepared to cope with a skunk exhibit just at that time so I decided to release it since it was not seriously injured. My question was "Is this youngster old enough to have developed his odor glands?" I thought not so I put my foot slowly on the spring of the trap to release my prey – and found I was mistaken. This left me with the problem of eliminating a definite dose of skunk odor which, in spite of many soap washings of my socks and trousers, it was days before I dared to wear them again.

With access to the Gun Club area, Dr. Roberts often took his bird class on field trips there. He had a small astronomical telescope that was set up on the hilltop near the clubhouse and the students could get good views of quite a number of marsh birds without wading out into the swamp.

Much farther up the Minnesota River valley, Goodman Larson and I were exploring what must have been the Upper Sioux Agency State Park. In hiking on the south bank of the river, we followed for some distance a granite ridge well above the Minnesota River. There we were surprised to find a number of rounded potholes in the hard granite bedrock. Since such potholes are known to be formed by the swirling action of gravel being whirled about by swiftly flowing water it seemed most unusual to find such holes 50 to 75 feet above even the flood water level of the present Minnesota River. This strange situation was, of course, simply a reminder of the really enormous size of the post-glacial River Warren. Some 15 to 20 thousand years ago this huge river was the only outlet of the glacial Lake Agassiz, which covered not only northwestern Minnesota, but also a large portion of the Dakotas and part of Manitoba in Canada. What today appear to be the walls of the present Minnesota River Valley were then the actual banks of this huge River Warren. The Mississippi River above Fort Snelling at the time was a minor tributary of the River Warren.

The skull and parts of the skeleton of a prehistoric inhabitant of Minnesota was unearthed in a gravel deposit of the River Warren near Brown's Valley, Minnesota. These are now in the collections of the Science Museum in St. Paul. This is my impression of what the Brown's Valley Man may have appeared like carrying a head of huge prehistoric bison while his mate was scraping the hide in preparation for clothing or covering for their primitive shelter. The melting glacier appears in the distance with the beginnings of the River Warren draining its melt waters. This illustration was photographed for my film, Minnesota Valley Saga. (Plate 22)

These few of many cherished recollections of the Minnesota River Valley experiences make it doubly satisfying for me to see that real progress is being made to preserve from the developers some significant segments of the valley's wildlife habitat for present and future generations to enjoy. The Minnesota Valley Wildlife Refuge has been very effective in this preservation work and is continuing to extend its efforts.

GROUSE

Sharp-Tailed Grouse

While waiting to photograph sandhill cranes at the nest on April 20, 1930, I located a group of sharp-tailed grouse dancing on a small meadow, surrounded by rather dense woods. It appeared to be a good setting for movies of their performances, so I placed a few aspen branches in a good spot for photography. The next day I enlarged the pile and on the third day I removed the pile of branches and replaced it with my blind. Then at 4:00 the next morning I slipped into the blind before any birds had arrived. This they did at 4:25 when in came 12 or 15 birds. I had the time of my life that day and the two following mornings watching, describing and photographing the strange courting performances of these grouse.

Each cock laid claim to a small area about 20 to 30 feet across and rushed to confront any neighboring bird that threatened to intrude on its territory. Each cock would droop his wings to the ground, erect his pointed tail and spread his under tail coverts to form a conspicuous rosette. He would then inflate the purple neck sacs an either side of his neck and begin to pound his feet on the ground, vigorously producing a sound like a sewing machine in action. The most unusual element of the whole performance was that every now and then all of the courting cocks would stop gyrating about and stand perfectly motionless for several seconds as though someone was calling the dance. I cannot recall of any bird performances where such well-coordinated actions occur. Occasionally a bird would suddenly bounce up in the air and utter a sharp chicken-like cac-cac-cac call. (Plate 23A)

Females usually were not present on the dancing grounds, but occasionally one or several would come in and circulate among the strutting cocks. They caused quite a stir, with a good deal of disregarding of territorial boundaries occurring among the males while pursuing the females in their attempts to copulate. Sometimes they succeeded, but often they were attacked by competing cocks. When the mated females left the grounds, the males resumed their positions in their territories and continued their competitive displays.

The spirited dancing usually subsided in vigor by 7 or 7:30 in the morning and gradually, one at a time, the cocks would fly off, leaving the grounds deserted by about 8 to 8:30. Once in a while a male or two might reappear on the grounds in late afternoon but no spirited dancing would occur.

Ruffed Grouse

While still delaying my attempts to get movies of the nesting cranes I found that ruffed grouse were drumming in most of the wooded areas of eastern Pine County. I was anxious to take advantage of this opportunity so I established a photographic blind near a drumming log to record, for future study, the much-discussed, exact source of the mysterious drumming sounds made by the grouse.

This species, like the spruce grouse, does its courting singly, not in organized groups as do the sharp-tailed grouse and prairie chicken. A male ruffed grouse will establish a territory by choosing a fallen, often moss-covered log on which to drum, announcing his presence to any females occupying the area. The drumming sound is a muffled thumping, the nature of which makes it difficult to determine the direction of its source. If approached too near by an observer it will leave the log quietly and disappear. The log can be easily identified, however, by the droppings that accumulate during the druming.

A blind can readily be concealed in wooded habitat and you can sit for several hours before your subject chooses to return and continue drumming. In this case I succeeded in getting movie shots with several different telephoto lenses, but no still shots. It is difficult to take both stills and movies of such subjects since the bird may sit quietly as you focus your still camera for still pictures, then suddenly go into the action and you get neither picture.

Much discussion often takes place among bird people as to just how the wings are able to produce the drumming sound. Many people insist that the cock bird pounds the log on which it almost invariably perches or that he strikes his breast in making the sound. After studying my movies as well as the drumming birds, however, I found that the wings did not touch the log nor did they strike together over the back when in action. At the start of the drumming, the bird appears to tense the wing muscles and puts considerable energy into the forward motion and the change of direction of the wing. Immediately after, the wing drops loosely forward. I often compare it with the not too vigorous shaking of a rug, which produces a similar thumping sound. Usually the thumping motion is repeated slowly at first, then the timing speeds up into a whirr just before the action terminates. The thumping will often speed up at the beginning, then slow down only to speed up again before the whirr. The drumming is really an announcement of the bird's ownership of the surrounding territory and an invitation to females to come for mating and for later nesting in his territory.

Few of our birds are loved and admired more than the ruffed grouse and it well deserves all the attention it gets. (Plate 23B) The striking patterns and camouflaged colors attract artists and photographers and hunters gloat over getting an especially striking cock bird in their bag. No wonder it is called the "King of Game Birds." But bird watchers simply cannot understand why anyone would want to shoot such a gorgeous bird. Fortunately, careful legal protection is given to this grouse in order to assure its

94

continued existence in our forests. Since it has a marked six to seven year cycle of abundance, hunting seasons are usually set to reduce the hunting pressure on them when their populations are low.

The spectacular strutting display shown in this painting occurs when a female approaches a drumming bird. Sometimes the male will strut when another male or even a person intrudes on the territory of the drummer. With the wide range of the grouse, occasionally an extremely aggressive individual has been reported. Although no attempt has been made to tame it, the bird will suddenly rush out at a passing person, demonstrate its strut, and even attack the intruder like a barnyard rooster might do in a poultry yard. I encountered one of these fearless grouse along the St. Croix River some years ago. I found the bird willing and anxious to fight my cap when I actually tried to strike it with the cap. It would aggressively strut right up to me and, as I reached out with my hands on either side of the bird, it flew only when I almost touched it in my attempt to pick it up. The only explanation of these surprising actions is that the bird has the trait of territorial defense developed to an extraordinary degree – one that would appear eventually to lead to its almost certain destruction.

The following actually took place according to a story related by an acquaintance of mine at a party where he felt it was a laughable joke. He had been visiting at a friend's forest cabin when he was surprised to have a ruffed grouse come out of the woods and strut right up to him in quite a friendly manner. Then, instead of commenting on what approachable wildlife his friend had living in his woods, he said that he reached down, grabbed it by the head, wrung its neck and brought it in to be plucked and cooked for their dinner. Needless to say, my so-called friend dropped several notches in my estimation after such a deplorable treatment of one of the most beautiful and attractive of our forest birds.

Prairie Chickens

I decided to wait still a few more days before disturbing the cranes, which gave me the time to photograph prairie chickens that were known to have a booming grounds within easy driving distance of my headquarters at Sheridan Greig's home. A couple of days were spent in preparing my blind for these birds, much as I had done for the sharp-tails.

Here I recall losing some of my valuable sleep time when a warden's cute daughter invited me to go to a dance at a local party. I – unwisely perhaps – accepted and didn't turn in until about two a.m. This gave me almost no sleep since I had to be in my blind a bit before four a.m. Of course one can get rest sitting in a photographic blind but you cannot doze for fear of missing important action by your subjects. In this case I did get into my blind just ahead of the first arriving birds at about 4:30 but I had trouble keeping my eyes open.

In reporting my observations of the prairie chickens, I will simply compare their social organization with that of the sharp-tailed grouse, already described in some detail. Both species carry on their courting dances communally with each of the numerous males establishing his own courting area about 25 feet in diameter. Here he will droop his wings, erect his tail and inflate his neck sacs as does the sharp-tail. But the prairie chicken's neck sacs are much larger and are bright orange instead of purple in color. (Plate 24A) The prairie chicken is also known as the pinnated grouse, referring to the "pinnae" tufts of longer feathers on the neck resembling miniature wings. These are moved upward and forward in the dance, taking a prominent part in the display. The booming call suggesting the syllables "Old-Mul-Doon" begins with the inflating of the neck sacs. The air producing the call passes through the syrinx (the voice box of a bird) and, with the bill closed, it passes back into the crop, expanding it to form the so-called neck sacs. As the call ceases, the bill opens and the neck sacs deflate.

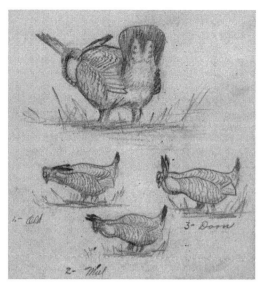

Prairie chickens drumming

The prairie chickens stamp their feet rapidly as does the sharp-tail, but I saw no coordinated stopping and starting as in that species. Females visit the courting grounds for mating as do the sharp-tails and, like them, they usually desert the dance grounds by about eight or eighty thirty in the morning and rarely dance in late afternoons.

I am sure that the Pine County expedition of April-May 1930 was the most exciting and productive of all the short trips I have taken throughout the state. This one pleased Dr. Roberts greatly and I was pleased to find he made extensive use of my field notes in his *Birds of Minnesota*. My observations of the sharp-tailed grouse courtship appeared on two and a half pages in the book; the crane nesting was reported on two full pages, and of my photographs, three of the sharp-tails, five of the prairie chickens, two of the ruffed grouse and five of the sandhill crane appeared in the book, all from the Pine County trip.

Spruce Grouse

I got a good many demanding assignments from Dr. Roberts during the final stages of his writing the *Birds of Minnesota*. One was to locate a promising habitat for the spruce grouse (Plate 24B) and to describe and photograph, if possible, the courtship that would correspond to the drumming of the

ruffed grouse as it had never been described adequately. After checking with the conservation officers, then known as game wardens, and the few knowledgeable bird observers we knew from northern Minnesota, we decided to concentrate our search in the Snowbank Lake area east of Ely near the Canadian border. Wardens from the area suggested that a Chippewa Indian named Jack Linklater, who was one of the wardens, would be an ideal assistant since he was as well acquainted with the wildlife as anyone in the region. This I found was true and I was happy to enlist his help.

Our first move was to follow the single-track logging road to its end where Mr. and Mrs. George Mackay, the warden for the area, lived. We could arrange for some of our meals with them. The isolated Fernberg Ranger cabin was located on the Kawishiwi River, not far from their home where we found reasonable shelter for the nights. While seated in front of the cabin one evening discussing our plans for the next day's search, we heard a clear whistling call, which was repeated several times from the surrounding woods.

"Do you recognize that call?" Jack asked. I didn't and his reply revealed his knowledge of the wildlife.

"That is the mating call of the saw-whet owl. You'll hear that only in May in this area." This was not the only happening that convinced me that Jack was one of the few Native Americans who still retained any extensive knowledge of the woods. Our plan called for each of us to go out in different directions, check for the presence of spruce grouse and report each evening on our finds. One evening I mentioned following a trail for a way when I turned off north for some unspecified distance through the dense woods. A fallen log induced me to sit down to listen for anything that might suggest spruce grouse. Instead I heard a small crunching sound of something just beyond my field of vision. It soon stopped and I did not investigate that particular sound except that I assumed it was a moose. This I reported to Jack and he made no comment. The following evening he reported, "You remember that sound you heard when you were sitting on a log over there?" Pointing in the right direction he gave the following detailed account of the noise I had heard.

"Well, I went down that trail to where you turned off north through the woods." The woods were dry, of course, in that season with no snow for tracking. "Following your track to the log where you sat down, I investigated the sound and found that it was not a moose but a place where a bear had stripped some bark from a log for grubs." Only a pretty keen observer could have made such a report.

Gradually over a period of days we accumulated a great deal of detail about the courtship of the spruce grouse by stalking quietly about in the spruce and jack pine habitat and listening intently for any whirring sounds of wings. No vocal sounds appeared to be involved in that stage of the breeding behavior, which announced the ownership of a territory. My first contact with a courting male grouse was finding a lone bird perched on a branch six or eight feet from the ground. Watching it quietly from a distance I could see it was undisturbed. Then presently it flew, not to disappear in the distant woods, but only 20 or 30 feet, where it arrested its forward flight and, with a whirring of its wings, it settled to the ground. There it flipped its wings a few times, suggesting the beginning of the ruffed grouse's drumming, but never continuing for more than two or three beats and producing little or no sound. Then peering upward, it suddenly flew straight up to alight on a horizontal branch. There it remained for 20 to 30 seconds when it then flew back to the ground, just below the branch where I had first spotted it. There it stood for a few seconds before repeating the upward flight as it had done at the other end of the opening. I began to realize that this was an established pattern of activity, which later I found was repeated many times, taking from one to two minutes for each circuit. Later I counted the bird repeating this round trip 50 times

between 5:15 and 7:40 p. m. The branches on which this bird perched repeatedly became smooth, even polished. By searching for these polished branches, we were able to locate a number of courting grounds. A dancing ground was used by only a single bird while its nearest neighbor had a similar ground about 100 yards away. These strange performances were used solely to announce the location of his territory and to attract susceptible females for mating and would not be considered courtship.

If a female grouse appeared, the male was immediately transformed from the quiet methodical bird into a spirited courting "show off." His tail was raised to a vertical position and the head cocked back as to almost touch his tail, thus appearing to be throwing out his chest. Then walking slowly in very dignified steps toward his mate, he would stop periodically and snap open his tail, fan-like, to form a nearly complete circle with the beautiful brown tips of the tail feathers forming a rich brown bar around the tip of the tail. The bright red mass of tiny tentacles over the eye was expanded and erected, adding a bright crimson dash to their black and white plumage. The neck and breast feathers were erected and spread in a very peculiar fashion to form a huge, black rosette an either side of the neck. Then suddenly the tail feathers would be snapped open like a fan, well beyond a semi-circle, and just as suddenly closed. With this surprising gesture he topped off his displays in a most spectacular manner, enacted for the benefit of the visiting female. Actual mating then took place if the coy female was so minded.

All of my challenging assignments were not as successful as this one, of course, but my report on this one pleased Dr. Roberts immensely. He included four whole pages of my field notes in his *Birds of Minnesota*, together with several photographs reproduced from the motion pictures I got of the entire series of performances.

SALT LAKE BIRDING TRIPS

Minnesota's Salt Lake, according to the Department of Natural resources, is the saltiest lake in the state. This little lake actually touches the South Dakota border a few miles southwest of Madison. We can credit Mrs. C. E. Peterson, wife of a local Madison pharmacist and an ardent bird watcher, with first discovering Salt Lake as a fine birding spot. For many years she reported to Dr. T. S. Roberts on the birds to be found in this area. Along with Franklin Willis, they often visited Salt Lake to check on the many species of migrants as well as resident birds they felt sure they would find there.

I first met Mrs. Peterson while on a trip with Dr. Roberts and William Kilgore in the late 1920's and soon after that I met another of her young birding friends, Goodman Larson. He and I often discussed the possibility of making a refuge of Salt Lake, but we encountered considerable opposition from local hunters who considered it their private duck and goose hunting lake and assumed that, if it became a refuge, they would no longer be welcome to its use. But after several years of negotiations, a compromise was reached in which its status as a "Wildlife Management Area" has pleased both hunters and birders.

Goodman and his wife, Marjorie, usually spend part of each year on their "Prairie Marsh Farm" only a few miles south of Salt Lake. Over a number of years, the Salt Lake bird trip for bird enthusiasts became an established Minnesota Ornithologist Union's official Spring Birding Weekend, with the Larson farm as its unofficial headquarters for many of the observers. And for a good many seasons Dorothy and I have been guests at their farm for the Salt Lake trip. Goodman has developed his farm into a real demonstration site for all kinds of conservation techniques. He frequently entertains and educates 4H Clubs, Future Farmers of America and other groups of all ages in the sustained agricultural methods that should be more widely used in our efforts to head off much of the environmental damage that is occurring in our farming areas.

We began as a small group of fairly well informed birders, but have grown over the years to over 200 enthusiasts. We now meet early on Saturday mornings at the VFW building in Marietta. There we split up into parties led by local birders familiar with the area for identification tours of the birding "hot spots," then we head back to Marietta for a lunch made available by the VFW members. After more field trips in the afternoon, we meet at the City Hall's large dining room for a chicken dinner served by the members of the local Sons of Norway. After dinner, a check is made of the total number of birds seen and identified on all the day's various trips in the area, with special reports on any rarities encountered. Most of those making the trip stay overnight for more birding on Sunday mornings before returning to homes scattered widely over Minnesota, Wisconsin and the Dakotas.

In recent years a small booth with information about Salt Lake and its bird life has been constructed at the parking lot overlooking the lake, as a memorial to Mrs. C. E. Peterson. Later I made a painting of the scene looking out over the lake which shows the Peterson booth. This painting is now in the Lac Qui Parle county Museum in Madison, Minnesota. (Plate 25A)

AMERICAN EGRET

Look carefully at the branch the egret is perched on. (Plate 25B) You will see that it is not a branch at all and you may not immediately identify it. There is a tale hanging on that perch.

On Prairie Marsh Farm, Goodman has deepened a couple of low areas that were originally marshy. These form small marsh-bordered lakes that are attracting nesting ducks of several species in addition to white pelicans, Canada geese, herons, cormorants, rails and yellow-headed and red-winged blackbirds and many others. When the dragline was dredging one of the ponds, Goodman saw something different and interesting projecting out of the mud where the machine was operating and, pulling on it, he unearthed a well preserved elk antler. "So," he thought, "we really had elk wandering about on our farm at some time in the past."

When Goodman later mentioned that he had just seen his first American egret on the shore of Lake Margie he asked me to paint a picture of the egret. Recalling his recent discovery of the antler, I suggested that I combine the two and paint the egret perched on an elk antler. This he agreed to enthusiastically, and so the accompanying painting came into being.

SWANS

As the name suggests, tundra swans nest in the far north of Canada and Alaska. They pass by the thousands through Minnesota on their spring and fall migrations. Large concentrations appear regularly in fall for extended rest and feeding stops in the Mississippi River and adjacent marshes enroute to their wintering grounds in the Chesapeake Bay area in Virginia and the Carolinas. This painting resulted from what was a rare sighting of these huge birds right over my home some years ago. (Plate 26A) Our area obviously is not on a much traveled route through the state, but this depicts part of a small flock that showed signs of dropping in on the river by our house but decided to continue on to join the larger flocks farther down river.

Another swan experience occurred when considerable numbers of the birds had been reported passing through western Minnesota along with large flocks of several species of geese. This induced me, along with a couple of other staff members from the Bell Museum, to go west for some movies of both swans and geese. We eventually located a small flock of swans on a marshy lake that promised good chances for photography, so we assembled my portable blind and set it up on the margin of the lake, planning to wait until the next morning for some pictures. On arriving about sunrise we found our lake already occupied by a fine flock of swans probing deep with their long necks

for aquatic vegetation that was abundant there. I unpacked my equipment hurriedly since I expected to remain in the blind for some hours. My companions then took off for observations elsewhere. After studying the situation carefully, I decided to lie down and crawl slowly to the blind as not to disturb the feeding flock. This plan I successfully carried out and I was much satisfied with my success. Then I began setting up my equipment and, on starting to load my movie camera, I was really shocked to find I had brought only exposed film. Here I was in excellent position for photographing and no film to record my observations! What to do! I knew my pals would not be back for several hours with the film needed. I had the idea that I might catch a ride back to town and get new film.

A poor chance, but at least I could give it a try, I thought. So, crawling flat on my belly, I left the blind hoping I could reach the shelter of a large boulder undetected by the swans. From there I could go on hands and knees far enough away without flushing the swans. After suffering some severely scraped knees and elbows, I succeeded in carrying out this plan. Now, "What are my chances of thumbing a ride in to town with this road having a minimum of traffic?" Here I had a stroke of good luck. My friends had decided to drive by to see if I had gotten settled in my blind without flushing the swans. Their arrival, of course, gave me the film I needed. I undertook the creeping and crawling act in reverse back into my blind. What a relief and a feeling of accomplishment when I did succeed in reentering my blind with my subjects still performing admirably, right where I wanted them. A nice series of sequences of their tipping and feeding followed. Finally they started stretching their necks in unison, which is their signal for a take off, and I got a fine few feet of movies as they made a long running start and lifted off on another long flight toward their arctic nesting. A greatly appreciated reward for a tough morning's work.

FOXES IN RED RIVER VALLEY

Whether or not you have a specific aim in mind, while in the field you can never be quite sure what Natures' diversity of wildlife you might encounter to arouse your interest. Some years ago I was driving about on the side roads of Mahnomin County on the edge of the Red River Valley, watching and listening for booming prairie chickens. In my travels I had located a four square mile area surrounded on all four sides by farm roads. It appeared to be virgin prairie and an ideal setting for booming grounds. Stopping and scanning about with my binoculars I spotted some sort of action on a low rise far off in about the middle of the tract. Studying the movements carefully I found they were not prairie chickens, but small red fox cubs playing about what I presumed would prove to be a den. I at once switched my interest to the foxes since this appeared to offer an unusual opportunity for photography. (Plate 26B) Since I already had my blind in my car, I packed it up and set off on foot toward the fox den. The cubs, of course, disappeared as I approached, but I studied the situation and decided to place my blind about 50 yards from the den, directly behind a small bush. Otherwise the area was without trees or bushes. Retreating as soon as possible, I allowed time for the foxes to become acquainted with the strange object behind the bush by leaving it over night. Or at least part of the night, since I drove back to the area before sunrise and hiked in the dark in the general direction of the blind. Several wet, splashy spots that I had avoided previously, I sloshed through in my hip boots before actually, spotting the blind and settling down to await the sunrise and the chance for pictures.

As soon as the dawn light appeared, a couple of cubs came out of the den and began snooping around, presumably chewing on fragments from previous meals and pestering each other. Then another head popped up and a fourth. Action pepped up considerably with the new arrivals. Mock fights erupted and tail pulling began. A fifth cub joined the company and, believe it or not, a sixth and seventh appeared. I began asking, "How many cubs can there possibly be in a single fox family?" Number eight finally appeared and what a happy, tumbling, wrestling, playful family it turned out to be. I fumbled a bit with my equipment in trying to catch as much of the action as possible before running out of film. I was continually smiling if not actually laughing out loud at all of the performances being enacted by these hyperactive cubs. The show went on for some time until suddenly the mother vixen appeared from over the rise beyond the den. Ever alert, she froze for a few moments, and, hearing the buzz of my movie camera she gave a sharp little bark – and every little cub made a dive for an entrance to the den. There turned out to be several of them. Such instant obedience was hard to imagine. The vixen, definitely alarmed, turned and disappeared over the rise. Every thing was quiet and the show was over.

SHREW

One winter, years ago, I was staying with the game wardens at their cabin in Grand Marais on the North Shore of Lake Superior. They told me about a deer yard along the highway near Cascade River where I might get some movies of deer browsing on white cedar that was common there. The term "deer yard"

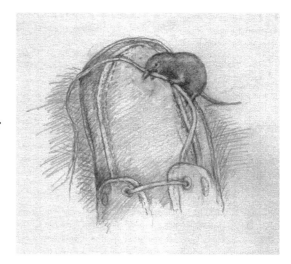

Shrew nibbling on Breck's shoelace

sounds like a fenced enclosure for captive deer but, no, this refers to an area where good browsing induced deer to concentrate during the deep snows of midwinter, where they beat down trails for easy traveling, especially when wolves might be harassing them.

Following their suggestion, I drove to the area, cut some cedar branches as bait, set up my blind in some brushy cover nearby and settled down on my camp stool anticipating a possibly long wait for action. The tedium was relieved after a while when I spotted a tiny little long-tailed shrew exploring around only a few yards from my blind. I almost forgot about the deer in my watching it dive down in the snow and reappear here and there, fortunately coming closer and closer to my blind. Most wild creatures fear the odor of humans, but it may have been the smell of my leather boots that finally lured it to actually come into my blind where he climbed up onto the toe of my boot and began chewing on the leather laces. I don't recall ever having had a more pleasant feeling of friendly companionship with a wild animal I had toward this curious little shrew, showing no fear whatsoever of me, only curiosity over whether or not this strange smelling boot might prove to be a source of food. My only regret was that the whole episode took place too close for my camera to focus and, too, the least movement on my part would have quickly ended the show. I never did get any deer pictures, but I felt far from disappointed in the day's efforts by the little show put on by one of the smallest of American mammals for my particular benefit.

DR. ABBOTT'S - NORTH SHORE TRIP

Back in the latter part of July, 1947 with our July 26th wedding anniversary approaching, we decided to take a trip along the North Shore of Lake Superior as an appropriate way to celebrate that important occasion. Furthermore, we recalled receiving an invitation to visit our friend Dr. W. P. Abbott at Grand Marais. We chose the somewhat longer scenic route along parts of the spectacular drive along the shore. On arriving

at his place I recalled that Dr. Abbott told us of seeing a moose cross his rather long driveway to his home. Perhaps we could see one, too. So we drove slowly, making little disturbance, but the moose failed to put in its appearance. Our youngest, Barbara, three and a half years old, was old enough to enjoy the trip and Betsy and Tom could explore the woods and shore to their hearts' content.

With Dorothy's interest in food preparation, she suggested celebrating with some Lake Superior fish, so Dr. Abbott took us to a fisherman's sales booth where Lake Superior herring fillets were available. And we really did have a wonderful 14th anniversary dinner. Dr. Abbott had an unusual drinking water source that we all found interesting. A long cable from the house was anchored to a huge rock well out in the lake. This supported a bucket tied to a rope which slid down the cable and, on hitting the water, it tipped over and was filled with cold, sparkling lake water which was then pulled back up to the kitchen.

The following day we enjoyed relaxing and I did some pencil sketching along the shore where one of my exciting subjects was a family of red-breasted mergansers riding the gentle wave along the rocky shore.

RED LAKE CARIBOU

After discarding the cumbersome 35mm hand cranked camera we got a much more portable, spring-driven-but-still 35mm Eymo model. It was much better adapted for field work and led me to attempt to locate and photograph the band of seven woodland caribou, the last of that species still existing in Minnesota. These were living in the very extensive black spruce bog country north of the Red Lakes. There, a seven-mile fence had been constructed from the lake, northwest, along the border of the Ojibwa Indian Reservation to prevent the caribou from wandering into the Indian country where the Indians could have shot them legally. Travel in that country was feasible only in winter when the frozen conditions permitted access on skis or snowshoes.

I first contacted the game warden, who described the trip we anticipated as a rather rugged undertaking. But he agreed to take his dog team and toboggan to carry our gear and to locate the caribou. Dr. Gustav Swanson accompanied me on this little expedition. I carried my new Eymo camera tucked under my heavy mackinaw jacket where it was kept warm to function properly. We spent the nights in heavy, eiderdown sleeping bags with one of the dogs curled next to our heads, keeping us cozy warm.

In the morning the warden set about tending his dogs only to be surprised to find the lead dog had disappeared. We wondered, 'How would his team perform without a lead dog?' After bemoaning our misfortune, we found that the warden and his aides had set a series of snares for wolves in the area. (This was when wolves were considered predators to be eliminated). He thought that it was possible for the dog to have gotten into one of these snares. Hoping he was right in his suspicions, he set out to make the rounds of the snares. Fortunately he was right. Caught securely in one of the wire snares, but still alive and well, was his missing dog. It had been accustomed to wearing a collar and did not pull the snare tight as a wolf would do in its struggles to escape, but it lay down, quietly waiting to be released.

After breakfast we set out again in our search for the caribou. We traveled for a good portion of our trip in the frozen drainage ditches that had been dug a good many years before in the ill-advised efforts to drain the area for farming. By following these ditches we could scan the areas ahead while keeping out of sight to the caribou. Several times we encountered fox tracks with dead shrews near the tracks, indicating that the fox had killed the shrews but must have found the poisonous secretions from the gland near the jaws to be distasteful and had tossed the prey aside.

We were really lucky in finally locating a group of five of the seven caribou known to be surviving in the area. (Plate 27A) Nice and warm under my jacket, my camera

functioned well and I succeeded in getting a few middle distant shots of the animals, adequate for proper identification.

CHUCK-WILL'S-WIDOW

After more than a century of bird watching by ornithologists in Minnesota, it is a real red letter day when a new species is located. The chuck-wills-widow (*Caprimulgus carolinensis*) (Plate 27B) is one of our latest such finds. And what is still more remarkable is that the evidence so far indicates that not just a wandering bird, but a fairly extensive population, may be involved.

I was led to investigate this possibility by my friend, Mrs. Rosela Gunderson, who in June 1981 told me about a whistling call similar to, but somewhat different from, that of a whip-poor-will that had been heard about her place in northern Sherburne County. Since the poor-will had been recorded once in Minnesota, she guessed that it might be that species. I visited the Gunderson farm on July 17-18, 1981 and found the bird calling, but only occasionally. I had heard poor-wills calls in British Columbia some years before and, at first, I thought it could be that bird, but an introductory note did not seem to fit into my recollections of this call. I tried to record the call but did not get adequate results for satisfactory identification.

Again in 1982, Mrs. Gunderson reported the bird calling very actively throughout the night. So I again visited the Gunderson farm on June 11-12 with my revamped recorder and got very satisfactory records of the calls. The preliminary note fitted perfectly into that of the chuck-wills-widow. On returning home I played the Cornell University's recording of the chuck-wills-widow, which was an exact reproduction of my recording. This left no doubt as to my identification. While in the field I tried to call the bird in by replaying the recording, but it failed to respond as the poor-will had done. I struggled through the underbrush, wet from an evening shower, in my attempt to see the bird and to my surprise I was able to approach quite near the call but I could not spot the bird perched.

When it finally flew, I was startled by a loud snapping or clucking sound, so entirely different from the usual call that I thought it must have been given by another bird or even a mammal nearby. However, on reading A. C. Bent's account of the bird in his *Life Histories of American Birds* I found an extensive statement of several unusual notes made by this bird. I now think that this sound could have been made by it clapping its wings together on taking wing. Bent further stated that the bird gave its calls at the rate of 25 per minute while I had checked them at 26 per minute. He further reported it giving 834 calls in an uninterrupted series. One morning I awoke at 4:00 a.m. on hearing the bird calling and it continued uninterrupted until 4:30. At 26 calls per minute this gave me the figure of 780 calls.

On June 22, 1982 I spent all day crisscrossing the wooded area (largely second growth oak with hazel undergrowth) hoping to flush a bird from a nest or at least from a perch, but without success. In the evening I played my recordings at intervals beginning at 8:00 p.m. but not until 9:15 did I get any response and that at some distance away. At this time, Terry Savaloja and I approached much nearer with a recording and then the bird flew overhead and alighted perhaps 50-60 yards away. As we approached nearer, it flushed and we followed. But again we were not able to spot the bird perched. This was repeated several times and we got fleeting glimpses of the bird in flight but no observations that would aid in its identification.

While recording the calls we heard a second call sounding as from a distance, suggesting a second bird's presence. I know that birds can vary the volume of their calls and this might have been the case here. Mrs. Gunderson stated that a friend interested in birds living about 8 miles north reported this same call having been heard along with the whip-poor-will. This strongly suggests that an extensive population of these birds may exist in northern Sherburne County.

On the evening of July third, Donald Bolduc joined me. Our plan was to spot the eyes of the bird with a strong flashlight and approach close enough for a flash picture. About 9:30 when it was light enough to see reasonably well, we heard a call nearby and I gave a few whistling imitations of the call. Within a minute or two the bird flew in and alighted crosswise on a branch about six feet high, silhouetted against the sky at a distance of 30 to 40 feet. In a minute or two it flew out into the road we were following and appeared as though it might alight on the ground. Then it flared upward, showing distinctly the white tail markings with the parallel dark margins, a good field mark distinguishing the male chuck-wills-widow from the whip-poor-will.

So we finally pinned down the identity of our bird visually as well as through the nature of its calls. Unfortunately, for several of the succeeding years, Mrs. Gunderson has not heard this bird calling and further attempts to get any responses from replaying the calls have been a failure.

GREAT BLUE HERON

This striking, big heron with its long neck, long bill, long legs and long toes is admirably adapted to be an excellent fisherman. (Plate 28) Recently I spotted one standing like a statue in the shallow waters of the river, watching intently for a fish to come within stabbing distance. I timed the bird with my watch and it stood absolutely motionless for three and a half minutes and after that entire wait, it moved on without success. They will take surprisingly large fish and swallow them whole. We are accustomed to chewing our food, but not so with herons. I have a movie showing the outline of a large carp on its unhurried way down the long, skinny neck until its final disappearance into its stomach. Again I recall stopping my car to study a great blue heron standing on the shore of a small northern lake. It had prey in its beak, but not the expected fish. This was kicking vigorously and it proved to be a chipmunk. Not perturbed by the active animal, the heron calmly swished it about back and forth in the water, time after time, until it finally stopped its squirming and the bird

103

swallowed this unusual prey whole. What a powerful digestive system these birds must have!

As suggested by the hazy background pattern in this painting, the species nests in colonies with the nests usually built far up in the tops of tall trees and are smaller and more fragile than one might expect for such a large bird. Being in this situation, they are exposed to extensive damage from storms. My attention was focused on this heron at the time of a tornado that struck the colony just north of St. Paul several years ago. I had visited the colony earlier in the season when we were building a habitat group in the Bell Museum. John Jarosz, our very skilled taxidermist, had mounted the fine specimens for the group and talented local artist Edward Brewer painted the background from photographic studies of this same colony. After the tornado we visited the colony again and were greatly distressed by the havoc the storm had inflicted on the nesting birds. The young were about half grown in most of the nests and only a very few had been able to hold on tenaciously enough to survive the tremendous blast of the winds. Many were lying dead on the ground or hanging among the branches beneath the nests. Others were still alive but suffering from broken wings or legs. It was a terribly decimating disaster for the whole colony and, on a later visit, we found the adults had deserted the area since it was too late in the season for any attempt at re-nesting. However, wildlife is amazingly resilient and the following year the herons were back and nesting in the same area.

NESTING LEAST BITTERNS

Palmer's Lake lay only two or three miles west of our Mississippi River home and the local Izaak Walton Chapter House. Soon after joining the group I found that the members were considering purchasing at least a small portion of the Palmer Lake shoreline. It was a small body of water with a wide border of cattails. While checking the ownership of some of the properties, I discovered that a pair of least bitterns was nesting in the cattails near the east shore

and I immediately began considering getting movies of the attractive little herons. (Plate 29A) I soon found the muddy bottom was too deep for hip boots, so returning home, I resurrected an old pair of skis tucked away for the summer and kicked my toes into the simple loops. I found them pretty clumsy to handle among the cattails, but they were really effective in preventing me from sinking dangerously deep into the slimy muck. My portable blind was constructed of aluminum tubes and wooden blocks assembled into a dome-shaped frame, which was then covered with burlap into which portholes were cut for photography. A number of stout forked sticks were cut and forced deep into the mud to reach solid footing for support of the blind frame. After considerable struggle, the burlap cover was draped over the frame and my blind was ready for occupancy. I then pushed my skis under the blind, readjusted my feet into the ski loops and settled myself on my campstool, also supported by forked sticks. Then, in this really quite comfortable setting, I spent several hours recording some of the birds' interesting activities, which included the male's returning to feed a small minnow to his incubating mate as she partially arose to receive his welcome donation. So after all of my arduous labors, I did succeed in getting quite an adequate record of these friendly little least bitterns.

The accompanying painting I did with help from the movie frames recorded on my film. I later exhibited this movie at an annual meeting of the American Ornithologists' Union and was not a little surprised to have Sewall Pettingill show a similar series of least bittern movies at this same meeting.

PASSENGER PIGEON

Beyond doubt, our private mini-wilderness at The Brackens hosted the now extinct passenger pigeon (Plate 29B) during the late 19th century. Dr. Roberts saw and collected specimens of this species in the Minneapolis area in the late 1800s. Since the last surviving individual of this species died in 1914 in the Cincinnati Zoo, we were obviously many years too late to have observed it at the

Brackens. Some late records, even up into the 1920s all turned out to be rare individual mourning doves that had slightly more brilliant markings than was normal for that species. So we are considering this as a "has been" on our Brackens bird list.

LOON FAMILY

Some years ago I made a trip in the BWCA with my 14-year-old daughter, Betsy. We frequently enjoyed hearing the varied calls of loon families and often saw these family groups, each with one or two tiny black young, cruising about, frequently carrying the young on their backs. Often while breaking for lunch or getting camp set up for the dinner hour, I made sketches of scenes or other details that attracted my interest. One of these sketches I ran across in my files when I was preparing to make a painting of loons. It showed admirably the habitat I associate with these birds and that is the scene that appears here with the loons added to the composition. (Plate 30)

One often notices while watching loons at a distance, that one of the birds may suddenly turn white. The bird in the painting shows the one bird rolling over on its side, revealing its white belly. Loons have their legs attached so far back on their bodies that they walk on land only with difficulty and often prefer sliding along on their bellies rather than assuming the upright position similar to that of penguins. In fact, they seldom attempt to travel on land more than just to reach the two eggs they may be incubating in a nest only a few feet from the water's edge.

Small vegetation-covered islands are their favorite nesting sites since there they are protected from most of the enemies that might prey on they eggs or young. Normally small lakes will have only a single pair claiming it as their territory, while larger lakes may harbor several pairs, each controlling a single bay. Intrusion into one's territory can often generate vigorous battles accompanied by numerous and varied versions of their loud, hollow calls that will echo and reecho

from the wooded shores. I often think of the calls of loons representing the stamp of genuine wilderness, like the word "sterling" identifies real silver.

RUDDY DUCK

I associate this little duck (that is Florence Jaques' favorite bird) with two small lakes near New Brighton, just north of St. Paul. One of these, Rush Lake, was only a couple of hundred yards across with a wide cattail border. I can see myself seated on a steep little hill, overlooking the lake with my spotting scope, studying and quick-sketching the various attitudes of several ruddy ducks competing over possible mates. (Plate 31A) Later in the day I circled the lake, walking through the wood, checking the birds I could identify. Then I made a second circuit with tubular water skis pushing through the thick cattails to flush some of the elusive species such as the least bitterns, common gallinules, rails and several species of sparrows. This effort produced for me a surprising 69 species – rather good for the limited number of different habitats I covered.

A few days later I visited the somewhat isolated Sullivan's Slough, only a mile or two from Rush Lake. There I found another small population of ruddies scooting and chuckling about in their curious courtship competitions. I had brought my canoe and 16mm movie camera hoping to get some good action shots o,f the cavorting males. I pushed my canoe through the dense cattails where I might encounter a performing male in one of the small openings cut by the muskrats. Time and again a bird would approach one of the openings only to dive and swim under the open water where I could get any pictures. I finally got so frustrated that, looking carefully around the margins of the slough and finding none, I peeled off my clothes and slipped out of my canoe into shoulder-deep muddy water. Finding the bottom fairly firm, I took my camera and, with only my head and camera above the water, I moved about slowly, trying to outwit the ruddies. I felt confident that without the disturbing canoe, I could plant myself at an opening for the action shots I was anxious to get. After nearly an hour of tiring efforts, the birds repeatedly outwitted me and I was forced to return to my canoe, completely defeated in my efforts.

Several days later I was attending an Audubon meeting, comparing bird sightings with some very competent lady field observers. I happened to mention my efforts to photograph ruddy ducks at Sullivan's Slough when one of the ladies exclaimed, "So that was you we saw with a canoe and a movie camera!!

HARLEQUIN DUCK

On April 10, 1932, my roommate, John Turner, and I were driving along the highway that parallels the North Shore of Lake Superior. We made frequent stops, scanning the lake for any interesting ducks, gulls, terns or any other water birds that might be attracted by the huge expanse of the lake. Almost every bay had a fisherman's cabin with a sturdy rowboat pulled up on the shore or perhaps still in action by their owners setting out nets for tulleby or other small lake fish. On one particular bay we spotted several ducks we had assumed would be American goldeneyes or possibly an old squaw or two. One bird proved puzzling and we sat down, steadying our binoculars on our knees, for better views. It was a neutral, brownish-gray bird with an odd pattern of light spots about the head. A couple of species of scoters have light head markings, but their arrangement appeared different on this bird. After checking our field guides, we decided, without doubt, that this must be a female harlequin duck, a western species that had never been reported in Minnesota. We had no telescopic lenses for possible photography to provide proof of our observations, and furthermore, an actual specimen would be a valuable addition to the Museum's collections. (Plate 31B)

So we made plans to collect the bird with the 16-gauge shotgun that I carried, just in case some thing rare, such as this, might come along. As a staff member of the Minnesota Museum of Natural History (now the Bell Museum), I had both state and federal collecting permits. The situation looked favorable for collecting the bird since the mouth of the bay leading out to the big water of the lake was narrow enough for a shot if the bird should try to swim out of the bay. If we alarmed the bird, it could easily fly out if it chose to do so. Hoping for success, we contacted the fisherman. He agreed to let us use his small rowboat to enable John to herd the bird out into the lake, if he could do so without forcing it to take flight. In the meantime, I stationed myself in the narrow passage into the lake. As soon as I was properly concealed in my position, I signaled John to begin rowing the boat slowly toward the duck. Fortunately the bird was not seriously disturbed and simply began avoiding the boat by circling about in the bay. John persisted, however, and gradually the bird became convinced that it should swim out of its quiet little bay for the safer waters of the big lake. But it made the mistake of cruising too near to my point of land and I succeeded in making a clean kill of the duck. I realized that it was not sportsman like to shoot a duck while it was sitting on the water, but this was not a sporting event, but a serious attempt to secure a valuable specimen for the Museum's scientific collections. So I felt justified in taking it in this manner. On bringing the specimen to the Museum later, I remember well that this was the first bird I ever delivered to my mentor, Dr. Roberts, that he did not immediately identify.

BLACK DUCK

My taking of the harlequin duck has reminded me of another duck collecting episode that caused me considerable trouble and discomfort. Two of us were on an early April, 1927 collecting trip driving my little Model T Ford along the North Shore of Lake Superior highway. With my special collecting permits I could take spring specimens in their best breeding plumages for the Museum's scientific collections. At a wooded point near Grand Portage I spotted a beautiful male black duck swimming near enough to shore for me to shoot it. An onshore breeze was blowing so I expected it to drift in to shore where I could easily retrieve it. However, I was disappointed to find that, instead of coming in to shore, it drifted parallel to the shore and well out from where I could possibly retrieve it. Having shot the bird I was in no mood to abandon it, even though the lake was freezing several yards out from shore every night that early in April. I waited and followed the drifting bird for quite a distance before giving up hope of its coming any nearer shore. So, sending my companion back to the car for a heavy bath towel, I peeled off my clothes and waded into the icy water and, with only a few strong strokes, I reached my prize. The lake bottom was strewn with head-sized boulders, covered with slippery algae. As I stumbled back to shore, I stubbed one of my big toes, which bled profusely, but since my feet were well anesthetized by the chilling waters, I was unaware of the damage. This was of little importance, however, since I had succeeded in securing my prized black duck specimen.

Ring-tailed cat in Arizona

Chapter 11: Travels Outside of Minnesota

MOUNTAIN SHEEP

While visiting with Major Allan Brooks, the prominent Canadian nature artist, we occasionally took time off for trips together but I also made several trips around Okanagan Lake by myself with suggestions from him about any special wildlife I might expect to encounter. On one such trip I planned to encircle the north end of the lake to investigate the mountains where I might find big horned sheep. This excited me, as I never had field experience with this majestic animal. One other species he warned me about was the Oregon rattlesnake but he said they were quite rare and he didn't think I would have anything to fear. Having had considerable experience with reptiles, I was not too much concerned. However, I did come across a small rattler and, after photographing it, I released it back into its rocky habitat.

After some hours of climbing I failed to spot any sheep and decided to spend the night there and continue the search the next day. I rolled out my sleeping bag on a small grassy patch and dozed off, planning to get up early when possibly the sheep might be active. I had not planned on what appeared as a substitute for an alarm clock. Just about sunrise, some sort of disturbance must have awakened me and I opened my eyes very much wider than usual to find myself looking directly into the elongated face, of all things, a horse. And I really mean, into the face. Since the animal had placed one foot on either side of my head and was about to sniff, if not to actually lick my face. The animal had found my nice grassy spot a fine grazing patch and, encountering me in my sleeping bag, had come over to investigate. Although I was much surprised, to say the least, I didn't make any rash moves but spoke to the intruder in as calm and quiet manner as I could muster, which evidently satisfied the horse and it calmly moved off and continued its grazing.

After my breakfast I took off again on my mountain sheep search and very shortly located a small band. They were calm and slowly climbing up the mountainside at, what looked to me, a very leisurely pace. Obviously it was a leisurely pace for the sheep, but was quite an exertion for me even though I was in excellent physical shape. The one really good view I got of the animals that has stuck in my memory for years was when the big ram stopped momentarily for a glance down to see if I was following. It had stepped out on a small promontory to get a good look at me. I'm sure it would never realize what an indelible impression it made by that momentary exposure. Actually it was many years before I finally put down on paper my recollection of that moment. (Plate 32A)

ELK OR WAPITI

On a conducted tour of the western Canadian provinces one fall, we thrilled at the beauty of the autumn colors contrasting with the deep greens of the evergreen forests, especially when set against the varied colors of the Rocky Mountains and skies. At one stop in Banff, we were in the middle of the range of the elk, or wapiti. (Plate 32B) There, with the protection of the National Park, the animals actually wandered about through the streets of the town during the early morning hours before the humans were stirring. Some of our fellow tourists took the opportunity to play a round of golf and reported that occasionally they had to loft their drives high off the tees to carry over bands of elk that were strolling through the course.

SECOND HONEYMOON – 1934

The year following our "scientific" honeymoon to Churchill, we felt we deserved a more traditional one by ourselves. Dorothy had had no experience with our marvelous National Parks of the Big West, so we felt it would be appropriate to allot my 1934 vacation period to following an extensive loop of the West to enjoy the much touted, scenic beauties of these remarkable parks.

On July 7, 1934 we set out in our Oldsmobile Coupe, equipped for camping, to enjoy getting acquainted with the Big West. Our route took us directly west, with our first stop at Huron, South Dakota. After checking in at a motel, we visited a carnival where we mounted a merry-go-round. As I swung my leg up over my pinto, I happened to kick Dorothy in the calf, causing her to limp rather painfully back to our motel. Fortunately, no lasting damage was done.

The next day our schedule called for a short loop through the Black Hills after a night in Rapid City. Finding a motel proved to be a problem since the launching of a stratosphere balloon was imminent, attracting large crowds of spectators. We did make what turned out to be a very short loop

through the Black Hills and we picked up the Old Mormon Trail with a brief stop at Fort Bridger. There the stables of some of the ponies that carried the mail for the historic pony express attracted our attention. Farther on we joined the Oregon Trail and enjoyed reading some of the signatures and dates carved in the Independence Rock by hardy pioneers on their way to still farther west.

At Great Salt Lake in Utah we, of course, had to take a swim in the lake and were much surprised and amused by how high out of water we could float, buoyed up by the high salt content of the water. With our bird-conscious eyes we quickly identified a dense swarm of thousands of Wilson's phalaropes whirling about on and over the water. Abundant populations of salt-loving insects must have attracted them to build up their fat contents in preparation for the long, migratory flights to their South American wintering grounds. The lake's smooth, firm-looking sand beach invited us to drive out on it, in spite of warnings not to do so. In trying to start up after a brief stop, our drive wheels spun around and immediately dug deep into the wet sand and left us stationary. After digging and planking the wheels to no avail, we called for help from a partying group nearby and we finally got moving and made no more stops until we reached firm ground. The magnificent Mormon Temple and Tabernacle attracted our attention and admiration for some time.

From there we drove to Bryce Canyon National Park and "oohed and ahhed" at the unusual shades of rust and pink of the spectacular, jagged pinnacle formations that make Bryce such an attraction to tourists. We stayed there overnight, then went on to Zion National Park where Dorothy's notes say, "We developed stiff necks looking up at the enormous 3000 foot cliffs including the "Great White Throne," perhaps the crowning attraction of this park's well-deserved status of National Park.

Then on to Kanab on the Utah-Colorado line where we came upon a fine grassy meadow leading into a canyon with red sandstone cliffs on either side. On inquiring, we found it was owned by cartoonist Charles Plumb, who drew the Ella Cinders cartoons. He cordially invited us to camp back in the canyon. This we did and enjoyed ourselves for three days hiking, birding, sketching and photographing. Mr. Plumb had assured us that there were no rattlesnakes there but, to our surprise, on the first day we had walked only a short distance from camp when we came upon a small rattler. I pinned it down with a forked stick. Dorothy wasn't too happy, but she held it captive while I ran back to the car for a container to capture and preserve it. Buddy Plumb took us on a long horseback ride to the neighboring Cottonwood Canyon for a look at where ancient cave dwellers had lived. Under some very wide overhanging rock ledges we found remnants of corncobs and pieces of squash rinds quite well preserved by being protected from rain for centuries.

While camped in Plumb's Canyon I collected several birds and small mammals for the Museum. When leaving our pleasant little canyon, we thanked the Plumbs cordially for all they had done for us, but they insistently refused any payment.

On driving through the Kaibab forests approaching the Grand Canyon, we were really thrilled to get good looks at a couple of strikingly beautiful Kaibab squirrels with their pure white, bushy tails. The grandeur of the Grand Canyon was so overwhelmingly impressive I will not attempt to describe the colorful cliffs or how hard it was to realize that we were looking almost a mile straight down into one of the world's deepest canyons. We stayed overnight in a small motel and, to cap off our sojourn, there an accommodating buck mule deer with huge antlers came close around our cabin and I got several shots of it with my Graflex camera. We were sorry that our fast schedule did not permit our taking a real hike down one of the Canyon trails.

Our long drive east from the Canyon into New Mexico found us stopping frequently for quick looks at some cliff dwellings, museums and Indian settlement stores and sales booths. Navajo hogans, dome-shaped dwellings made of branches covered with adobe, were common enroute to Flagstaff, Gallup and on to Albuquerque, New Mexico.

We spent the night there and headed back north. Things were going along smoothly when we encountered a small group of motorists gathered on the shoulder of the road, obviously discussing some sort of a delay they were having. We immediately saw what had happened. A small stream paralleling our highway had recently flooded and had completely washed away the bed of the tarvia road, leaving a real "unnatural bridge", supported by little more than the blacktop surface. We were told that a small truck had unknowingly crossed it without mishap but the question was, "How many more cars could dare to do the same?" We looked it over and I decided to make a try to cross it, since the alternative was to make a nearly 50 mile detour. Dorothy got out, lightening our load slightly, and with crossed fingers and holding their breath, the spectators cheered when I got up speed and succeeded in negotiating the bridge without incident. Just how many others decided to do the same, and just what eventually occurred, we never discovered.

From there we turned north to Mesa Verde National Monument. There we joined a tour of many of the 200 rooms, kivas (council rooms) and even turkey rooms, still with perches preserved. Numerous ladders had to be climbed and toe holes in almost-perpendicular-walls were pointed out to us. These left one wondering why these people chose to live in such inaccessible places. Protection from enemies was the most plausible explanation. The guide told us that, from tree ring evidence, it was determined that they had suffered a 23 year drought that ruined their crops and forced them to move south, perhaps as late as 1275 AD, and that the Hopi and Pueblo Indians are probably their descendents.

On our way on to Durango and north we drove over two passes of over 11,000 feet. Some heavy rains caught us before we reached Gunnison where several sporting events had taken up all the housing available to the public. We finally contacted a Reverend Upton of the Community Church and he cheerfully allowed us to roll out our sleeping bags in his church, which we appreciated immensely. I recall that I skinned a specimen of Say's ground squirrel on the secretary's desk (with plenty of paper, of course.)

Going on east we climbed for miles to reach Monarch Pass, 11,369 feet. There we stopped for a look around. A small chirp of a bird caught our attention and, hoping it might prove to be a rosy finch or some other rare high mountain species, we checked it out, only to find it was a chipping sparrow, one we knew well in our own yard at home.

Still farther east and north we passed through Pueblo and Colorado Springs and on to Denver. There we visited the Natural History Museum where we met its Director, Dr. Figgins, (Dr. Alfred Bailey's predecessor) and Mr. Neidrach, the ornithologist. He showed me his method of making leaves out of celluloid. I was interested but have continued making our leaves from various waxes.

From Denver we continued on east through Greeley to spend the night in Fort Morgan. Then, proceeding east over the Nebraska prairies, the weather became progressively hotter. By dusk we began seeing more and more people sleeping on their grassy lawns in their attempts to keep cool. We, of course, became terribly hot and sweaty (this was before air conditioning in cars was available) and about dark we decided to simply roll out our sleeping bags on a grassy spot on a side road, not bothering to put up our tent. After a hot and more or less sleepless night, we took off early as to make as many miles as we could before having to survive another 100 degree plus day. Finally we pulled up at my brother Harold's house in Fort Dodge, Iowa. There they were struggling to keep themselves and their two children cool. This was the beginning of the Dust Bowl days

Moose among the lily pads

we oldsters remember well. Fort Dodge was only an easy day's drive home, which we reached after a memorable, but at times frustrating, Second Honeymoon.

MOOSE

When traveling in the BWCA I have always disliked the sound of an outboard motor. I have the feeling that innumerable deer, moose, bobcat, lynx or even a fisher are standing along the shore just around the next point of land. Hearing the sound of a motor, they retreat back into the woods and stand hidden to watch me pass, unaware of their presence. Gliding along noiselessly with a paddle, my intrusion into the silence of the surroundings is far less objectionable and my chances of seeing interesting wildlife are greatly enhanced.

In all my contacts with moose in the field, one particular sighting I cherish as a choice memory. Frank Powell and I were stroking leisurely along, keeping close to a picturesque lakeshore and watching for whatever wildlife might appear. Occasionally, where the water was shallow, we glided through scattered groups of water lilies, both white and yellow, with our canoe gently pushing them aside, allowing them, undamaged, to drift back over the slight wake of our craft. This reminded me of a similar experience I had had while canoeing in the slow-moving headwaters of the Roseau River further west in the BWCA. We were cruising quietly, watching for moose, deer or perhaps even a caribou. At one point a baldpate duck allowed us to approach surprisingly close. I soon understood the reason for its actions. Instead of taking wing, it spattered along, running on the water and soon outdistanced our canoe, telling us that it was in its flightless period, having lost its old flight feathers, as ducks normally do, and had not yet grown new ones for actual flight. In one cluster of water lilies I spotted a small, white flower bobbing among the others, but only a fraction of their size and with only 6 or 8 petals. Steadying the canoe with our paddles thrust into the muddy bottom, I took several movie shots of this strange miniature. Then, suspecting that it might be a different or even a new species, I collected and pressed the specimen for later study. And it was found to be a rare relative of the normal water lily with only very few specimens in the Botany Department Herbarium.

As we scanned the distance we noticed a disturbance in the water. Our binoculars identified the movement as the head of a cow moose appearing suddenly from beneath the water in a bed of yellow pond lilies well out from shore. She appeared to take a deep breath, then plunge completely out of sight, reaching for the root of a pond lily which we knew was a favorite food. We stopped paddling so as not to attract the attention of the moose, although we realized its eyesight was poor. She repeatedly dived and came up with lily roots dangling from her mouth. Planning for a possible close approach, we spotted a large glacial boulder, almost haystack-size, projecting well above the water not far from the feeding animal. Seeing this as good protection, we circled about and made our approach in back of the concealing rock. Then, awaiting our chance when she dived, we paddled hard, realizing that we would be in the moose's full view when she reappeared. She stopped feeding, of course, and made rather slow progress toward shore in the deep, muddy lake bottom, thus allowing us to gain on her rapidly. Just how close we should go was something of a question but, as we pulled surprisingly near and found her still deeply submerged, we

took a chance and drew along side of the retreating cow and actually patted her on the rump with our paddles. Then showing good judgment in realizing the possible danger of the flailing hooves of such a huge animal, we backed away as soon as she reached solid footing and watched with great satisfaction as the startled moose disappeared back into the woods.

Our North American moose is the largest and most impressive of all the members of the deer family. Some huge bulls attain a weight a little shy of a ton and the spread of their antlers can reach over six feet. (Plate 33A) Unlike the elk or wapiti and the white-tailed deer, the moose is exclusively a browser, that is, it feeds on trees and shrubs while the former species tend to graze on grasses and other herbs, many of which include farmers' crops. This brings them into direct conflict with Man and they regularly invade cultivated fields for their foraging. The moose, on the other hand, tends to spend its entire life in the dense woodlands thus avoiding damage to crops. This habit has relieved it of much of the persecution aimed at the other animals. Its majestic appearance, however, has made it highly sought after by hunters in search of prizewinning game heads. Wildlife artists often paint moose as salable subjects. In fact the moose can almost be considered the trademark of one of the world's best big game artists, Carl Rungius. While I was working with the Canadian wildlife artist, Allan Brooks, he told me about entertaining Rungius on a moose hunt some years before. Rungius shot a fine bull, but instead of just taking the head and antlers as a prize as most hunters would do, he erected a huge tripod and, with a block and tackle, hoisted the animal into some semblance of a live attitude. From this he made innumerable sketches and paintings. This did not give him information on positions, of course, but he spent several days studying and recording how the light struck the moose's coat in various lights in different times of the day. Thus he profited more from his taking this animal than 99% of the hunters who might have shot a similar specimen. While traveling along a back road near the Canadian border north of Red Lake late one

Bison sketches from the Black Hills

fall I came upon evidence of the power of a bull moose. A fine, large, directional highway sign with deeply carved letters had recently been badly splintered by the charge of a huge, super-aggressive, well antlered bull moose. This was during the rutting season when one might anticipate such aggressive action by one of these animals.

BLACK HILLS TRIPS & BISON

In the late 1920s I got my first look at the Black Hills. I joined up with Ed Reinhart, a botanist and author of *The Witchery of Wasps*, a book for which I made a few small drawings. I recall how the pine-covered hills really looked black as we approached them from back on the prairies. We drove up on Mount Harney, the highest peak in the Hills, to the end of the road, then hiked on up to the very summit at 7242 feet where we got fine, sweeping views in all directions of the jagged landscapes of much of the Black Hills.

Several years later in the 1950s, Dorothy and her mother, "Mom" Shogren, Barbara and I took a vacation drive to the Black Hills where we stayed with a friend of Mom and Dorothy's from Madison, Minnesota for a few days. My keenest remembrance of that trip was when I drove down to the bison range in the Wind Cave National Park in the southern part of the Hills. A fairly large herd

of bison was grazing on a partially wooded hillside. I was alone in my car and watched them for some time at a distance. Then I decided to drive off the road and up the hillside where I could get a much closer look at the huge animals. They did not appear at all disturbed by my approach and I remained in my car and took some photos. I then settled down for numerous pencil sketches from almost within arm's reach. (Plate 33B) After a half-hour of getting acquainted, I noticed a car turn off the road and approach me. I recognized his uniform as that of a park ranger and I wondered if I was violating some park regulation. Much to the contrary, he greeted me cordially and asked if I was having car trouble since I had been there so long. He warned me not to get out of my car since the rutting season for the bison was approaching and some aggressive bull might attack me. In fact, he said, a small school bus was actually over turned by the charge of one of these one-ton animals. He was interested in my sketching, wished me good luck and went on his way.

Another bison experience pointed out how a wildlife photographer must be adaptable in taking advantage of opportunities when they arise unexpectedly. When returning from an Audubon lecture in Arizona and New Mexico, we were approaching Garden City, Kansas when we passed a ranch where quite a large herd of bison was pastured. Recognizing the possibility of getting some movie shots of bison herds that might somewhat resemble the primitive herds of our Wild West, I contacted the owner and explained my mission and asked him about how, when and where we might get the best pictures of the herd. The owner was very cordial and invited me to accompany him early the next morning when he went out to feed the herd. Then the animals would be moving in a compact herd toward the food being scattered on the ground. This fitted well into our schedule, so we stayed overnight in Garden City and arrived back at the ranch soon after sunrise the next morning. The bison responded much as he had described and, photographing from his truck, I got several suitable wide-angle as well as close up shots of what we could imagine were "migrating herds." These fitted nicely into a film I had on the making of the natural history of the Minnesota Valley. Thus these chance shots made it unnecessary to arrange a special trip for the rather difficult sequences needed for the film.

ISLE ROYALE TRIP

On July 26, 1963, Dorothy and Barby took me to a gas station near White Bear where I met Judge Hella, Director of Minnesota State Parks, and Thomas Savage. We then drove directly to Tom Savage's cabin on the North Shore of Lake Superior. We had been planning to hike the length of Isle Royale so we were fully equipped for spending a couple of nights and most of three days on the jaunt. Grand Portage was our next stop where we boarded a tour boat for the hour's trip over to the east end of Isle Royale. Our actual hike began at Daisy Farm, a short way west from our landing at Washington Harbor. We were surprised to meet long-time friends, Warren and Bette Nord, on the short boat ride to Daisy Farm. There we set off on what was called the Greenstone Trail, I believe, which followed the ridge of the Isle to Windigo at the far west end of the island.

We had hoped to see a good deal of the moose and possibly at least some glimpses

of the wolves that supposedly were keeping the moose population in check. We were quite disappointed in not seeing any wolves, but we did encounter a couple of moose. I got a few feet of movies of a young bull thanks to my carrying my camera around my neck in addition to my 45 pound pack. The first night we stopped at a shelter cabin where Tom and Hella rolled out their sleeping bags; I went down by the lake and slept with a mosquito bar over my head. While eating breakfast at a table near the shelter we were entertained by a snowshoe rabbit with a couple of young, playing about and hoping for some handouts, which they got as I recall. Near the west end of the island we passed through quite an area of beautiful, big yellow birch trees, some almost three feet in diameter. Also, some huge white cedars indicated, beyond doubt, that this was a virgin forest stand.

Judge Hella developed some foot trouble and finally decided to give up. He turned off our trail at Hatchet Lake, I believe it was, while Tom and I stopped at a lookout tower and had the ranger radio the park superintendent to helicopter in and pick him up. Tom and I were really footsore when we completed our last day's hike of 13 miles, but we made it by 3:00 p.m., just in time to catch the returning boat for Grand Portage. There we picked up our car and returned to Savage's cabin where we met Dorothy and Betty Savage who had driven up a couple days before. While we were there, a female red-breasted merganser with 7 young climbed out on the rocks and I got some movie footage of them and later made a watercolor painting for the Savages. (Plate 34A)

Tom and I had stopped at a Mr. Shemeld's cabin. He had a fine mountain ash tree in his yard and he told us he had shot a kestrel and a sharp-shinned hawk that had been pestering the evening grosbeaks feeding on the ash berries. But he added that he had shot 30 yellow-bellied sapsuckers to protect his mountain ash tree. I knew that these birds were fond of puncturing the ash trees for the sap, but I'm sure he had practically eliminated the sapsuckers for miles around in his efforts to protect his tree.

FAMILY IN COLORADO

Back in August 1974, we decided to arrange a three-generation family vacation. Our suggestion took root and the YMCA Snow Mountain Camp in Granby, Colorado was to be our gathering point. Tom and his family arranged to camp enroute. We became a bit concerned when we heard that a mountain valley where a good many tourists camped was hit by a flash flood and several people were drowned. We thought that Tom's family might have chosen to come by that route but we were relieved to find they had not and they arrived safely. Barbara and Bruce flew to Denver and we drove in to pick them up. While there the girls bought about $100 worth of groceries for our stay at Granby.

Our whole gang was housed in the large, multi-room log cabin where we had fine opportunities for visiting and we were able to cook and eat together. And we really enjoyed those very "yum yum" pancakes. Saddle horses were available and the younger elements got up early one morning and rode out one of the mountain trails for breakfast where they reported that the pancakes there were even more "yum yum."

I did a lot of birding, sketching, and photographing. A Japanese friend located us and came out to see if I might go birding with him to get more acquainted with mountain birds. I took a long hike with him and, among other birds of these high habitats, we succeeded in locating a white-tailed ptarmigan, which pleased him and me, too, since I had seen very few of these high mountain grouse.

One side trip took us to Mary Jane Mountain, which had a particularly high ski lift. A long ride up the cable car got us within a short distance of the top where I felt I could spot some of the typical high mountain birds. However, I did not find anything other than the more typical species such as gray jay, Steller's jay, mountain chickadee and red-breasted nuthatch. We did enjoy the sweeping views, we got of several of the 12,000 to 14,000 foot mountain peaks including Long's and Hague's Peaks in the Rocky Mountain National Park.

Breckenridge, Colorado was only a few miles away and we, of course, had to shop for caps, sweaters or sweatshirts with the name "Breckenridge" on them. I recall that the originally grass-bordered, rocky valley at the city had been worked over so thoroughly for gold that it no longer was a beautiful, grassy valley, but a barren mass of huge rocks.

I made several watercolor paintings of the mountain meadows near our cabin with horseback riders in the distance. In addition to much lively conversation one evening, we had special entertainment – Barby put on one of her belly dance routines in costume and a very professional job she did.

ARIZONA EXPERIENCES

Tucson – 1973

One Audubon program we gave in Tucson, Arizona in 1973 was where we encountered Kenneth and Maxine Peterson. Back in the 1920s I had known Ken as a teammate on the gymnastic squad at the University of Iowa. After graduation we both ended up in Minneapolis, he as gymnastic coach at Roosevelt High School and I as preparator in the Minnesota Museum of Natural History at the University of Minnesota. Years went by without our paths crossing until I found that he had remarried after his wife died. Our reacquaintance came about in the early 1970s when Ken and Maxine attended our lecture and invited us out to see their place and for a visit since both were interested in birds and in photography. His new wife, a widow, was left with a winter retreat near Tucson.

Their Arizona estate included a comfortable guesthouse and we have enjoyed several visits, one in April 1973, to their desert winter habitat. We found them surrounded by saguaro cactus and all the exciting desert plants, mammals and birds that were of great interest to me. Undoubtedly the most unusual of the many happenings while there was our getting acquainted with their almost tame coyotes.

"There comes Limpy." Our hosts recognized the individual coyote with a limp from a previous leg injury. It cautiously approached from the darkness into the lighted area and the small pool of circulated water surrounding their porch where a regular menagerie of Arizona's wildlife might be expected to appear. We waited impatiently for Limpy to come out into the more brilliantly lighted part of the dooryard. As he did, numbers two, three and even four soon emerged from the mass of darkness beyond. Being dedicated environmentalists, they had hoped to make friends of the whining howls they heard regularly coming from the surrounding hills. The coyote families soon located the pond they constructed. Ken and Maxine then added food scraps to increase the attraction and, before long, they developed a regular floorshow for their visiting friends. We certainly enjoyed getting acquainted with their coyote friends and immediately set up our cameras and tripods and tried our luck on pictures. The alert coyotes gradually moved in for the food, but a little too much activity on our part sent them scurrying back in to the darkness. But, still hungry, they soon returned and put on a fine show until the food was all consumed. We had rarely seen coyotes in the wild, even at a distance, and to have several give an excellent chance to study their activities within only a few yards was a real treat. Early in the evening on the next day, it was a different cast of characters in the show. Javelinas, also known as peccaries or wild pigs, showed up before dark. They were less easily frightened and even came up to the low brick wall bordering the porch and accepted ears of corn from Maxine's hand. They finally came in on the porch and I'm sure they would have actually come into the living room if they thought food might be found there. Although they were interesting visitors, they were not as welcome as were the coyotes since they did considerable damage to their choice cactus plants. These they had planted in their gardens after bringing them in from the far corners of their desert holdings. Such unwelcome damage is often encountered from wildlife that one might enjoy befriending. For instance, a sizable population of

pack rats moved in on the Peterson's property. They eventually found these mischievous rodents invading the garage where they climbed up onto the motor of their car. There, in addition to packing nesting material, they seemed to enjoy chewing at the insulated electric wires. This forced a campaign of elimination before the damage could be terminated.

While touring the Peterson's rather extensive premises, we had the chance to get acquainted with the big, columnar saguaro cactus that had been thriving there for centuries. I was interested to find that when a cactus finally died and toppled over, the fleshy parts rotted away leaving a pile of long, hard, very durable wooden ribs. (Plate 34B) These were an inch or so in diameter and sometimes as much as 20 feet or more in length with little or no taper throughout their entire length. I immediately saw the chance to use them as picture framing material and still have one of my paintings of one of these spectacular cacti framed in a rib.

Birds, of course, attracted much of our attention since we had had little experience with Arizona birds. One evening, after enjoying a delicious Mexican dinner with our hosts, we walked up the path to our guesthouse with a flashlight showing us the way when we spotted a bird sitting squarely in the middle of the path. We stopped abruptly only a few feet away and, strangely enough, the bird, which proved to be a poor-will, did not flush but gave us a wonderful chance to examine it in great detail. This is a close relative of the whip-poor-will and is one of the few birds in the world that is known to hibernate. The birds would squeeze into a little pocket in a rocky cliff surface where it would remain for as much as several weeks, camouflaged perfectly with the rock surface.

Cave Creek - 1990

As we have done several times since my brother Harold's death, we drove to Boone, Iowa for a brief visit with Ona May Breckenridge, his widow. This made an easy first day's drive on our way south to various destinations. This time, on February 25, 1990, we were heading for Arizona, partly to escape some of Minnesota's chilling winters – it was ten degrees below zero when we left home - and to get acquainted with the Cave Creek Valley near Portal in extreme southeast Arizona. We took Ona to dinner and found that she was definitely slowing down in her activity.

The next morning we took off to the south, rounded Kansas City and turned west across Kansas. We made a short stop at Emporia for a visit, then on to Wichita for the night. We saw numerous wintering hawks including a jet black red-tail. We had hoped to leave the snow in Minnesota, but it did snow some but then brightened up before we reached Deming, New Mexico. The next day we arrived in Portal, Arizona and immediately looked up John and Ginny Emlen. They had rented a rather large house surrounded by a long stone fence. Back at Cave Creek Ranch, we checked in at a Cabin #5, one of five adjoining motel rooms right on Cave Creek with a nice view across the creek. The next evening we enjoyed a meal at the Emlens and a long, exciting after-dinner "floor show," it might well be called, with the actors being gray foxes, ring-tailed cats and skunks! The long stone fence served as a highway for these visitors who posed obligingly for many photo shots. Several climbed about on the branches of the tree just outside the windows and even came down and walked along the low-sills of the full-length windows. Especially exciting to us were the ring-tailed cats with their foot-and-a-half long tails, ringed with black like a raccoon's, but much more bushy and flexible. (see chapter heading) And they were very active, climbing and crawling into the containers which held dog food and table scraps. One of the three skunks that came along the window sills had an all white back. I thought it must be the different species, the hog-nosed skunk, but the Emlens thought it was only a variation of the common striped species. I had never had such wonderful looks at gray foxes. These kept running along the stone fence, jumping off and back up, for lots of action. Especially exciting action by the visitors frequently interrupted our fine dinner. This most certainly was the highlight of the whole Arizona trip.

Also we were situated within walking distance of the Spoffords – enthusiastic birders who maintained about 20 bird feeders and who broadcast an invitation to all birders in the immediate area to come and watch the bird visitors. Several times during our stay I spent time at the Spoffords' studying and photographing Gambel's quail, curve-billed thrashers, Cassin's finches, Steller's jays, painted redstarts, and many others that came to their bird feeders. So many birders visited Cave Creek that they put out a welcome sign asking everyone to come, uninvited, to enjoy watching the birds.

The name Cave Creek came from the presence of numerous natural caves, mostly situated high on the nearly perpendicular walls of the Cave Creek Valley. On the protected inner cave walls were many Indian paintings of unknown ancient origin. John Emlen and I climbed up to a couple of these caves and photographed some of the paintings. The rugged terrain of the Chiricahua Mountains here in southeastern Arizona was the stamping grounds of the famous Apache Chief, Geronimo. We noticed a particular small valley was named "Geronimo Valley" and we hiked up it for some distance, looking for birds, not Geronimo relics.

GAMBEL'S QUAIL

The Spoffords had a number of bird accident victims in their freezers, and they gave me a Cassin's finch and a roadrunner, which I skinned and salted to be made into scientific skins later. I also spent a good deal of time photographing hummingbirds at our porch feeders and I also made several watercolor paintings of species new to me.

One day we drove south toward Douglas and hiked up the "Skeleton Canyon" and the "Devil's Kitchen" where the Apache chief, Geronimo, had a hide-away while terrorizing the area in the late 1800s. Now there is a roadside monument commemorating the site of his final surrender.

Recently (October 1998) Roger Breckenridge, our genealogical friend living in Apple Valley, called my attention to a book he had located entitled Helldorado. It was an autobiography written by a William Milton Brackenridge who had been a deputy sheriff at Tombstone, Arizona during the Civil War times. Among his many exciting and dangerous experiences were numerous encounters with Geronimo, and, if I remember correctly, he was involved in his final capture. Brackenridge had numerous visits with Geronimo during his captivity and became very friendly with him. And it was "Bill" Brackenridge who was called upon to conduct him by train from his prison in Arizona to his final confinement in Florida. A couple years later he paid him a visit and found he was teaching a Sunday school class in a church where he was being held.

While visiting the Emlens we met Bob and Mary Metz, Ginny Emlen's sister. Later, Bob, John Emlen and I climbed up to a couple of the caves where we photographed a number of Indian paintings on the walls. Nearly all of the caves along Cave Creek Valley were well up on the cliff sides and required a lot of exertion to get to them.

Several times during our three-week's stay at the Cave Creek Ranch we had visits from the local javelina, or wild pig population, but they were quite skittish and not nearly as confiding as those we saw at Ken and Maxine Peterson's place near Tucson.

A few miles west from our motel we enjoyed visits at the American Museum's Southwestern Research Center established for the accommodation of students interested in studying any phase of geology of the region. We met the director, Dr. Wade Sherbrooke, who showed us around the facilities, which obviously were invitingly adequate for students with varied interests to center their activities.

Baird's Sandpiper

Chapter 12: Arctic Trips

BACK RIVER

In the early 1950s, Robert and James Wilkie, owners of the Continental Machine Company of Savage, Minnesota, approached the Minnesota Museum of Natural History concerning their interest in travel, exploration and motion picture photography in the Canadian high arctic. Would the Museum be interested in cosponsoring a trip for the benefits the Museum might derive from it? I was actively using wildlife movies in the Museum's educational programs and such a trip could add much to that activity. Dr. Roberts, Dr. Warner, ornithologist, and Harvey Gunderson, mammalogist, were interested in adding to their collections of arctic birds and mammals, as well as extending their distribution and life history data of those forms from such little known areas; the University Botany Department could utilize collections of arctic plants. Favorable responses from the University set our preparations in action and our party left in early June, 1953 for the Back River region of extreme northern Canada.

Our party consisted of the Wilkie Brothers, Dr. Lou Larson, a physician friend of the Wilkies, and Museum staff members Harvey Gunderson, John Jarosz, preparator, and myself, plus Philip Taylor from the Geology Department who was interested in the study of glacial movements in that region. The area chosen was the lower reaches of

Back's Great Fish River, whose rocky course only two parties of white explorers had previously traveled in summer – Captain Back in 1834 and James Anderson in 1855. The latter was searching for the lost crew of 129 men of the Franklin Expedition of 1845. Dotted lines marked the course of the river on the best Canadian topographic maps with the entire area marked as "unexplored." However in 1950, the Royal Canadian Air Force (R.C.A.F.) had recorded most of the area by high altitude trimetrogon photography and although official maps were not yet available, the Canadian Department of Mines and Technical Surveys generously supplied photostatic copies to our expedition.

Churchill, Manitoba, on the western shore of Hudson Bay, straddled the tree line in that area and was our take-off point. Here we learned that carefully planned schedules into the Back River area didn't mean a thing. During the first week of July reports came in that the ice was beginning to break up north of Baker Lake and, finally, we took off on July 12. Three planes carried our party: a U. S. Fish and Wildlife Service's amphibian plane, a rugged Norseman plane piloted by bush pilot Charlie Weber and another Norseman of the R.C.A.F.

On our arrival at Baker Lake, Sandy Lunan, a ruddy-faced Scotsman who had been in charge of the Hudson Bay Post there for 17

Photographing at Wales, Alaska

years, met us and gave orders to his willing Eskimo housekeeper to "kill the fatted calf." But here, just before the annual supply boat from Churchill was to arrive, this meant opening a tin of canned beef. Scott McRae, the C.M. policeman did not, of course, wear his traditional red uniform. He was a well-conditioned physical specimen, friendly and cooperative. His pretty young wife was conspicuous in her white parka beautifully trimmed in red by the skilled Eskimo needlewomen. Baker Lake is a tiny disjointed sort of settlement sprawled out for a mile along the shore of a narrow inlet at the mouth of the Thelon River. A few official Canadian representatives, several missionaries and a few Eskimo families make up the population.

After a short night's rest in our sleeping bags on Sandy Lunan's dining room floor, Charlie Weber warmed up his Norseman plane and the first flight headed north toward the Back River country. Camp was finally located at 66 degrees, 10 minutes north latitude and 96 degrees, 57 minutes west longitude. Here our tents were set up on a boulder and gravel point that jutted out into the Back River, 15 miles below the mouth of the Meadowbank River. Two additional flights brought in the rest of the party and equipment, the last landing shortly after midnight. But night or day, work and flights could progress uninterrupted since July nights were like brilliant sunsets.

Geologist Spence Taylor determined that the river was 100 feet wide at our campsite. The river was important to us as a source of food and for scientific specimens. Hook and line fishing was good, but not phenomenal, and our short piece of gill net brought in a good many fish specimens including whitefish, tullibees, lake trout, char and graylings. The char with its bright red flesh was voted the best eating.

Although Back and Anderson in 1834 and 1855 found herds of caribou and musk ox, we were disappointed in seeing none of these. A few caribou tracks and a moldering lichen-covered skull of a musk ox were the only evidence of these we found. Gunderson, in his trapping of small mammals, took a few lemmings that were not at the low point in their 4-year population cycle, but definitely not at their peak. Geologist Taylor in his wanderings came across an arctic fox den about a mile and a half west of our camp. We visited the den and photographed a brief encounter with the adult fox. (Plate 35A) Then, finding the carcass of a Parry's ground squirrel near the burrow, we tied it to a stake a little distance from the den and succeeded in getting a short sequence of movies when the fox came from the den and attempted to take the bait back into the burrow. It was puzzled on not being able to remove it immediately and after several attempts it gave

120

up and dived back into the den. This squirrel and the remains of an arctic char lying about near the burrow gave us a suggestion of the diet of this predator. In its summer pelage, this fox was a mottled black, dark gray and white, not the pure white of the winter.

In the three and a half weeks of our stay, we identified only 30 species of birds, 14 of which were represented by only one to five individuals, including the willow ptarmigan. (Plates 35B & 36A) A crude map drawn by an Eskimo living not far from our base camp, published in the *Third Thule Expedition Report,* designated our area as the "very deserted area." No wonder we found wildlife scarce when Eskimos, so skilled at wresting a living from one of the world's most barren regions, called the area "deserted."

Fauna & Flora

One of the most abundant and least appreciated forms of life that kept us lively and wide-awake was the mosquito population. These little insects tended to land on dark surfaces, which presumably absorb heat. One day John Jarosz killed 66 of them with one swat on his knee. We came well-defended against these onslaughts with several types of chemical repellents which we were testing for the U. S. Army Quartermaster Corps. Several provided excellent protection against the bites. However, we soon found that they had to alight momentarily in order to be driven off by the repellent. This constant pelting was bothersome so we had to resort to head nets frequently for relief. Black flies put in their appearance late in July and, although they were of a species not known for their belligerence, their numbers were very annoying.

The scarcity of bird and mammal life gave us the opportunity to get better acquainted with the arctic flora. The very presence of so many varieties of tiny plants invited study as to how they could possibly survive. A Canadian botanist, Porsild, reported finding the big, rose-purple petals of arctic fireweed blossoms frozen as brittle as corn flakes, but an hour later, after melting in the sun, they

showed no ill affects whatsoever. One striking feature of the flora was that practically all were biennials. The short growing season simply did not allow time for them to blossom and produce seeds in a single season. Most of the arctic plants were very small but nevertheless many were beautifully colored. The gorgeous blossoms of fireweed, arctic poppy, Lapland rhododendron, moss pink and arctic arnica all were quite common and added a great deal of color to the otherwise drab and dreary tundra landscape.

While we were at our base camp, Charlie Weber with his Norseman plane came in and flew us downstream along the Back River for 25 miles on an inspection flight. Later, in a stretch of 130 miles, we encountered less than 50 Eskimos living in three widely separated locations. We landed at one of the camps, which was the largest settlement of ten families. The Danish ethnologist, Kai Birket-Smith, in a report of the Fifth Thule Expedition, had reported that the lower Back River Eskimos were the least altered from their primitive habits of living by the white cultures of any of the Eskimo stocks. This statement was made in 1924, but little change had occurred in the intervening years. In spite of their primitive and precarious state, they eked out a seemingly happy existence, spearing fish in summer and shooting caribou when they could during the rest of the year. On our visit to this main Eskimo camp about 30 miles below our base, a short, round-faced Eskimo named Ennikichik welcomed us. According to Scott, the Canadian Mountie at Baker Lake, Ennikichik was a great caribou hunter. These families were loosely gathered together at a rapids because of the good fishing for lake trout and arctic char. After the fishing season they would disband in their search for caribou. At this camp, one family was still living in a caribou skin tent while the others had canvas tents.

We knew practically no Eskimo words, but a small printed vocabulary was of some help in our efforts to converse with these people. It was immediately evident that our host knew no English whatsoever. Their obvious curiosity set the stage for some amusing exhibitions of sign language, picture drawing and exchanging of approving and disapproving gestures. Our most useful, and nearly our only, Eskimo word, "shoo-naah" they fortunately recognized to mean, "What is that?" or "What do you call that?" It was an excellent base word and we recorded a number of words that were added to our Eskimo vocabulary, although they made several guttural sounds we could not pronounce.

While visiting the Chantry Inlet Eskimos, Luke Anguhadluq, the oldest man in the tribe at 54 years of age, traded us a white wolf pelt for two pocketknives, cigarettes and several tins of tea and coffee. His wife gave us a letter she had written in Eskimo syllabic characters, and by hand signs asked us to deliver it to Sandy Lunan at Baker Lake. We made many guesses as to its meaning. On our return trip, Sandy's Eskimo housekeeper told us it reported several recent deaths in the village.

An interesting occurrence took place 40 years later in 1992. I got a letter from a research worker at the Art Gallery of Ontario in Toronto. She had read our report of this trip that appeared in the Hudson Bay magazine, *The Beaver*, stating that we had taken movies and photographs of this group of Eskimos. She was writing a thorough treatise on the life of Luke Anguhadiuq, a very noted Eskimo artist, and could she look at some of the movies we had taken. I sent some clips of the movies and she identified Anguhadliq as the person she was writing about. After a few months I received a copy of the elaborate report telling about his work and some exhibits they had arranged of his work in the art gallery in Toronto. One of our photos appeared in the report.

Back to our visit at the Chantry Inlet Eskimo village: We described the location of our camp to the Eskimos and explained that we would leave a cache of food and equipment for them when we left. Shortly after this visit with the Eskimos, Charlie Weber flew in with his Norseman plane and took Spence Taylor, our geologist, and me up the Back

River to Lake MacDougall, some 50 miles west as the crow flies, for an 85 mile return trip by small boat. On the flight we got good aerial previews of some of the really awesome stretches of wild, white water we would soon be navigating.

After launching our not-too-dependable folding canvas craft and taking aboard the equipment, we watched the plane disappear in the eastern sky. We started our little three-horse-power putt-putt and it purred along reassuringly, although the clouds began to thicken and left us wondering what kind of weather the Fates were whipping up for us.

The second day's travel set the pattern of our navigation for the trip. Although it was exhaustingly strenuous, we did make fair progress and had no accidents. With a sturdier boat and under conditions where our lives did not so completely depend on our equipment, we would have attempted shooting more of the rapids than we did. We had many rapids that could have furnished exciting sport. Tracking was a new experience for both of us, but we had anticipated the possibility and out came our nylon ropes at the next turbulent white water. Then, hopping from boulder to boulder along the shore, we soon gained some degree of confidence in jockeying the boat in and out of the racing channels with bow and stern lines. Usually we could keep up with the careening craft by running, jumping and scrambling over the rocks and in and out of the water. Frequently, however, we had to call a halt in a quiet eddy while we caught our breath, then detoured around some difficult jumble of jagged rocks or got out our tracking ropes for more dangerous white water. In fact, by the time we had passed our last rapids, we felt closely akin to that bird of the mountain torrents, the water ouzel.

The following day we felt a bit battered ourselves after three portage trips with our motor, gasoline, camping equipment, rock specimens, food, instruments and the already much patched canvas boat. Seventeen patches I remember were on the boat with some of the patches on other patches. At one point in the quiet water, below a falls, we spotted a loon swimming. I grabbed my binoculars. Could this be that long-hoped-for arctic species, the yellow-billed loon? Its pattern appeared to be the counterpart of our common southern loon but, sure enough, its bill was a shiny ivory! And the identification of another first field observation of a North American bird for me was verified.

On one of our tracking scrambles I turned my ankle and, on camping for the night, I had difficulty getting my hip boot off over my swollen ankle. I was worried about how I would function the next day, so I got up once in the night to exercise my swollen ankle. And, to my much-appreciated surprise, it felt almost normal the next morning and caused me no further trouble.

We were occasionally fooled by huge boulders looking like tents or houses before we spotted a particular group. When our binoculars proved that these were really tents, we hurried through a mile of tracking between us and the village. If our previous informa-

Breck as a tour guide at Great Bear Lake

tion was correct and no white men had ventured on these waters in the last hundred years, we certainly would surprise the occupants. So we approached with some doubt as to our reception. If they were astonished by our arrival they were most successful in concealing it. Some slight excitement was shown by the two women and five children, but the two men simply left their work, which appeared to be cleaning fish for drying, and walked slowly to meet us. We approached smiling and with open hands to assure them of our friendly intentions and were received with smiles in return. We were at once amazed at the simplicity of their living.

The group of nine comprised an extended family of three generations. They must have been as independent as any similar group to be found anywhere in the world. Their only contact with the outside world was a winter shopping trip made by the men and dog team to Baker Lake. Obviously, their major food was fish. In securing these they used a long wooden spear, tipped by a sharp point that appeared to be an old metal file.

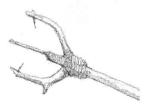
Hand-made Eskimo spear

Just below the tip were two points from a caribou antler; a sharp nail pointing backward near the tip was bound onto the spear in such a way that when a fish was speared, the antlers would spread slightly and grasp onto the fish – a very ingenious and successful instrument for securing their food. A few wing feathers of geese lying about indicated that they were able to get some of these birds, possibly with a rusty old 22-caliber rifle we noticed, although they could have captured molting adults as well as well-grown young.

After a brief visit we returned to our camp where I was anxious to get a small white-rumped sandpiper I had collected skinned and salted before evening. While I was at work on the specimen, the two Eskimo men came and watched me skinning the bird. Without language to explain what I was doing, it was difficult to give them the idea that I was skinning the bird to preserve the feathers, not to eat the tiny sandpiper. They smiled and nodded as though they understood and soon went back to their camp while I finished preparing the specimen. Before very long, however, the two Eskimos returned and presented me with a big dried fish mistakenly thinking we were running low on food. We thanked them as best we could for their generosity that was genuinely appreciated.

We later returned to the village and had another interesting conversation, again using our only Eskimo word "shoo-naah", which we had used with the Chantry Inlet Eskimos, meaning "What is that?" With this word we added a number of Eskimo words to our vocabulary. These people had their camp on a bluff overlooking rather violent rapids, which Back had designated as "Escape Rapids", evidently from some hazardous experience they had encountered there. We, of course, were portaging around this especially wild white water and the cooperative Eskimo men helped us with our transportation problems, which we greatly appreciated. I recall that we gave them some chocolate pudding as a bit of payment for their help.

Near the end of our stay on the Back River, Bob and Jim Wilkie decided to return early to Churchill when Charlie Weber came in with his Norseman plane. He took them aboard along with a part of our equipment and a good many of our specimens while John Jarosz, Harvey Gunderson and I were to stay a few more days. Since the experiences they had enroute back did not involve me, I am here reporting on them in only a very sketchy manner.

John Jarosz and Breck in the Artic preparing bird skins

Their flight back took them over Lake Kaminuriak, which was about 60 miles long. While over this lake their engine began to sputter and finally stopped. An oil line had ruptured, spraying oil over the engine, which immediately caught fire. Pilot Weber was able to pull on a fire extinguisher he had attached to the motor. This put out the flames, but the oil spread over the windows, cutting off his vision. Since he knew the altitude of the lake, he watched the altimeter until he thought they were down to about that altitude, leveling the plane to a very bumpy landing. Unfortunately, on the last bump, the plane hit a rock that was the end of a bar jutting out into the lake about a quarter of a mile long. It doubled up one of the pontoons and the plane settled down and began to sink. This forced the passengers to climb out on to a wing to prevent it from sinking. In this precarious situation they huddled together for several hours. They finally inflated several sleeping bags, cut out an emptied gas tank and, using these, they constructed a raft. They then chopped out pieces of metal from the plane for paddles and succeeded in reaching shore. There they stayed for two to three days waiting for rescue planes to find them. Finally they spotted a plane off on the distance and, using an aluminum specimen tray as a mirror, they signaled the pilot, who circled back, landed and within hours they were back in Churchill. Actually Charlie Weber's wife had come along for the experience and she really got more than she had bargained for.

For Harvey, John, and me, those of us who had remained at the Back River, a party came in for the return trip two or three days later but in a strange plane. Of course, we immediately asked, "What happened? Why isn't Charlie Weber here with his Norseman plane?" They were a little hesitant about telling us what had happened but we finally got the story out of them. Actually two planes came for us. One was an Army Air Force plane, as they were paying us for some reports on conditions along the Back River. We gave them notes and photographs and the results of experiments we had carried out on the effectiveness of some insect repellent we had used. A bush pilot had come in, too, thinking they should have had the business for their company. We were considerably embarrassed in making the decision as to which plane to choose, but we finally took the Air Force Plane for the trip. Thus ended the near tragic Back River Bell Museum Expedition.

The following data are from the final copy of our report to the Army of our Back River Trek 1953:

Our Back River camp was 15 miles below the mouth of the Meadowbank River at about 96° 57' north latitude.

Escape Rapids was about 45 miles above our campsite. This was where we encountered a family of nine members, consisting of one man and his wife, a younger couple, perhaps their son and daughter-in-law, and five children. This was at 66° 1' north latitude and 98° 5' west latitude. The older man was Ou-eye-eye.

Again another family of nine persons was reported on August 2. This family consisted of one man, Fel-Yuk, and his wife and five children. [My notes do not mention this family.]

On July 28 we visited a group of 30-40 Eskimos about 25 miles below our camp. The leader appeared to be an elderly man, En-niki-chik. It was here that we identified the artist, Anguhadlih, about whom a researcher from Toronto was writing her thesis.

GREAT BEAR LAKE – CHAR FISHING

Early in the spring of 1962, Jack Dow, President of the Louis F. Dow Company in St. Paul, called me. He asked if I would be interested in accompanying him and a group of his friends on a fishing trip to the Coppermine-Great Bear Lake area in the Northwest Territories of Canada. I would be the naturalist for the party with my expenses paid. Of course, I accepted with enthusiasm. This would give me the opportunity to take movies of the natural history of the area and collect some specimens for the Bell Museum. Suitable Canadian permits were arranged and the group took off on August 14 in their private plane for the North Country.

I profited considerably from this trip, but I very soon was somewhat irritated by the actions of several of the party that led me to classify the group as "ugly Americans." I informed Jack Dow of my objections to these actions and I felt a bit irritated throughout the trip, but it didn't disrupt our relations. My voluminous diary (45 pages) gave pertinent details of the entire trip, but I will relate only two of the major incidents I remember in particular.

White-eyed Robin

My hosts did not object to my occasionally hiking off by myself while they were fishing. Since my interests were mainly in birds and botany, I reveled in the chance to prowl aimlessly in this exciting habitat for whatever came to my attention. It may seem odd that one small bird should suddenly become my focal point since it was only a robin – but not exactly a common robin. Some years before, Mr. M. J. Magee, a banker and a very active bird bander in Sault Ste. Marie, Michigan, called my attention to the fact that he invariably encountered small flocks of late-migrating robins displaying a light gray plumage and having larger white eye rings than the local birds. These he felt sure must be a far northern race that was migrating after the resident birds had already gone south. I wondered if I was far enough north to find these birds here at Great Bear Lake. I had found that the robins in northern Canada and Alaska were far shyer than the door-yard birds I was used to seeing in the states. And these Great Slave Lake birds were also unusually shy. On this particular hike I ran across a small flock of 25 or 30 robins and hoped that I could stalk close enough for a telephoto shot to determine if it was this northern variation. But they were much too alert and I soon gave up. I had my collecting gun with me so I decided to take one of them, but even this proved difficult. After several stalkings, I finally succeeded in getting one. But instead of dropping to the ground, it lodged far up in the bristly branches of a spruce tree. I was, frankly, amazed to find 60-foot spruce trees this near to the tree line. I tried throwing stones to dislodge it, to no avail. I then thought I might be able to shoot off the branch, so I slipped a charge of heavy shot into one barrel of my 16-gauge shotgun. The first shot had little or no affect on the tough branch. Neither did the second or third shot. So my only chance of retrieving my choice specimen appeared to be to climb the tree. Have you ever tried pushing yourself through the bristly, thorn like branches of a spruce tree? Not a pleasant prospect! But I buttoned up my collar tightly, put on my leather gloves and twisted, squeezed and squirmed my way up and finally reached my goal. The bird proved to have the gray plumage and the white eye ring, so I very carefully carried it back to the cabin and made a small watercolor painting of it in its fresh condition for future reference in its identification. (Plate 36B) Later, in examining specimens in the collections of the American Museum of Natural History in New York, I found that they had so few specimens from the far north that a definite determination of such a northern race of robins could not be made.

We had just landed our sea plane at the mouth of the Tree River that flowed north into the Arctic Ocean, north of Great Bear Lake, with the party all set to fish for the particularly colorful arctic char known to inhabit this river. It was a stroke of luck that we met a couple of Eskimos with their boat and outboard motor who were fishing for food for themselves and for their dogs, who were back at their village. They spoke reasonably good English and, after a bit of good-natured conversation they agreed to take us up the Tree River to a rapids where the char were biting especially well. I had been taking some still pictures of our landing and, since they described our destination as "just upstream around a bend", I climbed in with the first load with my still camera. To my considerable concern, we went not "just around a bend" but around many bends, a mile or more to the fishing spot. I had planned to take some still pictures and then hike back for my movie equipment when the men started fishing. Not wanting to spend so much time riding down and back I asked our Eskimo friends to bring my camera along with the second load of personnel. I gave the Eskimo a detailed description of the brown leather case and just where I had left it. This would give me more opportunities to shoot pictures of the men pulling in the remarkably brilliant red char; I could get action shots when the boat returned with the second load of fishermen and my movie camera.

After some time the second load returned, but without my camera equipment. Here was all this spectacular fishing action taking place – the men landing what was undoubtedly the most brilliant arctic char to be had anywhere in all of the arctic - and I had no movie camera to record it. I knew there was not time enough to get my equipment since we had to get back to our plane and make the return flight back to Great Bear Lake that day. It would do no good to berate the poor, forgetful Eskimo, although I did make my displeasure abundantly clear to him. I later had to take movie shots of some of my still pictures and enlarge some very poor, amateurish, 8 mm shots taken by one of the fishermen to include this extraordinary adventure in my account of the trip, which I was expected to provide for the members of the party.

WALES, ALASKA – May 1964

I had been very interested in ornithological investigations in Alaska, particularly in studies of arctic birds that appear in Alaska merely as random visitors or as ones becoming established as permanent residents. On one of my lecture tours for the National Audubon Society I spoke at the Denver Natural History Museum. Dr. Alfred Bailey, the Director of that museum, was an alumnus of the same University of Iowa museum preparation course where I had taken my work several years after his graduation. He and his wife invited Dorothy and me to stay with them while in Denver. On hearing that I was anxious to do some fieldwork in Alaska, he pricked up his ears and made many valuable suggestions. One in particular was that I contact the Eskimo postmaster, Dwight Tevuk, who had helped him with collecting birds and with securing two Pacific walruses that he was to use in preparing a habitat group for that museum.

One of Bailey's stories that amused me greatly has stuck in my memory. Enroute from Point Barrow to Wales by dog team, he and his guide stopped at the guide's friend's home overnight. They spread out their sleeping bags on the floor where Bailey was not enamored with the strange odors in the room. In fact, he soon became slightly ill from breathing them. The idea came to Bailey that he could get a bag he had wrapped around the gasoline can to use as a pillow. He felt quite pleased with his idea. However, just as he was dozing off comfortably his guide tapped him on the shoulder and said, "I guess you'll have to get rid of the bag. It's making my friend sick."

Following Dr. Bailey's suggestion, I contacted Dwight Tevuk, who generously agreed to assist me in finding any Eskimo help we might need during our visit in Wales. Soon after my Denver visit I completed my plans for a museum-sponsored trip in early May, 1964 to Wales on Bering Strait. Our museum friends, Bob and Jim Wilkie, again agreed to supply us with financial help. Early in our planning, we found that a graduate student in wildlife management, David Cline, was more than anxious to visit Alaska and was well trained for just that sort of an expedition. He proved to make an ideal assistant for the trip.

A bird collecting and photography expedition into such a primitive area as Bering Strait required considerable planning and condensing of equipment, which included tents and cooking utensils, in addition to collecting and photography gear. With plans finally completed, we flew on May 8, 1964, on commercial planes as far as Nome, Alaska. Then we contacted a local airline about getting to Wales, located on the tip of the Seward Peninsula, with bush pilots delivering mail. Definite schedules for such flights were nonexistent, depending so much on the weather. The really pioneering character of the flight was impressed on us right at the start. After three days' delay, word came that a flight to Wales was in order. Our pilot, Jim Isabel, squeezed our dozen or more into the baggage compartment. The plane was a little red single-motor, ski-equipped model. Finally we started down the rather short runway, but didn't take off. An experienced bush pilot, Jim decided we could not be airborne, so we turned around for a second try, then a third and a fourth. Finally he persuaded an Eskimo to take his gear and wait for another day or two to make the flight. With that reduction of weight, we succeeded in getting into the air and headed northwest for Wales. There we landed on the still snow-covered sea beach in front of the village. What appeared to be the total population of 50 or 60 people, turned out to greet the plane, hoping for mail or just curious about who or what might deplane. I happened to be wearing an old, ordinary, narrow-brimmed felt hat that elicited the comment, "Look, a cowboy!" from one of the youngsters. Our numerous packsacks soon came out and, at first, we were a bit disturbed when the Eskimos, young and old, grabbed our bags and started toward the village. You never saw such friendly, helpful red caps – with no thought of tips - but just anxious to be helpful.

Our pilot, Jim Isabel, took us to the school to meet Mr. Greenup, the teacher with whom we discussed our housing problem. We had camping equipment, but we had contacted the Bureau of Indian Affairs in Nome and they had suggested that the old school building might be a good place for us. Greenup informed us that two well drillers were already established there and would have first choice. However, on talking with them, they suggested the upper room over the kitchen, which was heated from a register, and we were more than pleased with that situation. Later we met with Dwight Tevuk and he agreed that this would be fine. This settled our housing problem and we moved in. Later we met Greenup and his wife and two children and also Mr. and Mrs. Horton, who managed a weather station. They lived in a small house just south of the main Eskimo village. These people made up the total non-Eskimo population of Wales.

In checking over our varied equipment in our new home, we discovered that one important item was missing – our food bag. This being the case, I immediately went shopping for a bit of nourishment. I located the store and pushed open the squeaky door of the primitive looking establishment. As I stepped up to the counter I was a bit surprised to see, seated opposite me, a row of the wildest looking Eskimos I could imagine. Most of them wore parkas with fur collars, thin scraggly beards and mustaches, baggy trousers of untanned sealskin and oversized mukluks. I was a bit hesitant about turning my back, but this fear was entirely uncalled for. In fact, the following Sunday I entered the little Swedish Covenant Church to find one of them playing the ancient foot-pedaled organ for the service led by the Eskimo minister, Reverend Walter Emuck. One Eskimo mother attended the service with her fur-bordered parka hood thrown back and, leaning far forward, she shook out a baby well bundled up for the service in the rather chilly chapel.

After getting well settled in our "upstairs apartment" we spent nearly all of our time hiking about in the surrounding, rather rugged territory, photographing and collecting an occasional bird specimen. On one of

our trips we came upon the ancient cemetery. We had been previously warned not to disturb anything lying about. Due to the rocky terrain and the permafrost, the bodies were not buried, but the coffins were simply laid among the rocks. The caskets had fallen apart or had been badly disturbed by polar bears, wolverines or wolves. My notes listed "many human bones scattered about together with whale ribs and jaw bones, polar bear skulls, rusty shotguns and rifles, iron pots, boat oars, sledge frames and numerous unidentified items." It was evident they had left the dead with some of their choice belongings. I measured a couple of the larger polar bear skulls, which proved to be about normal size for the species. We took numerous photos, both movie and stills, before Dave spotted a yellow wagtail hopping about, quite unconcerned, exactly like an American pipit. This was our first sight of a Siberian species. (Plate 37A)

After one morning's collecting and photography, I was making watercolor sketches in my upstairs studio when George Kite, an old, much wrinkled, almost toothless Eskimo, came up the stairs. He handed me a small piece of equipment with the explanation that he had found it on the tundra near the Raven Rocks. Not knowing what it was, he guessed it must belong to me. I really pricked up my ears and opened my eyes wide since it proved to be my light meter. I hadn't realized I had lost it. My cameras had no through-the-lens exposure meter, so I would have been terribly handicapped without it. I thanked him enthusiastically and gave him a generous reward. He smiled broadly, of course, and was very pleased to find he had been able to help me.

Following is a quote from one of my numerous letters to Dorothy during our stay in Wales:

"...we are spending this morning in the house. The wind is 45 miles an hour and the temperature 30 degrees F. It seems the temperature stays within a few degrees of 30F all the time. This is the first day we have not gone out. We finished preparing a beautiful white rock ptarmigan Dave got yesterday and taking some interior shots of our 'apartment.' ... [Yesterday] I went up to visit Dwight Tevuk and his wife to ask some questions. He has a nice little house covered with red roofing. I walked around for the door but couldn't find it at first. Finally I noticed a hole in the snow about 20 feet out in the front yard and I realized his tunnel-like entryway, 20 feet long, was completely under the snowdrift. I walked down 14 steps cut in the snow to get to his door, which normally was at ground level."

It was mid May when Dave Cline and I accompanied Pete Seradlook, an Eskimo, who was just hitching up his dog team and sledge to make a run up north of Wales for a few miles where he knew he would have good luck hunting eider ducks. Eskimos, of course, are permitted to hunt ducks on a subsistence basis in spring. After a spirited ride of a couple of miles behind the willing dogs, we decided to part company. The ice pack had shoved up a particularly high ridge of ice a couple of hundred yards out near the open water that would give us good protection for photographing the migrating flocks of eider ducks. So with Pete's warning not to go beyond the ice ridge, Dave and I climbed, slipped and slid over the huge, jumbled ice cakes to find a nice pocket in the 29-30' high ridge of ice cakes that was out of the wind. There we watched and photographed the long chains of ducks. They were continuing their migrations to lands still farther north, to nest either west along the Siberian coast or east on the arctic rim of Alaska or Canada. These birds had been wintering along the Pacific Coast near the Aleutian Islands, 400 miles to the south. The flocks were probably made up of king, Pacific, spectacled, and Steller's eiders, along with Pallas murres and horned and tufted puffins, although they were skirting the shore ice too far out to make positive identifications.

After an exciting few hours of photography, we returned to Wales to find Pete Seradlook had arrived back home with a good bag of eider ducks. He and his family were interested in the birds as food, of course, but we were glad to deal with him for a few birds as museum specimens. We were especially excited about the beautiful male king eiders that were at the peak of their gorgeous spring plumage. (Plate 37B) I soon retired to my field studio in the upper room above the old school house (It was scheduled for removal soon since the new building had just been completed.) We had adequate heat coming through the register opening from the kitchen below. There I spread out my pencils and watercolors and proceeded to make color notes on the fleshy parts of the bills, eyes, eyelids and feet. These were necessary records since the colors of these parts changed greatly on drying as museum specimens. These birds were then skinned and salted for return to the museum to be made into scientific skins or mounted for the permanent collections of the Museum.

Even at this late date of May 15, many deep snowdrifts remained while the windy conditions left some areas completely clear of snow. There were places where the deep snowdrifts covered completely the rapid streams of snow melt water that undermined the drifts. One had to be constantly alert to the possibilities of breaking through these snow bridges.

During the following few days we made the acquaintance of Silas Komonoziak. Like most of the homes, Silas's home had a front door leading into an unheated entry compartment which opened into a second partially heated area where food was stored, then a third door opened into their living quarters. I remembered counting 14 steps cut into the snow bank leading down to the level of the front door. Here, in their very congested home, Silas had a tiny one by two foot table immediately adjacent to a window where he did his ivory carving. He was busy at the time of my visit working on a very nice polar bear carving. I asked to purchase it but he told me it was for one of the two white workmen who had been in Wales for several weeks drilling a well for the village. I was disappointed since it looked like an especially fine bear carving, but he said that he would make another and send it out to me

Eskimo ivory carvings

later. Just before Christmas, 1964, I wrote him asking about his progress on my polar bear carving. Following are some quotes from his very well written letters:

"I have been quite busy trying to hunt seal on nice days and carving ivory for the store on stormy days. Have just finished carving ivory for the day and have been working on your bear and have it about half done. Working by gaslight, my eyes are not as good as they used to be. Some times I think I make nice looking bears and other times I think they do not look as good as I think they should look but I will try my best on your bear....On the 9th of December I saw two polar bears on the front side of Cape Mountain. They were not very far away but I was not able to get them for being afraid of going through the thin ice....Have gotten a few seal. Have been getting too much southeast wind. We always like the north wind for hunting. I hope to have your bear finished this week."

He did finish it and it is the very best looking polar bear carving I have ever seen. I sent him the payment for it and I received another excellent letter from him in reply:

"The money you sent went to buying two dresses for my daughters. Thank you very much....We had a nice Christmas here having had a Christmas program at the school and one at the church. We also had a nice village Christmas feast with reindeer stew as the main dish and lots of Eskimo ice cream along with berries, rolls, donuts and coffee."

I might explain here that Eskimo ice cream is seal oil whipped up very vigorously with the hand into a fluffy material something like whipped cream. Silas continues:

"All of the people still remember you as the Eskimo people do not forget nice people. I still get a smile from remembering how all the young boys were calling different birds by fancy names after you were here. Before they were just plain "birds" or "snipe."

Here I should add that I left a copy of Roger Peterson's bird guide for the library of their school when I left. I was very pleased to find that some of the boys were beginning to learn the names of the birds after an experience with me on this trip. More of Silas's letter:

"It would be nice if you could come up here when we have a nice spring. Last spring was so poor being bad weather all of the time. I wish you could see the people here bringing in walrus by the boat loads. I guess any one of the boats would take you along on one of the walrus and seal hunts. You could take many pictures as there are many seabirds of different kinds.
Sincerely, Silas Komonoziak."

Well drilling here faces serious problems due to the permafrost. This makes it necessary to keep a well constantly in action to prevent it from freezing. Two sets of pumps were needed, one in reserve to take over the work when the first pump was inactivated for any reason. On discussing their work with the drillers, we found they had drilled their first well too close to the shore. They then drilled a second well farther back and this too was salty. They were then working on a third well, still farther from shore, hoping to finally get fresh potable water. The villagers got their water supply from chopping out ice from a flowing spring a couple of hundred yards up the mountain side and melting it in huge oil barrels kept by the kitchen stove. Their primitive sewer system was a so-called 'honey bucket' that was carried well out from shore and dumped on the ice in the hope that there would not be an onshore wind blowing when the ice broke up in spring.

The Swedish Covenant minister, an Eskimo Reverend Emuk (Outwater) and his wife very kindly invited us to have dinner with them one evening. We were served a rather normal meal for us except that the meat was oogruk liver. An oogruk is a huge, 700-pound seal. This they kept in a hole in the snow bank just outside their door, covered by a large wooden cover to prevent any stray sledge dog from sampling it. The liver tasted much like beef to us with no liver taste, and Reverend Emuk surprised us when he mentioned that he spent much of the nicer days hunting seals. The oogruk we had for dinner was no doubt taken by him personally. After dinner we told him how much we appreciated their preparing such a palatable meal for our special benefit, but that sometime we would like to enjoy a typical Eskimo dinner. Their reply was "Oh, no, you probably would get sick if you tried one." She was no doubt right, we decided, after glancing over a few of the recipes in a small cookbook assembled by a school teacher in Shishmaref and printed exactly as some of her pupils had reported their home recipes as follows:

"Owl"
Take feathers off from owl. Clean owl and put into cooking pot. Have lots of water in pot. Add salt to taste.
Bert Tucktoo

"Oogruk Flippers" (Ooshak)
Cut the flippers off from the oogruk. Put the flippers on the seal in fresh blubber. Let them stay there for about 2 weeks. Take the loose fur off the flipper. And then cut them in small pieces then eat the meat.
Raymond Seetomona

"Eskimo Ice Cream"
Grate reindeer tallow into small pieces. Add seal oil slowly while beating with hand. After some seal oil has been used, then add a little water while whipping. Continue adding seal oil and water until white and fluffy. Any berries can be added to it.
Morris Kiyutelluk
Stewart Tocktoo

In checking numerous recipes, I find these Eskimos recognize a good many low-growing tundra plants and many of their berries, leaves and roots are preserved over the winter months in blubber or seal oil. I recall once picking 80 crowberries (*Empetrum nigrum*) from an area covered by the palm of my hand.

On June 4 our plans called for a Muntz plane to take us out to Nome, but considerable confusion developed as two planes came. One plane landed on the old metal-matted landing field two miles from the school. This was a military field used during World War II to ferry planes to Russia. We finally decided to have Tevuk take our ten packs down to the beach to be loaded onto the Muntz plane – when and if it arrived – while Dave and I were to hike the two miles to the other field. This required splashing through a quarter of a mile of knee-deep water with rough ice beneath, terrible footing, in which Dave fell and filled his boots with ice cold water. We had already packed our hip boots, so Dave borrowed a pair, waded the quarter mile and had an Eskimo return them for me to slosh my way to the plane. So our departure from Wales turned out to be a really unique and a very tiring experience.

From Nome we flew on a commercial plane to Fairbanks where we had a visit with Brina Kessel, biologist at the University of Alaska, and her two very well trained, big white Samoyed dogs. After looking over their largely ethnological museum, we boarded our plane for home.

WALES, ALASKA – June 1965

In 1965 plans developed with Jim Kimball, the Minneapolis outdoor writer, to make a repeat visit to Alaska. Jim was anxious to write a series of articles about some of the far off parts of Alaska such as I had made with Dave Cline in 1964. Such a trip would give me another chance for more wildlife movies for our educational series, as well as, more bird specimens for the Museum Collections. It could also provide more valuable data on bird movements across the Bering Strait from Siberia. So early in June we took off by commercial airlines for Nome.

There we again arranged with bush pilot Jim Isabel of Muntz Airline to fly on a mail run to Wales.

We landed on the ice just offshore, in front of the village. A crowd of 50 or 60 Eskimos greeted the plane and I was able to recognize several of them from my stay there in l964. I certainly should have greeted Silas Komonosiak, the carver who made the excellent polar bear for me, but I did not, and my friend Dwight Tevuk later told me that Silas was very disappointed that I did not recognize him. Tevuk took Jim and me up the beach a short distance to a small tarpaper shack whose owner was on a temporary job in Nome, making it available to us. After numerous introductions and chats with friends, we took a short hike out into the hills adjacent to the village to get our bearings and lay some plans for the future. We then spent a few days collecting birds. I made watercolor sketches while Jim wandered about getting acquainted. Fortunately for us, a group of Eskimos from Little Diomede Island, 30 miles out in Bering Strait toward Siberia, had just come ashore to shop at the Wales store. After a short chat with them Jim asked if we could get transportation to the island with them. Their answer was, "We don't know when we might be coming back to Wales. If you want to go on that schedule we can take you."

Hoping that the stay wouldn't be too long, we accepted their offer and rushed about packing suitable gear and food for perhaps a week's stay. The transportation was a 29-foot umiak, or women's boat, with a driftwood frame and walrus skin cover from which they had hunted walrus enroute to Wales. Several bloody walrus heads with tusks were piled in the craft. A biologist who had been on the Island studying walrus populations was returning to Wales with them, bringing his report to his headquarters in Nome. Originally this remarkably seaworthy umiak was propelled with oars and a sail. Now a 75-horsepower motor did the work. A fair wind was blowing when we got under way. A tarpaulin, held in place by oars wedged between the ribs of the boat,

protected us from the cold spray. We appreciated this not only for our comfort, but to protect our cameras from the salt spray when we removed them from beneath our rain gear for quick shots of any action that might take place. Part way to the island, ice pans (small circular ice floes) began to appear and all hands became alert, looking for walrus riding on the pans, which was their means of travel north through the straits. Suddenly an arm popped up, pointing ahead at some walrus and the motor was throttled down for a slow approach. I was surprised to learn that they used only 22 caliber special rifles and that it required a hit in the ear to kill an animal.

For what happened at this point I am turning to Jim Kimball's account of the exciting action:

"The walrus threw up their heads and their long white tusks glistened against their dark brown eyes. I started shooting pictures. The gunners lay low and motionless. The walrus saw us, and probably having poor vision appeared to be unable to make out what was approaching. At about 150 feet the guns opened fire and the big animals panicked. The lucky and the wounded slid into the water and one lay dead. As the bow of the umiak slid up onto the ice, two Eskimos jumped out, drew their knives with their foot-long blades and started to cut off the walrus' head. Just then we spotted a herd of 12-15 walrus near by on a block of ice apparently not sufficiently alarmed from the melee to flee. As the guns roared again a large tusk snapped in half from a bad or unlucky shot. The broken tusk flew high in the air as the startled bull plunged into the water. Another bull, dead, slowly slid off the ice. The hunters started for him with their harpoons but too late, as he sank into the sea. While this was going on, one Eskimo, tall and wiry, stood on the ice scanning the water in all directions. A more alert man I had never seen. Then he shouted, "Get paddle into the water." Realizing he was shouting at me I looked into the water beside me and saw three pairs of shining tusks backed by tons of ferocious young bull walrus com-

132

ing full speed at the very spot in the boat where I was sitting. Waylaying the onslaught with a flimsy paddle seemed as ridiculous to me as elephant hunting with a BB gun. The long lean Eskimo bounded off the ice and into the boat and was pumping lead into the water beside me. It was none too soon either because the walrus were within five feet when the bullets changed their course and prevented a pair of tusks from hooking over the gunwale of our umiak."

Only one walrus lay dead on the ice pack although bloody patches in the water indicated there were other nonlethal hits. When the action subsided, several Eskimos jumped onto the ice pan to examine the kill. They had considered taking the hide and some meat but they took nothing but the head with its valuable tusks. The reason they gave was it was a female and the females had already migrated north leaving only males to follow. This situation suggested that this must have been a diseased animal so they passed up eating any of the meat. I thought, "What a waste to kill a ton-sized walrus without taking at least the hide." DuPont had offered them $200 for a walrus hide but the hunters' reply was, "Too expensive and too much work to skin, prepare and transport the hide to Nome." If the umiak had needed a new covering they would have taken the hide.

We saw no more walrus on the rest of the trip to the Island. I admired their navigational ability as with only a large compass they zigzagged through the fog and some snow to hit the Little Diomede O.K.

The precipitous rocky terrain of the Little Diomede Island was highly attractive to many sea birds. Huge colonies of several species of auklets, murres, gulls and cormorants were established there, but I also found a number of small songbirds appeared in this unlikely habitat of jagged rock cliffs. These were probably resting on their migrating flights from Siberia to Alaska. Whatever the explanation for their presence might be, the fact remained that, since I found them there, I was anxious to get at least a few movie shots of them to fill out my records of the avifauna of the Little Diomede Island.

After arriving at Little Diomede Island, we found that we could bunk very comfortably in the second story of the school building. The Eskimos lived in really unique houses built of drift wood or wood imported from Nome. The only land available for building was so steep that the downhill side of the house might be 16 feet high while the uphill side would be only a few feet above ground level. They entered through a door into the lower level. Then one climbed a ladder through a hole in the floor to the second story, their living quarters. A seal oil lamp supplied heat, but some had connected small electric heaters to the generator for heating and lighting the school building.

One activity that kept several of the Eskimos busy was the netting of auklets to replenish their larder for future use. This required a ten-foot pole with a net like a small landing net. The netter would hide among the rocks and swing at the auklets as they flew by, like catching butterflies. The three species of auklets - least, paraquet and crested - were small chunky birds, only 6 to 10 inches, that stood upright like miniature penguins. They were so abundant that the Eskimo take probably had little effect on the population. The birds taken were packed away in holes in the permafrost, the year around refrigerator of these people. I was surprised to see two Catholic nuns sitting on the rocks cleaning auklets. They were living with the Eskimos and helping them in any ways they could. I asked if I could take their pictures but they refused.

On one of my solitary jaunts along the shore of the Island, I encountered an attractive little Siberian yellow wagtail that was either quite friendly or very tired. At least it allowed me to approach it within a few yards, so I set up my movie camera in anticipation of some fine shots of this colorful little bird as it started up the rocky cliff. However, each time I set up my tripod it would flit on up a few yards, forcing me to make the same move. The surface was rugged enough to

133

afford me safe footing, so I followed after it. I finally succeeded in getting a short sequence of movies, but still the bird kept tantalizingly close without being unduly disturbed. Time after time I kept climbing higher and higher without getting the longer series of shots I had hoped for. After many moves, I finally admitted defeat and decided to return to the beach. But on looking down I found I was much farther up the cliff than I realized and I further discovered that to find dependable footing down was much more difficult and uncertain than picking my way on up. Not too far above me I could see that the surface was somewhat less steep leading on up to the top of the cliff so I decided to try for the top and to explore from there for a safer way down to the beach. Unfortunately I found that several of the little gullies leading down were filled with snow. Crossing one of these ribbon-like snow fields could readily set off a miniature avalanche with me riding with it. Fearing these prospects, I climbed still higher in my search for a route down. Finally I felt assured that one really did exist when I saw my pal, Jim Kimball, and an Eskimo named Iapana, approaching from around the mountain. They had been concerned about my long absence and, fearing an accident, they were searching for me. So with their competent help I made my way safely back to camp, but without the adequate series of movie shots of that very friendly but elusive yellow wagtail I had hoped for.

While on the Island we cooked our own meals and found that we could get walrus meat. To us it tasted much like rather dark, tough beef. After a week of exciting and productive collecting and photographing, we were settled down to sleep in our second story school building bunkhouse. About 4:00 a.m. there came a rap at our window and a voice informed us that the crew had decided to go to Wales, and if we wanted to go along we would have to hurry. A wild scene of packing our belongings and specimens followed and we boarded the umiak for our return trip. Enroute we stopped at Fairway Rock for lunch and the collecting of a tufted puffin. One of the Eskimos offered to climb up the cliff to where he could get within

range of the bird and he returned with a fine adult specimen of that striking bird. No walrus were seen on this trip and we arrived at Wales without incident.

On landing, I found a husky Eskimo woman skinning and cutting up an oogruk, a 700-pound seal with her ulu, a crescent-shaped knife with a T-shaped handle, an excellent type of knife in my opinion. She told me she had helped Alfred Bailey prepare a walrus for mounting in a group in the Denver Museum some 20 years before. Bailey, the Director of the Denver Museum had been my original contact in Wales. He had taught Dwight Tevuk, the local Eskimo postmaster, how to skin and prepare bird specimens for the Museum.

Soon after returning to Wales from the Little Diomede Island, Jim Kimball and I flew back to Nome and then on to Point Barrow. Enroute we stopped at Shishmaref where we ate at a small cafe claiming to be "The Best Restaurant North of the Arctic Circle." I recall watching fishermen carrying one by one, some remarkably large fish, presumably salmon, from their boat to the refrigeration plant for storage. We noted with approval that the local liquor store advertised that they shared their profits with the city for youth activities.

I had my most exciting experience with snowy owls while at Point Barrow. When arranging for lodging at the research center, we met Dr. Pitelka from the University of California whom I had met at the American Ornithologists' Union (AOU) meetings. He was there to study the lemming populations that were just reaching the peak of their 4-year cycle of abundance. His interest was to determine what disease would be involved in the sharp decline of their populations. During his stay he had spotted a curlew sandpiper, a Siberian bird. We were successful in finding the bird again but it was just too shy for me to get any movie shots of it. Petilka also found a snowy owl nest. While we were photographing the birds they proved to be unusually aggressive, almost hitting my camera lens as they dived repeatedly at our intrusion. Fortunately the eggs had already hatched and the parents were doing an excellent job of providing food for them. The nest was circled with lemmings waiting to be fed to the young. I was surprised to find a fine, undamaged specimen of the tiny least weasel in the circle, the same species found in Minnesota. You might say that I stole the weasel from the young owls for the U. of Minn. Museum.

THELON RIVER TRIP

Back on July 6, 1970 just after retiring from the directorship of the Bell Museum, I joined two other wildlife enthusiasts on a visit to the Thelon Wildlife Sanctuary in about the center of Canada's Northwest Territory. This was not a scientific expedition. Our primary interest was to get acquainted with whatever wildlife we might encounter. Instead of traveling continuously, spending time pitching and taking down camps, we established a base camp on the Thelon River some 300 miles east of Yellowknife (104° 25' W longitude, 63° 45' N latitude nine miles below the mouth of the Hanbury River), and there we stayed for 16 days. Each day we would set out either individually or together finding and photographing whatever proved interesting.

Soon after Wallace Dayton and I began discussing the possibility of a trip to the Thelon River area, we took a preliminary tune-up trip to the Voyageur National Park in northern Minnesota. For 2 or 3 days we paddled our canoe for some good physical preparation and we exercised our photographic equipment on bald eagles, mergansers and herons to get ourselves into a good frame of mind for our northern trip. Knowing we would be isolated from civilization for a couple of weeks, we had invited Dr. George Rysgaard to come along. He was a family physician recently retired from a practice in Northfield, Minnesota who, like us, was an enthusiastic wildlife photographer. This made us a very compatible trio for the trip as well as giving us some skilled help in case of any illness or accidents.
After a great deal of preparation, we finally

took off in Wally's car with our 17 parcels of baggage, headed for Winnipeg. One of our bags contained a knocked-down kayak since bush pilots often objected to carrying a canoe on their pontoon. At Winnipeg we boarded a commercial plane for Edmonton, Alberta and then transferred to a local plane to Yellowknife, the capital of Northwest Territory on Great Slave Lake. There we contacted a small chartered plane to fly us in to some still-undesignated point on the Thelon River in the Thelon Wildlife Sanctuary, designated as a refuge primarily for the protection of the musk ox, a few of which still survived in this favorable habitat.

We took off on July 10, flying over innumerable lakes including Artillery Lake to the Hanbury River which we followed to the Thelon. About 9 miles down the Thelon we finally chose a favorable spot for our camp.

On arriving there our pontoon plane glided to a smooth landing on the Thelon River and taxied as near shore as the water depth permitted. We then hopped off into the shallow water and, tossing the anchor onto the beach, we began unloading our gear. A fine drizzle was falling, though not enough to be of any threat to our pitching our tents. But, just in case of more rain, we tossed a plastic sheet over our packs and began exploring for tent sites. We needed four sites, one for each personal tent plus the cook tent. As the plane zoomed away we didn't anticipate being out of touch with civilization for 16 days since the pilot promised to stop by in about a week to check on us, but he forgot. We worried as to what our spouses would think when they received no word from us, but we learned later that a mail strike in Canada, which they learned about, seemed to be a reasonable explanation for the missing mail.

Rough-legged Hawks

While getting settled, I couldn't help but pause to sweep the surroundings with my binoculars. To my great satisfaction, I spotted an American rough-legged hawk wheeling about and landing on the cliff just across the river. Could this be one of a pair that was

135

nesting so close at hand? After setting up camp, I sat down and intently watched the gyrations of the two hawks. The mate had just appeared and I finally decided that yes, there undoubtedly was a nest just below and slightly to the right of a patch of bright green grass, an excellent key for us to locate the nest from the top of the cliff. What a great start for our stay on the Thelon! I had seen many of these hawks in migration or wintering back in the states and had made extensive food studies of birds that had been shot and brought in to the Museum by hunters. This was back in the days when all hawks were considered unprotected vermin. But I had never seen a nest even though I had been in the subarctic habitat of the hawks several times before.

The next day we assembled our knockdown kayak, crossed the river, climbed to the crest of the cliff and had no problem locating the green grassy spot part way down the precipice. The first ledge we investigated had what appeared to be a year-old nest and the feathers scattered about were of ptarmigan. Rough-legged hawks would rarely if ever take ptarmigan, which indicated that this could have harbored a pair of gyrfalcons or peregrines the previous year. We then climbed to another ledge farther down and there it was: the rough-legged hawk nest with four fuzzy, gaping, fist-sized young, just the size that would be demanding quantities of food, which meant numerous visits to the nest by the adults.

The temporary blind I had brought consisted of a frame of aluminum rods and wooden blocks that could be rigidly assembled, placed in an accessible position and covered with a lightweight camouflaged canvas. Without any planning ahead, I had colored it as to blend perfectly with the lichen-covered rocks. After getting the blind situated and anchored firmly, we left the area, hoping the birds would accept the new rock as an integral part of their rocky habitat.

Our spirits were high as we paddled back to camp with the feeling that our investigations here on the Thelon were getting off to a

great start. Our enthusiasm grew still higher when we ran across arctic wolf tracks on the sandy beach, almost the size of one's hand. In this, however, we were to be disappointed since our only contact with this predator was a distant view of one across the river that George Rysgaard reported a few days later. Arctic terns along the river, Harris sparrows and Lapland longspurs on the rocky uplands, and an occasional pair of one of the smaller races of Canada geese flying over, kept us planning all kinds of reconnoitering trips into our little arctic empire over which we were to rule for the next couple of weeks.

The decision as to when to get one's rest is a puzzling problem in these higher latitudes where there is no night to tell one when to roll in. Here on the Thelon, the sun dips low in the northwest and a colorful sunset overruns the entire sky, changing slowly from pink to orange to red, not fading out to darkness but lingering on until the sun rising in the northeast brightens up the colors into a sunrise of another day. Then, too, when you are in strange surroundings with new birds, plants, mammals and insects to get to know in a limited number of days, you can't afford to spend many hours sleeping. Still, one must spend a few of the 24 hours resting in order to be wide awake enough to see and appreciate all the new contacts you are anxious to make.

All three of us had photographic ambitions, so we each planned to spend a full day in the blind at the rough-legged hawk's nest. My turn came first, so Wally and I paddled across the river early in the morning and climbed the cliff to the blind, disturbing the hawks considerably in doing so. According to plan, Wally remained for a while, attracting the hawk's attention from the blind. Then, walking conspicuously in the open, he returned down to the kayak and back to camp. My getting settled as comfortably as possible in such a jumble of rocks in the blind was the first requirement. Then came the long wait for action.

Usually the hawk would circle around several times before alighting on a rock about 50 feet beyond the nest. If it had prey in its talons, it would gaze inquiringly at the blind. Then, reassured by my keeping perfectly still, it would take off and swoop in to alight at the nest. Still, not too trusting of the intruding blind, it would wait a bit before feeding the clamoring young, struggling to be first in line for the mouse or small bird to be served. Unfortunately I could only guess at what species they might be as they all were plucked of their feathers before being brought in to the nest. I expected that lemmings would be a conspicuous species to appear in their diet. But after I trapped some small mammals around camp and taking several red-backed mice of the richly colored northern race, but no lemmings, I decoded that the prey taken by the hawks were the red-backed mice. Of the birds brought in, several were the size of Lapland longspurs and one small shorebird of unknown species. The older nestlings were able to dismember these into swallowable portions, but the adults fed the smaller young on tiny morsels. Frequent stops interrupted the feeding, as the adult would stare at the blind, especially when I started the buzzing of the movie camera. Between feedings I scanned the valley, hoping to see some action of caribou, musk ox or some other wildlife, but life is scarce in these northern latitudes, and I had no luck. Even if I had felt bored or sleepy at times, a jagged rock pile is not a very inviting bed for napping.

However, the day was long and no fading dusk gave me any signal as to when to give up my vigil and the hawks kept right on feeding. I never determined whether they actually took any lengthy rest period during the colorful sunsets or not. They probably took short "cat naps" during the day. I finally interrupted the proceedings by packing up my cameras, leaving the blind and climbing down the cliff to the shore where Wally met me in the kayak for camp and supper.

On a later occasion, hiking out from headquarters, I encountered a small stream tributary to the Thelon which was partially dammed by brush to form a small pond. In it was a family of scaup ducks, an adult female and a number of downy young. Among them were several northern phalaropes, spinning about, feeding on the tiny insects they stirred up with their actions. I examined the adult duck with my binoculars, trying to decide whether it was a greater or a lesser scaup. I knew that the tooth on the tip of the bill of the greater was wider than on the other species, but I never could decide which it was. I didn't think it was important enough to collect the bird since it was protecting its family. Also, I could simply contact Dr. W. Earl Godfrey, the ornithologist at the National Museum in Ottawa, when I returned for the information as to which species is known to nest in this area. This I did and to my surprise, I received the following letter.

Dear Walter:
While abstracting data from some local lists yesterday for our bird distribution files, I discovered to my chagrin that I apparently overlooked thanking you for your thoughtfulness in sending me, last September, a copy of your Annotated List of Birds, Thelon Game Sanctuary, N.W.T., Canada

Regarding the identification of the scaup in the frame from a 16 mm film, I was not able to be quite sure, although I thought that the bill looked like that of a greater scaup.

Please accept my belated thanks for your list of the birds observed. We are delighted to have this for our files.

Sincerely yours,
Signed
W. Earl Godfrey
Head, Vertebrate Zoology Section

Musk Ox

On July 19, Wally and I were reconnoitering across the river from camp when we spotted a tiny, moving, black speck on Grassy Island in the distance. Even by sitting down and steadying our binoculars on our knees we could not decide whether this could be a moose, a caribou or a musk ox. We decided to wait until the next day to investigate our black speck on Grassy Island. Continuing on down nearer the river, we encountered what we thought might interest the archaeologists: an ancient grave, presumably Eskimo or Indian. It was a small mound of flat rock in an oven-like arrangement. By removing a couple of rocks in the side, the interior could be examined. Only the cranium of the skull remained obvious. In this the sutures were not coalesced at all, indicating that the individual must have been a teenager. Near the grave we photographed a circle of rocks, no doubt a campsite, stating as well as we could the position of the material in relation to Grassy Island that appeared on our maps of the area.

The following day, all three of us followed the north bank of the river to a point where it curved around Grassy Island. We were approaching a number of large boulders when we suddenly realized that one of them was a sleeping musk ox. It was partially in the shade of some eight-foot willows about 50 yards from us. It soon stood up and stared at us for a few moments, turned and sauntered down the beach, finally walking out into the shallow water for a drink, then back into the willows. We approached it again and were photographing it at about 60 yards when it began pawing the ground. With this threatening move we expected a charge, but, there being no trees to climb or get behind, we were definitely at a loss to decide how we should respond if it did charge. But there was no charge and surprisingly enough, the animal lay down! What in the world did this mean? Then we realized that it was a hot day (in the 70's) and it had pawed away the hot surface sand to expose the cool, damp, underlying sands on which to lie. It was breathing heavily and was obviously uncomfortably warm. We moved slowly and took several movie shots without disturbing the animal. After resting for a few minutes it stood up and began browsing in the willow leaves. We spent the next hour or so thoroughly enjoying watching and photographing this very accommodating musk ox, without seriously disturbing it. Occasionally it would trot off a short distance

if we approached too near. In doing so its coat of extremely long guard hairs swished back and forth, reminding us of the swishing grass skirts of Hawaiian dancers.

We puzzled over why such a big, healthy looking bull should be wandering about away from a herd. But this probably was an aging bull that had been dispossessed of its harem by a younger, more vigorous animal. Whatever the reason, we were certainly thrilled to have such an exciting hour or more getting acquainted with this very accommodating animal, undoubtedly one of the major aims of our entire trip.

Archeological Observations

We reported the grave and ring of stones we found while searching for musk ox to Commissioner S. M. Hodgson of the Northwest Territories in Yellowknife. Still later we received the following letter, which I quote verbatim.

Archaeological Survey of Canada
Bells Corners, Ottawa, Ontario
September 24, 1973
Mr. W. J. Breckenridge
James Ford Bell Museum of Natural History
Minneapolis, Minnesota 55455

Dear Mr. Breckenridge:

Mr. Ted Boxer, Secretary, Historic Sites Advisory Board, Northwest Territories, has forwarded to me a copy of your letter to Commissioner Hodgson dated Dec. 12, 1970. In your letter you included three 35mm colour transparencies taken by Mr. Wallace Dayton showing a grave and a stone tent ring just upstream from Grassy Island in the Thelon Game Sanctuary.

A two-year field party under my supervision was surveying in this area in 1970 and 1971, but missed both grave and tent ring. One of the curious facets of our work there was the absence of rings and graves, and it is gratifying to know that these exist. Several questions are posed by your findings, which are of high interest to me. They are:

a. Were any artifacts of stone, metal or bone found in conjunction with grave or ring? Ethnographic evidence supports both as indicative of the Chipewayan Indians in this area.

b. Did you bring any of the one material, especially the skull, out? Osteometrics would help us in determining whether the skull was male or female, robust or slight, etc.

c. Do you have any additional slides of either feature? The Museum shall reimburse cost of copying either.

d. Did you notice whether anything peculiar was present on the skull? i.e., cranial sutures open or fused, presence of teeth, condition of teeth, grave goods such as wood or bone, etc. The sutures appear open in the photo and may indicate a young individual. Any historic materials such as metal, buttons, cloth?

I hope the 3-year interval since you were there will not prevent you from remembering the fine details. As a matter of interest my project located sites dating back to 4-5000 years B. C. in this area. The sequence includes at least 8 cultural levels with 24 carbon dates.

Yours sincerely,
[Signature]
Bryan C. Gordon, Arctic Archeologist

Caribou

One day I was picking my way among some boulders along the shores of the Thelon River. I stopped now and then to study some possible compositions, shaped by the nodding heads of the cotton grasses, or to admire the yellow cups of the arctic poppies struggling to survive in the sterile gravel, recently pushed up by ice cakes shoved ashore by the tumbling melt waters of the river. I was hoping to spot some pictorial excuses to toss off my pack, heavy with photographic equipment. Just ahead were numerous large boulders, scattered about on the wide sand and gravel bar. Why my eyes happened to focus on one particular rock, I do not know; they all appeared to be made of the same gray stone. But suddenly, a strange, ungainly

head began to jut out from that stone and the stone slowly stood up on long spindly legs to become a perfectly normal cow caribou. Its color, when crouched, matched exactly the tones of the surrounding boulders. Some tense moments ensued while I slipped off my pack and set up my tripod, all the while hoping that the animal would not take off. In fact, much to my surprise it calmly laid down again. However, my movements, although slow, appeared to arouse its curiosity rather than fear. It stood up again and calmly studied me carefully before taking off with the caribou's characteristic long swinging gait and I got some fine movie shots for my records. A real thrill, since a week had passed in our vain search for caribou in what was prime caribou country. Yes, it really is a wonderful feeling that goes with one's first sighting of an animal you have heard of and dreamed about since boyhood, but had never seen. Actually, on the long, sweaty, two mile hike back to camp, the black flies swarmed about my head and crawled up under my cuffs and around my hat band but, in spite of all these discomforts, I was happy and feeling well repaid for the day's efforts.

A real migrating herd of barren grounds caribou was the one exciting event we hoped to encounter, but we realized that it was possible that we might miss the migrating herd entirely. Actually, this is just what happened for the first fourteen of the sixteen days of our stay. That wandering young cow was the only caribou that put in its appearance during that period. However, on our awakening on the fifteenth day, Wally arose first and we were aroused by his shout, "Wake up! The caribou are here."

And he was not kidding. A long line of them was stringing along the beach toward our camp. We literally leaped out of our sleeping bags. The welcoming weather was not exactly to our liking. It was a drizzly morning but we loaded up our photographic equipment and set out to cover the exciting event as best we could under the circumstances. Just as the head of the line arrived opposite our camp, the leaders spotted our little kayak lying on the beach. This strange object seemed to puzzle them and their movements were halted as the herd waited for the leaders to decide whether or not this strange object threatened any harm. No harm, the decision was and a portion of the herd continued along the beach while the remainder of the herd split off, climbed the bank and circled close around our camp, giving us a wonderful opportunity to examine individual animals closely. Both males and females bore antlers that were still in the velvet, but fully-grown in size. A knowledgeable person in Yellowknife had commented that the cows without calves had larger antlers than those with calves. An occasional big, mature bull appeared with an enormous rack of antlers, carrying an unusually large triangular brow palm on the forward pointing brow tine. Ordinarily only one of the brow tines had a well-developed palm, which would be serving it later in scraping away snow from the lichens, its favorite food.

The herd had first approached the Thelon River about a half-mile down stream from our camp, coming down from the north over a huge sand dune that formed the riverbank at that point. The herd then split with one part traveling upstream along the wide sandy beach while the other plunged into the river, which was perhaps a hundred yards wide at that point. The still quite small calves swam strongly right along with the adults. On reaching the far shore, they moved up the bank where apparently they were frightened and began to scatter. We hoped it might have indicated the approach of wolves – but no such luck! They soon settled down and continued along the south shore of the river.

The animals, all intent on traveling, were not noticeably alarmed by our presence. They allowed us to sit down on the sand beach, set up our tripods and take close up movie shots of the peculiar swinging gait of individual animals or of curious ones as they stopped to stare at us.

We actually missed a meal or two during that long day of photography as the straggling herd of several thousands continued passing throughout the day and still came the next day and the next.

We continued photographing caribou at camp, along the beach and down the river a mile or more to get those crossing the river. Small groups kept coming all day on July 24 and on into the 25th some stragglers were still arriving. That was the day we were expecting our plane to arrive for us. Intermittent drizzly rains had been falling during both days of the migration, which interfered considerably with photography, but on that last day of our stay, a really dark mass of storm clouds was looming up on the horizon. There were still some possible movie shots of caribou as we were breaking camp, and, carrying our considerable luggage down to the beach, we were really on edge as we waited anxiously to see which would arrive first – the storm or our plane. Fortunately the plane did arrive first and we piled on our luggage and boarded the plane without incidents.

During our 16 days on the Thelon we observed and identified 39 species of birds and 10 species of mammals. We collected no specimens of birds, 6 species of butterflies, 4 species of mammals and 100 specimens of plants of 64 species. These were donated to the various collections of the Bell Museum and the botany Department at the University of Minnesota.

Tropic birds

Chapter 13: Galapagos and Latin America

GALAPAGOS ISLANDS

"Be careful and don't step on that iguana that just crawled under the table." Where else but in the Galapagos Islands, 600 miles off the coast of Ecuador would you be apt to make that comment? We had just sat down for a snack in the outdoor restaurant in Academy Bay on Santa Cruz Island.

We might truthfully say that the island was literally crawling with wildlife and nowhere on our planet will you be able to associate so closely with the abundant wildlife as here on the Galapagos Islands. Most of the world's iguanas are terrestrial, but here, one of the island's three species has adapted to a life in the sea.

Of the world's remarkable travelers, the 20 odd species of albatross may very well "take the cake." After fledging on their nesting grounds, most of these birds leave their natal homes and take to the open seas where they wander throughout the oceans of the tropical and temperate waters, entirely circling the globe over a period of three to four years. After attaining sexual maturity, they return to their natal islands for nesting. Galapagos has but one species, the waved albatross, which nests only on Hood Island. The fine, wavy gray pattern of their plumage gives the bird its name. We found them going through their strange courting performances facing each other, bowing and crossing their bills in a whetting action, producing loud clicking sounds as the bills strike together. Single eggs were being laid in depressions in the ground and little or no nesting material was collected. Their extremely long wings made it difficult for them to take to the air from level ground. We often saw individuals walking for some distance to reach the brink of the precipitous cliffs bordering their island. There they spring off into the air, spread their enormous wings and, with a minimum of effort, become airborne.

Regarding the bird life of the Galapagos Islands, we now turn from the larger, exciting species, to one of the most drab and colorless ones, the Darwin finches that, scientifically, are probably the most important birds on the islands. These were the species that originally gave Charles Darwin the ideas that resulted in his theory of evolution. Evidently a small group of songbirds managed to cross the 600 miles from the South American mainland several thousands of years ago. These birds thrived and, over the years, spread to all the islands. They encountered food and habitat differences and eventually evolved into what is now recognized as 14 different, but closely related, species. The most obvious changes that occurred were in the structure of the bills; they now vary from a small narrow bill to a huge almost parrot-like one. One species, the woodpecker finch, even developed a bill capable of manipulating a tool, a cactus spine, in probing into holes to retrieve insect larvae. In our visits to eleven of the islands I was lucky enough to photograph seven forms of the Darwin finches. In doing so I spent much more time than one might expect creeping about in low bushes and rock crevices to get recognizable pictures of such undistinguished looking birds. But I did so since they have become such important figures in the whole field of biology. There were a number of other finch-like birds, including the red-throated parrot finch. (Plate 38A)

The word Galapagos refers to the giant tortoises found on these islands. For many years the islands were uninhabited by humans. At first they were known only to seafaring buccaneers and whalers who used them as hideouts and as a source of fresh water and meat in the form of the giant tortoises. Literally thousands were stowed away in ships' holds where they survived for months without food or water.

Today the populations on some islands are being threatened by the damage to the nest, eggs and young by all of the introduced enemies. This situation was recognized in the early 1960s and efforts were initiated to slow down and reverse this man-made damage. Financed by UNESCO and various other organizations, the Charles Darwin Research Station was set up on Santa Cruz Island. In the years that followed, the National Parks Administration of Ecuador began working on many aspects of the Island's conservation. In cooperation with the Darwin Station, it is rearing, in captivity, the most endangered races of tortoises and land iguanas in order to repopulate their home islands.

We got our first contacts with these giants while on Santa Cruz Island. We drove our jeeps to stables where we mounted horses for a ride of several miles up to the high portion of the island. There we found a number of the tortoises. Their huge size amazed us but they were not at all active or disturbed by our presence. Tui Moore mentioned hiding and waiting for some time before the

animals would become active and resume their feeding and drinking in small rainwater pools where they drank huge quantities of water. They are vegetarians and the enormous numbers of them must have taxed the growth of the plants, shrubs and small trees in their habitats.

Enroute back, my horse encountered one of the tortoises and refused to walk past it, in spite of all of my spurring and slapping it. I finally had to dismount and lead it past the tortoise barrier.

In trying to pick the one, big highlight of our Galapagos visit, I found that there was no single one, but several. The one where the most photographs were taken was undoubtedly the frigate bird colony on Tower Island. There actually were two species in the colony, the "great" and the "magnificent," with the "great" being far the most numerous. Their differences were so difficult to determine in the field that we treated them as a single species. In the colony, the birds perched on the low salt shrubs within easy photographic range. The huge, red inflatable air sacs of the male birds makes their courtship displays one rarely equaled by any other bird in the world. Here they repeatedly inflated their brilliant red air sacs in their attempts to lure any receptive females flying over. They have good control of these and will deflate them while resting or when no females might be visible. Protected nesting territories are small, allowing several displaying males to appear in a single camera field. (Plate 38B) The displaying males, besides inflating their air sacs, spread their wings widely while quivering them with a vibrating motion and uttering what Tui Moore describes as, "a concert of clear cooing warbles." Presumably these add to their visibility and to their chances of success in attracting mates.

On the wing, the frigate bird is an acrobatic performer par excellence. It has the greatest wingspread of up to 8 feet for its weight of 3 to 5 pounds of any flying bird. This feature, together with its strikingly long forked tail and its long hooked beak, makes it a predator feared by all of the sea birds. Much of the frigate birds' food is secured by pestering gannets, gulls, shearwaters and others, forcing them to drop any fish they might have secured. Then with barrel rolls, twisting and turning the frigate bird will invariably retrieve the fish before it strikes the water. One can spend a lot of time watching and admiring these aerial gyrations while trying to photograph the most exciting episodes.

The breeding of the frigate birds is somewhat seasonal although eggs, chicks and nearly fledged young can be found throughout the year with the young remaining in the nest up until they actually take wing.

Even though the islands lie astride the equator, there usually are two somewhat ill defined seasons, one cool and dry during July to December, the other warm and humid in January to July. These seasons are controlled in a rather complicated manner by several oceanic currents as well as changing trade winds.

MEXICO - 1974

My first trip to Mexico actually originated through our contacts with Chester Lyons when he was a lecturer for National Audubon and stayed with us back in the 1970s. He had conducted several trips to Mexico and we were intrigued by his accounts of the birding in that subtropical region. We found that Bob and Ann Gammell, friends from Kenmere, North Dakota, also were interested in a trip to Mexico so we arranged to make the trip together. They could fly to Victoria, British Columbia where Ches lived. There, with another passenger, Nora Beeson, the four of them drove his VW van to Tucson, Arizona where we were visiting with Ken and Maxine Peterson. From there our party of 6 took off for Mexico on March 3, l974. We made frequent birding stops and stayed in motels for the two weeks of our trip.

The farthest south point we reached on this trip was at San Blas on March 12, which was about half way to the Guatemala border. At San Blas, Ches contacted a Mexican with a

boat who took us several miles up the Tobara and the Estero El Christobal Rivers. On this exciting side trip we actually penetrated, we might say, dense mangrove forests and, farther along, into areas of huge tropical fig forests. Here we tallied such exotic birds as bare-throated tiger bitterns, boat-billed herons, rufous-crowned motmots - which pull out portions of their long tail feathers to leave tufts at the ends (Plate 39) - and happy wrens as well as the gorgeous hooded orioles and citroline trogons. Some areas were overgrown with 12 to 15 foot cattails.

At Tepic we turned about and started back, making numerous birding stops where our birds were mostly repeats, but a few new ones appeared on our lists. We commented on the numerous beehives that were painted various bright colors, quite in contrast with ours that were all white.

TRINIDAD – 1976

This trip was not a conducted tour under a designated leader, but just a friendly group of birders from the Minneapolis-St. Paul area that included Fran and Gus Knubel, Torry and Bill Davidson, Rachel Tryon and Dorothy and me. We had heard from Dr. Horace Scott and others about the wonderful tropical birding at the Asa Wright Center in Trinidad. It was an island about 100 miles across, lying within distant view of Venezuela on the north coast of South America.

On getting up the first morning, we thrilled on finding ourselves set down in spectacular green hills, almost mountains, clothed with strange tropical trees, vines and flowers, too many to even try to learn their names since we were mainly interested in the new birds we were finding. A wide porch with numerous bird feeders attracted many colorful tanagers, orioles, euphonias and hummingbirds and brought them close enough to identify and photograph. On leisurely strolls in the yards, we passed orange, grapefruit and tangerine trees where we could pick up any on the ground for sampling. The birds (129 species we recorded) were too numerous to list in this report; we were almost overwhelmed as we tried to identify and remember them.

The Wrights, who originated the Center, had located a native man, Lawrence Calderone, who had learned the birds surprisingly well while netting them for cage birds as a boy. They recognized his ability and hired him as a birding guide. We found him to be a remarkable imitator of the birdcalls and could attract them for us to add to our lists. On numerous occasions he would stop the van and say, "Well here we have a good chance to see a yellow-throated spinetail," and, giving its call, out would hop the spinetail into the roadside shrubbery.

On one such trip he took us to the north shore of the island and on another to the eastern shore. On another side trip we saw flocks of Trinidad's most striking bird, the scarlet ibis. It was truly exciting to see hundreds of these flaming red birds flying in to pass the night in a grove of large trees on the western coast of the island. To get the best view one must get access to a small boat and oarsman, available commercially nearby. Traveling a short distance to a point west of the concentrations of birds, where the evening light is best for viewing, the long streams of scarlet birds pour into the trees, decorating them with myriad scarlet spots like lights on a Christmas tree. A light misty rain was falling during our visit, but still it was a memorable experience in spite of the lack of the sunset light to illuminate the birds.

Still another of our exciting side trips was the visit to the Oilbird Cave. This involved quite a long hike over often slippery trails, wet by the frequent rains. To actually enter the cave we had to wade through shallow water and cross a small stream on a tipsy ladder which was laid down for our convenience. Our guide had a large flashlight and, after penetrating a short way into the cave, he directed its beam up onto narrow ledges where the birds were perched, quite undisturbed by our presence. The birds left the cave at night to gather the palm nuts to feed their young. His light allowed me to focus my camera before shooting the flashes and I

got numerous, quite good pictures with the birds' large eyes showing bright red. These birds were relatives of our nighthawks and whip-poor-wills, but a good deal larger.

Oropendolas

One spectacular Trinidad bird, which I saw and photographed in an Immortelle tree but was able to spend very little time studying, was the Oropendolas. (Plate 40) Our visit obviously must have been during their courting period since I was lucky enough to get an excellent shot of one of the largely black courting males when he tipped far forward, pointing his tail skyward and displaying his bright yellow tail and undertail coverts.

COSTA RICA

We have made three trips to Costa Rica, which lies adjacent to Panama and is really the narrow neck of a funnel for migrating birds enroute to South America. A student, Steve Herje, who had spent part of his college years in Costa Rica and was well informed to be our guide to good birding territory, led our first trip in 1980. In the party were Ruth Carter, Torry Davidson, Karen Eastman, Fran Nubel, Jo and Mel Herz, Sewell Pettingill and Dorothy and me.

From San Jose we took a small plane to Palo Verde Wildlife Refuge on the northwest coast. A remarkable concentration of water birds met us there including whistling ducks, roseate spoonbills, wood ibis, several species of egrets and others. The wooded surroundings of the lodge attracted me one day and I strolled down a trail, not looking for anything in particular, when on a tree capping a distant ridge I spotted a couple of rather large birds, too far to get anything of color or pattern with my binoculars. Suddenly they flew - not away, but directly toward me - and to my surprise, they alighted in the tree right above me. Their gorgeous scarlet, red and blue plumage was wonderfully visible in the bright sunlight. Then, to further amaze me, one of the birds flew down to a cavity in one of the larger limbs and, propping itself with its tail like a woodpecker, it tipped up and entered its nest cavity. I was lucky to have had my Pentax camera with a 200mm lens already mounted with me. And the birds, obviously feeling at home, hopped about for some time giving me great opportunities for pictures. (Plate 41)

Thinking I had made a wonderful discovery, I hurried back to the lodge to tell the others and I was considerably deflated but pleased to learn from the resident manager that that was the only pair of scarlet macaws still nesting in the refuge. Poachers had trapped all the others for the cage-bird trade and the refuge staff members were watching this pair carefully to make sure that they raised a family. The sad thing about the situation is that the poachers often ship the trapped birds in such inhumane containers that a large percent of the birds die enroute. If we could only persuade the public not to pay the high prices demanded by the cage-bird trade, the profit for the poachers could be cut down and the poaching could be stopped. Let's wish the enforcement personnel the best of luck in their attempts to curtail this despicable trade.

Quetzal or Resplendent Trogon

Most birders visiting Central America have the quetzal or resplendent trogon (Plate 42) as the number one species they would like to see. This was true with me. While on a couple of trips to Costa Rica we visited the nature preserve of Monte Verde in the north central part of the country. We succeeded in locating a couple of quetzals very high in some fruiting trees where the dense foliage prevented our getting good views or photographic shots. Again, in the Cordillera de la Muertes south of San Jose, I recall seeing a male quetzal on a steep mountain slope where, looking up at the bird, it appeared to me as a deep, iridescent green and later, looking down at the bird, it appeared as glistening blue. Most observers record it as green, so this is the color I show the bird in my painting. The quetzal is normally found in mountainous areas at elevations of four or five thousand feet up to ten thousand feet

where Skutch and Stiles state that they prefer damp, epiphite-laden mountain forests. At Monte Verde, several of our group spent time about the headquarters building and got quite good views of some of the birds but I went out on the trails where I thought I would have better chances to find one, but failed.

One would presume that the long feathers appearing like tail feathers were actually that, but these are really rump feathers, sometimes referred to as streamers. The real tail is much shorter and concealed by the streamers. Some observers, thinking that the long streamers would interfere with their nesting in hollows in tall trees, reported that the nesting cavity had two entrances to accommodate their coming and going, but photographic records prove that the male occupies a normal cavity with only a single entrance. The streamers, being very flexible, simply curve about when he is incubating.

We spent several days in Monte Verde with considerable success searching for rain forest species in addition to the quetzals. We hiked the narrow, rough trails as well as the road leading up to the continental divide where we got a spectacular view of the Atlantic side of the country. We took these opportunities to photograph many rain forest plants, including the huge tree ferns. On one occasion, Karen Eastman was being photographed just off the road on the edge of a steep drop-off when she was asked to step back slightly in order to include some vegetation we wanted in the picture. She suddenly disappeared from view. We dashed over, expecting to find her unconscious or at least badly injured from her fall. However, to our great relief, we found she had fallen directly into a tangled mass of tough vines that cushioned her fall perfectly and nothing more than her pride was damaged.

145

"Migration Mysteries" announcement illustration

Chapter 14: Audubon Lectures

My years as a lecturer for the National Audubon Society constituted one of my major contributions toward educating the public in the field of conserving our natural environment. I was invited to join the staff of lecturers on the strength of our successes with our Sunday afternoon lecture series. Wayne Short, director of the Audubon Screen Tour Series, invited me in the late 1940s to lecture for them. At first I refused since I was a full time member of the Minnesota Natural History Museum staff. But when Short insisted, I applied to the U. of M. administration for permission to make a two to three week's tour each winter. They approved this as constituting a part of my educational work with the Museum. So I undertook this tour arrangement and continued it through the 1960s. My records indicate that I gave at least 595 lectures to Audubon audiences that varied from about 50 to 1200 in attendance. Estimating an average audience of 180, I must have spoken to over 100,000 people on these movie-illustrated lecture engagements. The accompanying map shows where I spoke in all but two of the 50 contiguous states, Mississippi and Nevada having been missed, plus all the provinces of Canada and several of the West Indies Islands. Dorothy, acting as projectionist, accompanied me on the great majority of these trip. (Plate 43)

We experienced numerous exasperating, amusing or even exciting happenings on all these thousands of miles of car traveling. Our western Canadian talks took us as far north as Edmonton where Edgar and Jeanie Jones, Audubon lecturers whom we had also entertained back in Minneapolis, entertained us. Edgar had taken excellent movies of far northern wildlife and had just begun watercolor painting of the wildlife he had photographed. Our lecture visit with the Joneses preceded the construction of their famous Edmonton Mall in which we stayed while on a conducted tour a few years later. On that visit we stayed in a luxurious apartment with excellent accommodations and with an additional Jacuzzi bath (125-gallon capacity) in the outer room. On touring the Mall we found it had 19 movie theaters, an 80-foot slide into the swimming pool, and a full-sized replica of Columbus's ship, the Santa Maria, floating in an enormous pool where one could go on a conducted underwater tour to view many kinds of sea fishes, corals and other marine materials. It was in my opinion a vulgar display of our modern affluence, an excellent example of doing what we could do, not what we should do, with our excess wealth. I later wrote a short letter to the *Minneapolis Star Tribune* when I heard that the Ghermezian Brothers were planning an even bigger Mall of America in the Twin Cities, stating that I hoped that no such Mall would ever be built in Minneapolis. The article was published, but it had no effect on our public's craving for the remarkable and ostentatious. We asked our hosts, the Jonses, if they visited the Mall very often and their answer was, "Only when we have guests who want to see it." And this is my attitude today toward our grandiose Mall of America.

Another of our memorable happenings in the Canadian area was our being entertained by Dr. William Rowan of the University of Alberta in Edmonton. He was the biologist who carried out extensive experiments with juncos and crows in which he first proved that a bird's response to the migratory urge was instigated by the length of days it was exposed to. With artificial light lengthening the days for the birds in midwinter, he induced individual birds to move north from Edmonton in winter, long before the normal spring migration. On our visit with him, Dr. Rowan served us roast trumpeter swans. They had been shot illegally, confiscated by Conservation Officers and donated to the museum at the University.

At Regina, Saskatchewan, we visited a museum where we were pleased to find they had several large habitat groups with backgrounds painted by Clarence Tilenius. Dr. Rowan told us that he had been stimulated to build the exhibits after seeing our large displays in the Bell Museum. Tilenius and his wife had entertained us at their home in Winnipeg previously when he told us the touching story of his early ambitions to be a wildlife artist. While still a young man, he wanted to travel out west where he could see big game animals in the wild so he hired out as a crew member on a railroad that traveled through the Canadian Rockies. While uncoupling some cars, the train started unexpectedly and ran over and severed his right arm - his painting arm. But undaunted, he succeeded in retraining himself to be left-handed and has become an outstandingly successful painter of wildlife. Many large background paintings in Canadian museums are his work.

During World War II, I was assigned to a tour in California and, in order to save gasoline, I went by rail for a program in El Paso, Texas and then on to Los Angeles. There I took a car belonging to National Audubon for the several short jumps up along the west California coast and back home by rail. Later when our youngsters were small I took a midwestern lecture trip on which I drove by myself. Except for these two, Dorothy went with me on all the rest of the tours.

We had very little mechanical troubles with our 16mm projector other than an occasional burning out of the projection bulb. However, on one of these occasions in Dallas, Texas when I saw Dorothy was having difficulties, I went down to help. There I found that not only was the bulb burned out, but also it had expanded, making it necessary to break it to allow it to be removed. But worse than that, the broken bulb had become welded onto the condensing lens. The question then was what effect this would have on the projection of the pictures? The only thing to do was to try it and see and, to my great satisfaction, it had no detrimental affect at all. And the show went on unimpaired.

The only program I actually missed on all my years with Audubon was another West Coast tour supposedly starting in Portland, Oregon on New Year's Day. This meant a midwinter drive across the Plains and over the Rockies and Cascade Mountains. We encountered much snow, of course, in the mountains but experienced no serious delays except for one morning. With the temperature standing at -20° we had to get garage help in getting our car started. However, on starting across Oregon we faced rain and sleet and finally, at "The Dalles", the police stopped us with the warning that farther west the roads were closed due to bad, icy road conditions. So we phoned our Portland contact person who reported that the Audubon Program had already been cancelled since the whole city was shut down under a very serious sheet of ice. In this situation we took a motel in The Dalles and stayed through that night and the next day, New Years, and watched the Rose Bowl Football game before moving on south on the remainder of our tour, which proved essentially uneventful.

On another northwestern tour we ferried out from Seattle to one of the Puget Sound islands for a program. We then ferried again south to Port Angeles and on through the Olympic Forests of Washington. This introduced us to the magnificent virgin conifer trees so famous in that area. We made numerous stops for pictures and some quick birding. Particularly, I recall, we spotted some fox sparrows. The local race there was so dark that at first we thought they were cowbirds. The seaside highway along the Washington\Oregon coast presented frequent, most exciting views of the sea waves breaking over the rocky points jutting out into the Pacific. Without doubt, this was the most spectacular shore scenery we have ever experienced anywhere.

On still another winter Audubon trip, police stopped us up in British Columbia. The report was that a family in their car had been buried recently in an avalanche on the highway on which we were traveling. The road crews were blasting some additional hanging masses of snow that threatened another avalanche. So we were quite willing to wait an hour or so until the snow was removed for traffic to resume.

My movie-illustrated lectures on the Audubon "Screen Tours" (later Audubon Wildlife Films) made use of films I originally produced for use in the Minnesota (later the Bell) Museum of Natural History's public education programs.

While traveling on these Audubon circuits I made use of six different films of about 70 minutes in length:

1) On my first assignment I used the film *Paul Bunyan Country*, a heterogeneous combination of Minnesota wildlife shots which centered around the courtship of the four Minnesota grouse: the prairie chicken, sharp-tailed, ruffed and spruce grouse, together with sequences of the nesting of sandhill cranes.

2) *Sand Country Wildlife* concentrated on various sequences of plants, birds and mammals, but with emphasis on the life cycles of numerous insects adapted for survival in the sand dune habitats of east central Minnesota.

(3) *Island Treasure* dealt with many phases of the ecology of our home, three-acre mini-wilderness plus the 20-acre island in the adjacent Mississippi River. Included were sequences of the life cycle of the wood duck and the formation of some remarkable concretions with diagrams explaining their origin.

(4) *Migration Mysteries* presented a worldwide treatment of the still rather mysterious accomplishments of migrating birds climaxing with a series of shots of Sandhill Cranes migrating across Bering Strait to nest in Siberia.

(5) *The Far Far North* showed experiences from five arctic and subarctic trips into Canada and Alaska with travel, camping, wildlife and Native Americans one might contact in these incompatible regions.

(6) *The Minnesota River Valley Saga* focused on the remarkable history of the glacier-formed valley with animated diagrams explaining its origin together with concentrations of migratory water fowl in spring and fall and mammals, past and present, that found favorable habitats there.

Chapter 15: Art Work

Pioneer cabin from The Ghost Tree Speaks *(scratch board)*

This chapter is devoted to a brief resume of my art training and experiences including details of some of the techniques I experimented with and used extensively in the production of the several hundred pictures I have drawn and painted. Those that have been published I have listed in the Chapter 17. Publications. I have an extensive file of 35-mm color slides of a large number of my paintings, many of which have been reproduced, scattered about through the various chapters of my life accounts.

My mother was an amateur artist and always had some art materials in our home. She worked mainly with charcoal pencils and pastel, but she used both watercolors and oils at times. She was interested in family history and I remember she found a tiny engraving of the old, pre-revolution Breckenridge home in Bennington, Vermont, which she very carefully enlarged to perhaps 18 by 24 inches. This was framed in a wide gilded frame and hung in our parlor. A few large oils she copied from the paintings of well-known artists of deer and moose. I have no recollection of her doing many original paintings direct from Nature other than oils of Minnehaha Falls and the Round Tower at Fort Snelling, which she did during the few months that she and Dad lived in Minneapolis.

While still in grade school I recall doing some drawing and painting, first in copying the work of some recognized artists. Louis Agassiz Fuertes was one whose bird paintings I most admired and I still do. In high school, any classes requiring drawing, such as biology, always interested me greatly.

During my college career at the University of Iowa, I found that Professor Dill's curriculum in Museum Preparation included extensive training in the Art Department. So I took all of the courses offered in that department during the four years of my undergraduate work. Soon after settling in my position at Minnesota, I registered for some additional art training at the Minneapolis Art Institute. Along with this, I continued actively practicing bird art as my principal hobby.

The year after I arrived in Minnesota, Dr. Roberts asked me to drive his car for him to the annual meeting of the American Ornithologist Union at Salem, Massachusetts. At this and some subsequent meetings of the A.O.U., I exhibited several of my bird paintings, which attracted the attention of the Canadian bird artist Major Allan Brooks. He very graciously invited me to visit him at his home and studio in Okanagan Landing, British Columbia. In April, 1932 I finally made arrangements to accept his invitation during my vacation. On this trip, Northrup Beech, an enthusiastic Minneapolis birder, accompanied me. I keenly remember the long drive over the hundreds of miles of mainly graveled roads, so often deep with dust. The two of us checked in at a local hotel only a block or two from Major Brooks' home and he cordially permitted us to come to his studio whenever we chose. We found him busy on a series of watercolor paintings of herons for the *National Geographic Magazine*.

I had often wondered how Major Brooks got the rich colors that appeared in his paintings. He was very generous in not only telling me his so-called secrets, but also demonstrating his entire process of painting. I found that he used dark gray watercolor paper rather than the white that most artists use. His colors were transparent watercolors mixed with Chinese white to a creamy consistency, which gave him an opaque color to produce light colored areas on his dark gray paper. After sketching in his subjects, he immersed his drawing in water. Then he taped his drawing around the edges onto his drawing board with ordinary gummed tape. After completing his painting and allowing it to dry thoroughly, he cut the painting off with a razor blade. The drying stretched the paper to a perfectly flat surface, ready for matting and framing. This technique I have followed ever since, with a few modifications, and I have been ever thankful to Major Brooks for this and other helps he gave me on that memorable visit.

In my early years with the Minnesota Museum of Natural History I experimented with numerous artistic techniques such as transparent watercolor, opaque watercolor (gouache), acrylic, oil, pencil, pen and ink, and copper etching. I was intrigued for some time with the wide variety of effects one could get by simply using various pens with India ink on white paper. Arthur Guptill's excellent book *Drawing with Pen and Ink* published by Pencil Point Press Inc., New York, 1930, really inspired me to exert much effort with this technique.

Later I discovered scratch board, a rather stiff drawing paper with a heavy coating of white clay on which one could block out solid black areas with black watercolor or India ink. Using a sharp stylus, one could secure white lines on the black areas by cutting through the black coating, thus exposing the white clay surface beneath. This gives one the choice of white lines on black or black lines on white. I used this technique in producing a series of full-page illustrations for Richard Dorer's book of poems *The Ghost Tree Speaks* in which he followed the entire life history of a tree from its beginning as a seedling, through the uses the maturing tree might have served, before ending as a rotting log lying on the forest floor.

This drawing used as this chapter heading was included in the book. It might arouse memories for many outdoors persons since there are a few old, deteriorating cabins scattered throughout the forested parts of the country. This particular drawing is a close resemblance to a cabin in a somewhat overgrown clearing among dark pines just above Lake Winnibigoshish in north central Minnesota. I wish I had taken the time and effort to probe into its ownership and history, which might have revealed some interesting happenings the original inhabitants could well have experienced. Looking in through the creaky, half-open door, I couldn't help but wonder how the hardy pioneers could possibly have fought off the winter winds and snow piling high about the doorway. I thought of the contrast between them and my comfortable house when I arise at 6:15 a.m. and ask my wife, still in bed, how warm she would like me to tell the thermostat in our oil-burning furnace to heat our house by the time we get up at 7:15.

The following is what Mr. Dorer imagined the tree might have seen as the years took their toll on the efforts of the hardy pioneers who cleared the small opening in the woods for crops and then deserted it for a better life elsewhere:

The wilderness has crept across the lands
Reclaimed by fearless hearts and willing hands.
And yonder cabin where, at eventide,
The loved ones gathered by the fireside,
Has fallen to decay.
Beneath its floor
A marmot dwells, while thru the open door
The graceful swallows unmolested fly
Into the azured vastness of the sky.

Francis Lee Jaques was a great master of the scratch board technique and, with his superb composition ability, he produced many wonderful illustrations for numerous books, particularly those by his wife, Florence. While working with pen and ink as a hobby, I was invited to join an art group, "The Attic Club." One of the members of this group was doing copper etching. I had always admired the super-fine lines and strong contrasts that this process produced and so, with his help, I took up copper etching. Over the next few years I produced a good many etched plates with the resulting prints giving me considerable satisfaction. Later I found that S. Chatwood Burton of the U. Engineering Department was doing some etching and I worked with him for a while using his press for my printing. Soon after, I met Dr. Henrici of the Medical School, who also did some etching. He mentioned that he was giving up etching for photography as his hobby and he offered me his press if I could get it out of his basement. The two large steel rollers made it so heavy that at first I thought it was bolted to the floor. However, with the help of a couple sturdy friends, we removed it and installed it in my basement.

The long, tedious process of producing the plates and then the prints tried my patience, but I persisted and found that it was well worth the while. Briefly, the etching technique involved the following steps: An eighth inch copper plate was polished smoothly and covered with a thin layer of black wax. Previously I would have made a careful pencil drawing on thin tracing paper, the exact size of the plate, with considerable detail of my subject. I wanted the finished etching to have the same left to right facing as my sketch. Consequently the drawing on the plate had to be the reverse of my sketch. To do this I placed the sketch on carbon paper placed upside down and drew around the major parts of my composition with a dull point, thus getting my sketch in reverse on the back of the paper. I applied a light dusting of talcum powder to the original drawing and, laying this powdered side down on the wax-covered plate, lightly traced the outlines of the drawing onto the waxed plate, trans-

ferring the lines in white. This gave me the proper placing of the major features of my composition to guide the sharp stylus, which cut through the wax coating, exposing the shiny copper surface. After I completed the details I applied a solution of nitric acid to the plate. This slowly dissolved tiny grooves where the stylus had exposed the copper surface. Then the wax was removed and the plate was ready for printing. Rather viscous printers ink was then rubbed onto the plate and wiped off by careful rubbing with a coarse cloth. The plate was placed on the press and a damp paper laid over it. It was then run through the press and the finished etching appeared on the paper, reversed back to resemble the original sketch. After some experience, I found removing the ink from the plate was the crucial part of the process. Too little rubbing gave too dark a print and too much tended to remove the ink from the tiny grooves and the print would be too light. The plate, of course, had to be re-inked for each print. The biggest disadvantage of the whole process was that one never knew until the print was drawn from the press whether or not it was a success.

I did some experimenting with aquatint added to a plate. This process consisted of shaking finely ground resin particles in a box and immediately inserting the plate, allowing the particles to gradually settle on the copper surface. The plate was then heated, melting the resin particles onto the plate. A nitric acid solution was then poured over the plate, biting the minute spaces between the particles. This gave a smooth gray affect, like a half tone print, to those certain areas treated by the process. Several of these came out very satisfactorily, but I used the technique on only a few plates. Copper plates deteriorate slowly with use and usually about 50 to 100 prints are made and the plates destroyed. I was never in the business commercially and only a relatively few prints have ever been made from my plates.

After perfecting the copper etching technique, I made several bookplates for friends. I pulled perhaps a half dozen prints of each. The owner could then choose the print he liked best and make as many photographic prints as he wished from that print. One can identify an original etching from a photo reproduction by feeling the depressed edge of the etching where the copper plate was pressed into the damp paper by the pressure of the press.

LEIGH YAWKEY WOODSON ART MUSEUM EXHIBIT

In the late 1970s I heard that the Leigh Yawkey Woodson Art Museum in Wausaw, Wisconsin, had sponsored a rather prestigious "Bird in Art" exhibit since 1975 and I submitted a couple of slides for the competition in 1979. Included was a watercolor of "Wood Ducks" which was accepted. A selection from that year's paintings was later forwarded for exhibit at the Smithsonian Institution in Washington and my "Wood Ducks" was not only in the selected group, but also appeared in their catalog. I continued submitting slides of my work for several years and in 1982 I was lucky to have a "Ruffed Grouse" accepted and in 1983 a watercolor of a "Loon Family."

During the openings of the exhibits each year, the Forsters, significant supporters of the Museum, were very cordial and invited the artists for a social picnic afternoon at their luxurious summer home, Hazelhurst, north of Wausau. I remember particularly that among other prominent artists, there we met the well-known Canadian nature artist, Robert Bateman and his wife, and had a friendly chat with them about their work.

Peregrine Falcon (copper etching) from Logbook of Minnesota Birdlife

Arthur Allen Award Medal

Chapter 16: Awards and Honors

A. A. ALLEN AWARD

One pleasant July day I was working in the garden when Dorothy called me to the phone. I answered in my usual, casual manner, but the answering voice quickly brought me to attention. He identified himself as Dr. Douglas Lancaster, Director of the Ornithological Department at Cornell University in Ithaca, New York. Why would he be calling me? His answer dumbfounded me when he reported that the Cornell Department of Regents had just voted to award me the very prestigious A. A. Allen Award for my contributions to the field of ornithology. I thought it might be someone playing a practical joke on me, but my informer assured me that it was genuine. Dr. Lancaster was making sure I would reserve a few days around October 4, 1975 for a visit to Cornell to receive the award in person. Of course I would cancel almost any sort of engagement to attend such a presentation.

The time arrived and Dorothy and I took our daughter, Betsy Norum, with us by plane to Ithaca where we would meet our younger daughter, Barbara Franklin, and her husband, Bruce, who drove up from Ellicott City, Maryland. Also our friends Chuck Reif and his wife, Carolyn, came from Wilkes-Barre, Pennsylvania for the occasion. A fine banquet was served at the Statler Inn at Ithaca where I was presented the award, a real

bronze medal. I spoke briefly in acceptance and showed a 20-minute segment of my film, *Migration Mysteries*, as my part of the evening program. I actually felt much out of place to be honored along with such previous recipients as George Miksch Sutton, Sewell Pettingill and Roger Tory Peterson.

The following day Tom Cade gave us a conducted tour of the peregrine falcon rearing enclosures, which I had read about but had never seen. Some young falcons from their establishment were later liberated in Minnesota as part of our efforts to reestablish the species in our Minnesota area.

CHRONOLOGY OF AWARDS AND HONORS

1. College scholarship from Brooklyn High School - 1921.
2. Elected to Phi Beta Kappa, Honorary Scholastic Fraternity, U. of Iowa - 1925.
3. Won 1st in Big Ten Gymnastic Tumbling - 1925.
4. Elected Captain, U. of Iowa Gymnastic team - 1925.
5. Appointed Preparator, U. of Minn. Museum of Natural History – 1926, Advanced to Curator - 1936, Director - 1946.
6. Wilson Ornithological Society President - 1952-53. Life member.
7. KMGM. TV Outdoor Award - 1957.
8. Minnesota Academy of Science, President - 1947-48.

9. Elected to Gamma Alpha Scientific Society - 1930.
10. American Ornithological Union, Elected Member, Elected Fellow - 1950. Life Member.
11. Minneapolis Junior Chamber of Commerce Robert G. Green Conservation Award - 1964.
12. Thomas Sadler Roberts Memorial Award. For outstanding contribution to Minnesota ornithology - 1964.
13. Minnesota 4H Clubs. Recognition Meritorious Service - 1965.
14. Northwest Sportshow, Special Award as Communicator Conservationist - 1985.
15. Fur, Fins and Feathers Club. Sportsman of the Year - 1987.
16. American Museum of Wildlife Art - Contribution to the *Birds of Minnesota* - 1988.
17. National Audubon Society Citation for 23 years of lectures for Audubon Wildlife Film Programs -1984.
18. Minnesota Wildlife Heritage Foundation - Trail Blazer Award for Inspiration, Outstanding Achievement and Leader ship in the Field of Wildlife Art.
19. Minnesota Section Wildlife Society - The Minnesota Award Outstanding Contributions to the Profession of Wild life Management - 1967.
20. Mayor of the City of Birmingham, Alabama declared Dec. 11, 1980, Walter J. Breckenridge Day for his Audubon Lecture given on that day for its educational value to the city.
21. Izaak Walton League of Minnesota - The Ed Franey Award for Contributions to Conservation through written, spoken and visual media - 1988.
22. Audubon Chapter of Minnesota - Conservationist of the Year - 1995.
23. Izaak Walton League (Formerly the North Minneapolis Chapter) renamed the Walter J. Breckenridge Chapter - 1996.
24. Minnesota Herpetological Society Award and Life Member for contributions to Minnesota Herpetology - 1995.
25. University of Minnesota established the "Breckenridge Chair of Ornithology" - 1995.

Chapter heading from Market Hunters

Chapter 17: Publications

I have puzzled considerably over just how to present an appropriate resume of my 300+ published articles covering the 68-year period from 1929 to 1997. The confusion over classifying these articles stems from the fact that some were simply written texts, while others were paintings or drawings without texts, and still others a combination of both text and illustrations. A large majority of these articles were simply reports on observations of the fauna or flora or reviews of the work of others. My conclusion is to give detailed references of the few that I consider of some scientific value, or particularly interesting publications selected from the 43 books, journals, magazines, and pamphlets in which my writings, drawings or paintings have appeared.

My first published article was "Actions of the Pocket Gopher (Geomys bursarius)." *American Journal of Mammalogy* 1929, 10:136-139. Illustrated with two pen and ink drawings (See Chapter 1. Boyhood) "Nesting Study of Wood Ducks." *Journal of Wildlife Management* 1956, 20:16-21.

"Observations on the Life History of the Soft-shelled Turtle (Trionyx ferox) with Especial Reference to Growth." *Copeia* 1955, No. 1:5-9.

"An Ecological Study of the Marsh Hawks (Circus hudsonicus) of a Minnesota Sand Plains Community." M.A.Degree Thesis. Library, Univ. of Minn. 1934.

"Amphibians and Reptiles of Minnesota with special reference to the Black-banded Skink *Eumeces septentrionalis* (Baird)." Ph. D. Degree Thesis. Library, Univ. of Minn. 1941.

"Growth, Local Movements and Hibernation of the Manitoba Toad bufo hemiophrys." *Ecology* 1961, 42:637-646 (with J. Tester).

"Winter Behavior Patterns of Bufo hemiophrys in Northwestern Minnesota." *Annales Acad. Sci. Pennicae* 1964, Series A. Biologica IV 71/31:423-431 Finland (with J. Tester).

"Population Dynamics of the Manitoba Toad Bufo hemiophrys in Northwestern Minnesota." *Ecology* 1964, 45(3):592-601 (with J. Tester).

"Ecology of Mima-type Mounds in Northwestern Minnesota." *Ecology* 1968, 49(1):172-177 (with J. Tester).

While Dr. Roberts was working on his book *Birds of Minnesota* he had contacted several outstanding bird artists including F. L. Jaques, Allan Brooks, Walter Weber and

George Sutton. Dr. Roberts was anxious to have me represented in the book although I knew that my work was not up to the standards of those artists at that early period of my art career. But I practiced and, with some late hours of hard work, I finally produced some acceptable pictures. I was much pleased when 14 of my plates of woodpeckers (Plate 44), shore birds and shrikes appeared in the book and nearly all of the scores of pen and ink drawings in the book were my work.

Dr. O. S. Pettingill published a book *Ornithology in Laboratory and Field* 1946, Burgess Publishing Company, which went through five printings and three revisions. The majority of the 127 pen and ink illustrations were my work.

Through many years (1935-75) of the Minnesota Department of Resources' magazine *The Volunteer*, I wrote an even 100 articles, many of which were accompanied with full-page pen and ink illustrations.

The *Minneapolis Sunday Tribune* (1942-45) published eight full-page color plates of Minnesota birds and mammals on the front pages of the photogravure section of the paper that were my work.

The U. S. Bureau of Biological Survey's *Wildlife Research Bulletin* No.1 on the "Food Habits of the Shorebirds: Woodcock, Snipe, Knot and Dowitcher" was illustrated with three of my full-page color illustrations. In a later bulletin, in the same series on "North American Wolves" my color painting showed the three-color variations of wolves.

Birds of Colorado by Bailey and Neidrach published by the Denver Museum of Natural History, 1965 used ten of my full-page color plates.

Reptiles and Amphibians of Minnesota 1944, University of Minnesota Press. 202 pp.

"Birds of the Lower Back River, Northwest Territories, Canada" *Canadian Field Naturalist* 1956, 69:1-9.

"A Bird Census Method." *Wilson Bulletin*, 1935. 47:195-97.

"Life History of the Black-banded Skink." *American Midland Naturalist* 1943, 29:591-606.

"Weights of a Minnesota Moose." *Journal of Mammalogy* 1946, 27(1):90-91.

"A Century of Minnesota Wildlife." *Minnesota History* 1949, 30:123-134 and 220-231.

"William Kilgore Jr." *Flicker* 1953, (Obituary) 25:136-138.

"Naturalists on the Back River." *Beaver* 1955, Summer, 9-15. (Also in *Outfit* 285:42-45 and *Outfit* 286:9-13. A Canadian publication.) (with R. J. Wilkie).

"Birds of the Lower Back River, Northwest Territories, Canada." *Canadian Field Naturalist* 1956, 69:1-9.

"Comparison of the breeding bird populations of two neighboring but distinct forest habitats." *Audubon Field Notes* 1955, 9:408-412.

"Mammal observations at Lower Back River Northwest Territories, Canada." *Journal of Mammalogy* 1955, 36:254-259 (with H.L.Gunderson and J.Jarosz).

Revision of Thomas Roberts' *Manual for the Identification of the Birds of Minnesota and the Neighboring States*. Minneapolis: University of Minnesota Press, 1955. 362 pp. (with D. Warner).

"A Virgin Prairie in Minnesota." pp. 269-275 in. O. S. Pettingill, ed., *The Bird Watcher's America*. New York: McGraw Hill Book Co. 1964. 441pp.

"Sandhill Cranes and other Spring records of Birds from Bering Strait, Alaska." *Auk* 1957, 84(2):277-278.

"Francis Lee Jaques" Obituary. *Auk* 1971, 88(2):478-479.

"Common Loon" painting printed in Cornell's *Living Bird* 1968.

"Pinnated Bittern (Botaurus pinnatus) and male Altamira Yellowthroat." Colored frontispiece in article by R.W. Dickerman. *Wilson Bulletin* 1961, 73(4):332.

Twelve full-page scratchboard illustrations for *The Ghost Tree Speaks,* a book of poetic stanzas by Richard Dorer of the Minnesota Department of Natural Resources published by Ross and Haines, Inc., 1963. 73 pp.

The German wildlife magazine *Das Tier* printed two of my photos of newly hatched baby wood wucks jumping from a house. 1962.

"Back's Great Fish River." pp. 189-196 in *Flyways, Pioneering Waterfowl Management in North America.* U. S. Fish and Wildlife Service 1984.

Twenty black and white illustrations for Charles T. Flugum *Birding from a Tractor Seat* 1973. 435 pp.

Colored cover illustration "Warblers." *Conservation Volunteer* March-April 1975, 38.

"Spruce Grouse" colored frontispiece in *Minnesota Birds, Where, When and How Many.* J. C. Green and R. B. Janssen. U. of Minn. Press 1974.

"Chuck-wills-widow – First Known Occurrence in Minnesota." *Loon* 1982, 54(3):139-141.

"Maintain the Environment" *No. Hennepin Post.* 5/12/88.

"Upland Oak Forests." 4 separate articles. *Audubon Field Notes* 1948-51.

"White Cedar Bogs." 6 separate articles. *Audubon Field Notes* 1948-54.

"An Exciting Visit with a Barred Owl." *Loon* 1993, 65( ):51 (with D. Breckenridge).

"Moving Day for the House Finches." *Loon* 1996, 68(3):177-78.

"Dr. Breckenridge Remembers a Nuthatch and a First State Record Western Sandpiper." *Minnesota Birding.* April 1997, 34(2):1967+

Notes used in "New Bird Records from Alaska and the Alaska Highway" by Stuart Keith. *Canadian Field Naturalist* Sept. 1967, 81(3):196-200.

"Minnesota Nesting of White Pelicans." *Loon* Sept. 1968, 40:100.

"Letter on Kingbirds." *Loon* June 1968, 40:56.

"Common Loon (*Gavia immer*)" drawing in *Living Bird*, 1968.

"Science and Parks, Links to Leisure and Life." *Conservation Volunteer* May-June 1969, 32(185):14-20.

"Migratory Birds" in *Appraisal of the fish and wildlife resources of the proposed Voyageurs National Park.* March 1969.

Twelve chapter headings in David & Jim Kimball *The Market Hunter.* Mpls.:Dillon Press, 1969.

The following articles are not on Natural History but deal with the world's over-population (See Chapter 18, Overpopulation)

"To Heed the Population Threat." *Minneapolis Star-Tribune* Editorial Page 7/14/87.

"Our Population is one Expert's Concern." *Minneapolis Star-Tribune*, Outdoors Section 3/27/96.

"Population May Be Past Level that the Earth Can Sustain." *Minneapolis Star-Tribune* 11/23/91. With illustration of globe.

"Human Race Not Exempt From Natural Laws." *Brooklyn Park Sun Post*, Editorial Page Guest Columnist 11/30/94.

"Are You A Realist or a Happy-Go-Lucky Optimist?" The keynote address at a section of a workshop sponsored by the Non-Game Section of D.N.R at Bell Museum April 12, 1997.

"Are We Over-valuing the Human Individual?" *St. Paul Pioneer Press* Editorial Page 11/18/88.

"Alternative to Killing." *St. Paul Pioneer Press*. 10/14/97.

"World Over-Population Is the Real Problem" (my own title) *Minneapolis Star-Tribune,* no date.

"What My Religion Means to Me" *Minneapolis Star*. April 1, 1952. This article appeared on the front page with my photograph at the head of the article.

Complete chronological listing of Breck's publications can be found in Appendix 1.

NASA earth photo from Minneapolis Star *editorial*

Chapter 18: Overpopulation

For a good many years I have been interested in the subject of human over-population as the underlying cause of so many social, political, economic and religious problems facing today's world. This interest has urged me to compose many articles for public consumption. Following is a list of the titles of some of these many articles, most of which have been submitted for publication in various newspapers, but less than half have actually appeared in print:

1. "World Over-Population Is the Real Problem," (my own title) *Mpls. Star,* nd
2. "How Valuable is a Human Individual?" *St. Paul Pioneer Press*, 11/18/88.
3. "To Heed the Population Threat," Mpls. Star 7/14/87.
4. "Population May Be Past Level the Earth Can Sustain," *Mpls. Star,* 11/23/91.
5. "Human Race Not Exempt from Natural Laws," *Brooklyn Park Sun Post*, 11/30/94.
6. "Overpopulation Issue Grossly Under Reported, he says..." *St. Paul Pioneer Press*, 6/10/97.
7. "Our Population is One Expert's Concern," Mpls. Star 3/27/96.
8. "Alternative to Killing," *St. Paul Pioneer Press*, 10/14/97.
9. "Are You a Realist or a Happy-go-lucky Optimist?" Keynote speech at D. N. R. Workshop at Bell Museum.
10. "Attention Anti-abortion Factions"

11. "Enough is Enough – Too Much Leads to Disaster"
12. "How Best to Protect Our Environment"
13. "How Dense Can We Get?"
14. "Human Over-Population"
15. "Humans Vs. God as World Managers"
16. "Is Abortion Our Real Problem?"
17. "Natural Laws and Human Populations"
18. "Of Geese and Humans"
19. "Pro-lifer's Multiplication Problems"
20. "Too Many People"
21. "Sharing the World"

One of the first published articles on population:

TO HEED THE POPULATION THREAT
Minneapolis Star - Editorial Page
July 14, 1987

This month the population of the world will exceed five billion. The next billion will arrive within 10 years. The population threat is the most serious problem facing our planet, yet political leaders seem unmoved.

Nobel Prize winner, Norman Borlaug, has spent his life developing higher producing varieties of wheat and rice in an attempt to relieve malnutrition. In his article "The Human Population Monster," Borlaug ridicules society's attempts to solve its social, political and economic problems as "ugly symptoms." "This approach will not solve the underlying problem," the article says. "We must not be afraid or unwilling to recognize, confront and effectively struggle with the primary underlying cause, "The Human Population Monster." The longer we wait before attacking the primary cause of this complex, worldwide problem, the greater will be the deterioration of the quality of life and the fewer of the present species of fauna and flora will survive. Continued neglect will eventually lead to the destruction of civilization or even the disappearance of Man."

The article continues "Those of us who work on the food production front, have the moral obligation to warn the political, religious and educational leaders of the world of the magnitude and seriousness of the arable/food production problem that looms ahead. The imminence of disaster is closer than most people realize or are prepared to admit."

Such concerns of authorities such as Borlaug should arouse our political leaders. They should go a step past treating the symptoms of the disease and pay more attention to curing the basic cause of so many of the social, political, religious and ideological problems. President Reagan for one fails to realize the dangers of allowing humans to exceed the carrying capacity of our finite planet.

Statistics justify the use of the term "population explosion" and should convince pro-lifers that world wide family planning is an absolute must. Continence, contraception and sterilization, the best controls, are not being used adequately through the world. Until they are, abortion must be condoned as a necessary, but far less desirable method of population control.

(Signature)
W. J. Breckenridge, Brooklyn Park
Director Emeritus, Bell Museum of Natural History

"How Valuable is the Human Individual?" was published in the *St. Paul Pioneer Press* and was considered by many as very controversial. I am reproducing it in full since it has some well-stated support for my stand on the subject.

HOW VALUABLE IS THE HUMAN INDIVIDUAL?
St. Paul Pioneer Press - Outdoors Section
November 18, 1988

The recently publicized medical research using fetal tissues has received vigorous opposition from persons criticizing the action as just another violation of the sanctity of the unborn whose value to society is inestimable. This brings into focus the whole question of the value society places on the individual. Strange as it may seem to many persons, there is a great deal of evidence supporting the stand that society is definitely over valuing human lives. This does not mean that a life already existing should be considered less valuable but that millions or billions more will make individuals progressively less valuable to society.

Few biologists dispute the fact that humans are animals with a great many similarities to many other animal forms. Nearly all existing animals have reproductive potentials well beyond that needed to sustain their optimum populations. Excess individuals of all these species have been, and still are being, eliminated by Nature through diseases, predators, parasites, starvation and direct competition. Optimum populations are defined as that number that can find food and shelter in their habitats without significant damage to those habitats. This being the case it becomes plainly evident that Nature definitely does not place a high value on individuals where eliminating excess numbers results in benefit to the surviving populations.

The human race is not a favored, separate and distinct form of life that can continue to reproduce indefinitely far beyond the carrying capacity of its finite habitat-the Planet Earth. The human is the only animal that recognizes that this is true and that we are rapidly exceeding the carrying capacity of our habitat. We are also the only animal capable of planned reduction of our reproductive rate.

Primitive humans striving for survival placed a high value on the individual but our present over-population makes this not only unnecessary but detrimental to the welfare, if not the actual survival, of the human race. Realizing this fact, there is no tenable reason for us to place such a high value on humans as to insist that every ovum that happens to become fertilized should be carefully preserved to become another human. If techniques such as continence, contraception and sterilization could be more universally used the desired population reduction could be accomplished without the actual taking of lives which, of course, abortion does.

However, the changing of attitudes toward population control is, no doubt, an even more difficult reform facing humanity. Improved education for women and the raising of their status in the Third World is essential. The desire of minorities to become majorities disregards the long-term serious results of "too many people." Various religions that promote the sanctity of unlimited reproductive rights appear not to recognize that for the first time in human history over-population of our Planet poses a serious threat to the very survival of humanity. The changing of such attitudes must eventually take place but this hoped for change is far too slow of accomplishment to hold any hope of preventing Nature from stepping in with its often violent techniques such as the presently incurable AIDS. This is already taking place and can be expected to worsen in the near future.

Humans do not usually back away from problems because they are difficult but this seems to be the case with the population problem. All the recent marvels of medical research that result in longer survival of more humans are making it even more urgent for researchers to put forth more effort toward removing the obstacles to solving the over-population problem if we are to succeed in reducing our rate of births to more nearly balance with our rate of deaths.

(Signed)
W. J. Breckenridge

I received some interesting critical responses to the previous article that the Pioneer Press saw fit to publish soon after its appearance.

The editor of the Brooklyn Park Sun Post complimented me by designating me as Guest Columnist for the following article:

HUMAN RACE NOT EXEMPT FROM
NATURAL LAWS
Brooklyn Park Sun Post
Editorial Page Guest Columnist
November 30, 1994

With greater and greater controversy developing about the world's rapidly increasing human population, it seems reasonable for people on both sides of the issue to study a careful presentation of the reasons for one person's support of more effective control of these exploding numbers. It appears that a certain segment of our society is proposing legislation that aims to place governmental restrictions on physicians; advice to patients regarding their reproductive activities. It is appalling to realize such regulations would actually interfere not only with a physician's advising his or her patients regarding treatment vital to their health, but also would infringe on the physician's constitutional right of free speech. This aggressive insistence on such action is deeply seated in the backgrounds of the persons involved.

The source actually goes back over the last few centuries, during which a large segment of humanity has drifted, mainly through religious fervor, into placing a vastly exaggerated value on an individual human being. This statement will seem to many as an almost blasphemous comment, but there is much in the history of animals on our planet to support it.

Those persons with the biological education now accepted by educators could readily imagine one of our prehuman ancestors struggling with a saber-toothed tiger attempting to carry off his infant son while his mate was away gathering berries or digging roots as their major food supply. Under these circumstances the infant son would have been infinitely valuable as a contributor to the very survival of this prehuman society. Such struggles continued with gradually increasing success until, after several millions of years, Homo sapiens emerged through the evolutionary process to populate our planet with its first billion humans shortly before the year A. D. 1900.

Now, returning to those persons with conservative religious backgrounds: They will point out that, only a few thousands of years ago, Adam and Eve were created and, through direct communication from God, were instructed to "Be fruitful, and multiply, and subdue the earth." One must remember these instructions were supposed to have been given when only two humans were on the earth. Through the next few thousands of years, humanity has been "fruitful" to the extent of reaching the first billion by a few years before 1900.

Whichever of these accounts you choose as the origin and development of humanity, from A. D. 1900 to the present, our explosive increase is a matter of record.

During my lifetime this number has exploded to five-plus-billions, a figure that obviously is above the carrying capacity of our planet. The ecologists' phrase "carrying capacity" refers to the populations of animals that a habitat can support without damaging its future productivity. Would that we could establish direct communication with God today for advice under the present very different circumstances than in Adam and Eve's time. Let's now look critically at some known facts regarding the lives of all of our world's animal species, including humans.

There are hundreds of thousands of species of animals sharing the resources and living space on our planet. An inadequately understood complex of forces that we will refer to as "Natural Laws" or "Nature" is controlling the conditions faced by these animals. Each successful species can reproduce more individuals than are needed to sustain its population at an optimal level. To prevent

populations from building up excessively, natural laws have brought about controlling forces such as diseases, parasites, predators, starvation and violent individual, tribal, and national competition. Individuals are given little consideration by Nature when the survival of the species due to overpopulation is at stake. In our present case, the earth is the habitat under consideration, where natural laws have been operating since the beginning of time. The human race is simply one of the species involved in the process. It is not a separate and distinct entity exempt from the operation of natural laws.

Humans' advanced intelligence has resulted in remarkable scientific accomplishments, many of which are in the medical field. These have partially overcome many diseases and parasites. Accomplishments in the agricultural and transportation fields are coping to a limited degree with malnutrition and starvation. As a result, more babies are surviving, and more adults are avoiding death for longer periods, thus resulting in populations that are demanding more resources and living space than exists on our planet.

We have the intelligence to at least partially understand the natural laws we are opposing in our efforts to sustain ourselves. We have the intelligence to realize our populations are becoming excessive. Many people still contend the United States is losing population, despite the oft-published reports of demographers that we are gaining 2½ millions annually through excess births over deaths plus legal and illegal immigration. We have been intelligent enough to consciously devise methods of slowing our rate of population growth. The controlling techniques already in use are:

(1) Refrain from sex
(2) Use contraceptives
(3) Use voluntary sterilization; and
(4) Apply abortion

It is evident we are not willing or able to limit our control methods to numbers 1, 2 and 3. These three alone with worldwide application could accomplish our goals.

The world's population could be stabilized at an appropriate level. The detrimental results of overpopulation, such as wars, genocide, malnutrition and starvation, could be avoided. The spread of many contagious diseases could be much reduced. And surprisingly, people for and against abortion could join in opposing abortion as a population control.

Wouldn't this view of the future justify our putting much greater emphasis on population control?

The following article probably got more attention than any of my other publications on this subject since it appeared in the Minneapolis Star Tribune under an illustration of the globe.

POPULATION MAY BE PAST LEVEL THAT THE EARTH CAN SUSTAIN
Minneapolis Star Tribune
Editorial Page (with illustration of globe)
November 23, 1991

Since so much argument and confusion exists concerning the many facets of our reproductive activities such as abortion, family planning, sexual orientation and population it seems appropriate to consider some of the basic reasons for these differences of opinion.

Biologists long ago gave up the idea that the human race is a separate and distinct form of creation but that humans and the several human-like apes are similar in so many that without doubt they have descended from similar ancestral forms. The hows and whys of our development of such extreme intellectual superiority over other animals is still the basis of much discussion.

One obvious but seldom discussed point of difference is the simple fact that the human animal early in its evolution invented heat-conserving clothes and heated homes. These inventions have enabled humans to occupy practically all of the vastly differing habitats on our planet, Earth. Also these skills have enabled us to give our young better

care, which in turn developed our 12-month breeding season, something that most other vertebrate animals do not enjoy.

Most animals have reproductive potentials greater than needed to sustain a stable population under favorable conditions. However, there exists in Nature lethal factors such as diseases, parasites, predators, starvation and territorial competition that prevent unwanted increases in their numbers. This results in maintaining their populations within the carrying capacity of their habitats, in other words such numbers as can be continuously sustained over indefinitely long periods of time. This natural law must be observed by humans as well as by other animals.

Humans have controlled most serious predators. Our medical researchers are making important progress in controlling parasites and diseases. Our food production has at least delayed some starvation. Territorial competition resulting in wars has to some extent neutralized these gains in population. Also our problems in the distribution are hampering our attempts to eliminate starvation. However, our positive accomplishments are neutralizing to a large extent the natural and necessary removal of excessive populations.

No doubt the total gains in our attempts to thwart Nature's lethal controls over our populations have resulted in an overall improvement in our living conditions, to the extent that we are rapidly exceeding, if we have not already exceeded, the carrying capacity of our one and only habitat, Earth. With all of our intellectual successes that have rewarded our attempts to increase our populations, does it not appear logical that we use this same intelligence to limit our reproductive rate, thus avoiding having to resort to wars and starvation to keep our populations within the carrying capacity of our Planet?

Modern methods of preventing unwanted pregnancies are well known to most readers but in many areas, including the U.S., personal, religious, political and sociological taboos often stand in the way of their application. These impediments to the control of our numbers admittedly present tremendous problems but we humans have faced and overcome other seemingly impossible problems. Are we going to back away from this one simply because it is difficult? We can hope that reasonable and logical thinking will eventually govern our actions after the catastrophic results of over-population are pointed out and thoroughly understood and appreciated.

W.J.Breckenridge
Director Emeritus, Bell Museum of Natural History,
University of Minnesota

The following is the keynote address I delivered at a section of a workshop sponsored by the Non-Game Section of D.N.R at Bell Museum April 12, 1997 that is typical of my most up-to-date stand on this subject.

ARE YOU A REALIST OR A HAPPY-GO-LUCKY OPTIMIST?

It is not just my opinion but that of a rapidly increasing group of concerned citizens that our society is moving, not so slowly, but surely toward a catastrophe of an only partially known nature. Naturally those of us with this view of the future are considered by many as being pessimists of the first order. But I think that when we examine our overpopulation and certain technological developments, critics will admit that we are actually pessimistic realists.

Few biologists dispute the fact that humans are simply one of the many species of the world's mammals and that nearly all existing mammals have reproductive potentials well beyond that needed to sustain their optimum populations. Excess individuals of all these species have been, and still are being, eliminated by Nature through disease, predators, parasites, starvation and direct competition in order to keep their numbers within the carrying capacity of their habitats. The human race is not a separate and distinct form of life that can continue to reproduce indefinitely far beyond the carrying capacity of its finite habitat, the Planet Earth. The human is the only animal that realizes that this is true and that we are the only animal capable of planned control of its reproductive rate. The tragedy is that we appear to be unable to put this knowledge into action.

Many humans are recognizing that our excessive numbers are threatening to exterminate many species of plants and animals that our Creator has evolved to share the space and resources of our Planet. I am receiving in my mail almost daily requests for contributions to save the Gorillas; save the Florida Manatees; save the fish populations of the Newfoundland Banks; save the remarkable Lemurs of Madagascar; save the California Condors, save the Rhinos of Africa; save the Swainson Hawks wintering in Argentina. (4000 of these "Hawks that eat the Locusts" died in 1995 from pesticide sprays) and save the Albatross and other sea birds, mammals and fishes (tens of thousands are hooked and drowned annually by ocean fish nets scores of miles long.) The list of species threatened by humans goes on and on emphasizing the fact that we humans, beyond any doubt, are occupying a great deal more than our share of our world's space and resources.

Primitive humans striving for survival placed a high value on the individual but our present over population makes this not only unnecessary but actually detrimental to the welfare, if not the survival, of the human race since for the first time in human history the world's population has exceeded the carrying capacity of its habitat. If population control techniques such as continence, contraception, and sterilization could be more universally used, the population reduction could be accomplished and abortion could be eliminated.

Serious problems involve our excessive production of ozone-destroying gases that tend to eliminate the ozone layer of the stratosphere allowing excessive amounts of the sun's ultra violet rays to reach the earth.

164

This causes increased cancers in humans and also is responsible for trapping much of the infrared heat rays that normally are reflected off into space. Our excessive population's burning of wood, coal and gasoline adds greatly to the carbon dioxide which also tends to block the escape of this heat. Many scientists now believe this will markedly raise the temperature of the world's atmosphere. As little as 3 to 6 degrees rise in the average annual temperature can have detrimental effects on our production of food crops since significant portions of our best lands could become deserts.

In the face of all these detrimental developments is it not reasonable to feel pessimistic about the future of our society? Norman Borlaug, Father of the Green Revolution and Nobel Peace Laureate, who has spent most of his life developing better producing grains to feed the world's populations, now considers that relatively soon it will be impossible to produce sufficient food to support our increasing human populations. Three to four billion, a number suggested by several of our most competent ecologists as a world population that would have the best chance to survive indefinitely without serious damage to our environment and assure future generations much healthier, happier and safer lives.

I do not mean to belittle our many present projects to preserve our natural environment such as preserving our wetlands; reducing our uses of resources; cutting our over use of pesticides; encouraging the use of biological controls of pests; recycling our mountains of trash and protecting the habitats of threatened species. We should continue and increase these efforts. But I do want to identify and call your attention to the race that is now being run between our attempts to control our inborn ambitions to reproduce our kind against Nature's attempts to keep our populations from exploding far beyond the carrying capacity of the Planet Earth. If we humans fail to win this race within the next few decades, all our conservation projects will fail and Nature-sponsored catastrophic starvation, incurable diseases, masses of pollutants and wars will take over to drastically reduce our exploding human race.

W. J. Breckenridge
Director Emeritus
Bell Museum, U of MN

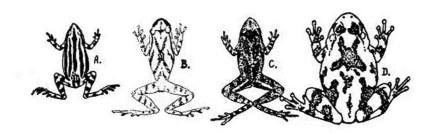

Frogs from Reptiles and Amphibians of Minnesota

Appendix 1: Chronological Bibliography compiled by John J. Moriarty

Walter John Breckenridge (Breck) lived to see his 100th Birthday in 2003. During those 100 years he published over 300 articles. His first publication, "Actions of the Pocket Gopher", was published in 1929 by the *Journal of Mammalogy* at the age of 26. His last publication, "Obituary of Harvey Gunderson", was published in 1999 by the *Loon* at the age of 96. Breck also illustrated 18 books for others during his 70 year career.

Breck's publications covered a variety of topics, but the majority (180, 60%) of the publications were bird related. He also published 34 papers on reptiles and amphibians, 12 papers each on mammals and museum studies, 8 obituaries and 45 papers on general natural history topics.

He published in over 30 different journals or books. The majority of Breck's articles were published in the *Conservation Volunteer* (78 articles) and *Flicker* (*Loon*) (83 articles). His publications also included the major ornithology (*Auk, Condor,* and *Wilson Bulletin*), mammalogy (*Journal of Mammalogy*), and herpetology (*Copeia* and *Herpteologica*) journals.

Breckenridge was the sole author of most of his publications. He only had 37 publications with co-authors. There were 31 different co-authors with John Tester being his most regular collaborator, with 10 publications. Breck had two publications with his wife, Dorothy, both were late in his career.

Many of Breck's articles were also illustrated by him. The majority of the illustrations included in his publications were black and white line drawings or scratch boards. His book illustrations included line drawings and scratch boards, as well as watercolors. His best known watercolors are in Robert's *Birds of Minnesota* and Bailey and Neidrach's *Birds of Colorado*.

Breck also regularly contributed drawings to the *Minneapolis Tribune* newspaper in the 1940's. He also contributed a number of op ed and letter to the editor pieces on the environment and population control to the *Minneapolis Tribune* and other papers. His newspaper contributions are not listed in this bibliography.

1929
Actions of the Pocket Gopher (Geomys bursarius). *Journal of Mammalogy* 10:336-339(first publication).

Nelson's Sparrow nesting in Minnesota. *Auk* 46:548 (with William Kilgore).

Connecticut Warbler Nesting in Minnesota. *Auk* 46:551-552 (with William Kilgore)

The Booming of the Prairie Chicken. *Auk* 46:540-543.

Cover Art -Flicker Version 1. *Flicker* 1(3) to 8(4).

Imitating Water in Habitat Groups. *Museum News* 7:7.

Museum Craft – Suggestions on the Construction of School Extension Groups. Minnesota Museum of Natural History, Minneapolis, MN 13 pp.

1930
Breeding of Nelson's Sparrow (Ammospiza nelsoni) with special reference to Minnesota. *Bell Museum Occasional Paper* 3: 29-38.

A Hybrid Passerina (Passerina cyanea and Passerina amoena). *Bell Museum Occasional Paper* 3: 39-40 (color illustration).

Two Notable Minnesota Duck Records. *Wilson Bulletin* 42:59.

Notes on the Reproduction of Cattails and Sedges. *Museum News* 7(19):9-10 (with A.H. Bulbulian).

1932
Harlequin Duck in Minnesota. *Auk* 49:345.

1933
Pomarine Jaeger in South Dakota. *Wilson Bulletin* 45:79.

1934
An Ecological Study of the Marsh Hawks (Circus hudsonicus) of a Minnesota Sand Plains Community. M.A. Thesis, University of Minnesota 85 pp.

1935
An Ecological Study of Some Minnesota Marsh Hawks. *Condor* 37:268-276.

Status of Minnesota Caribou. *Journal of Mammalogy* 16:327-328.

Trailing the Red Lake Caribou. *Minnesota Conservationist* 26:10-11.

A New Deal for Minnesota's Hawks. *Minnesota Conservationist* 30:8-9.

Science Judges the Owl. *Minnesota Conservationist* 31:5-6.

A Bird Census Method. *Wilson Bulletin* 47:195-197.

1936
Food Habits of Marsh Hawks in the Glaciated Prairie Region of North-Central States. *American Midland Naturalist* 17:831-848 (with Paul L. Errington).

Mammals collected in Northern Manitoba. *Journal of Mammalogy* 17:61- 62.

Minnesota Hawks and Owls: An Editorial. *Minnesota Conservationist* 36:1.

1937
Feather Feud. *Flicker* 9:8 (with E.H. Deller).

A Correction in the Range of Potamophis triatulus. *Copeia* 1937:231.

Cover - Flicker Version 2. *Flicker* 9(1) to 23(4).

Watch for reptiles. *Flicker* 9:3.

1938
Food Habits of the Buteo Hawks in North-Central United States. *Wilson Bulletin* 50:113-121 (with Paul L. Errington).

Food Habits of Small Falcons in North-Central States. *Auk* 55:668-670 (with Paul L. Errington).

Predator Control. *Minneapolis Public Library Museum Nature Notes.* 1(12):1-7, 1(13):8-11.

Minnesota Lizards. *Minneapolis Public Library Museum Nature Notes* 1:10-12.

Additions to the herpetology of Minnesota. *Copeia* 1938:47.

A Review of Predator Control. *Minnesota Conservationist* 57:10-11, 23-26.

The Search for Natural History Areas in Minnesota. *Proceedings of the Minnesota Academy of Sciences.* 6:20-25 (with A.N. Wilcox, R.L. Donovan, T.B. Magath, H.E. Stork, and G. Swanson).

1939
More Minnesota American Egret News. *Flicker* 11:13.

Further Progress in the Search for Natural History Areas in Minnesota. *Proceedings of the Minnesota Academy of Sciences.* 7:17-21 (with A.N. Wilcox, R.L. Donovan, T.B. Magath, H.E. Stork, and G. Swanson).

1940
Wildlife Photography. *Minnesota Wildlife Conservation - lst Short Course Proceedings.* pp 52-55 (with R. Woolsey).

Reptiles and amphibians of Minnesota. *Minnesota Wildlife Conservation - lst Short Course Proceedings.* pp 36-40.

Reptiles and amphibians of Minnesota. *Minneapolis Public Library Museum Nature Notes* 3:411-418.

1941
Record Flight of Sandhill Cranes. *Flicker* 13:2-4 (with W.H. Nord).

Minnesota rattlesnakes. *Conservation Volunteer* 1(6):10-12.

Minnesota turtles. *Conservation Volunteer* 2(7):11-16.

Beltrami's Beaver Story. *Conservation Volunteer* 2(8):10-13.

Snake myths versus facts. *Conservation Volunteer* 3(13):11-14.

Pinnated Grouse. *Conservation Volunteer* 3(13):60-61.

Pheasant Population Good. *Conservation Volunteer* 3(14):20-21.

King of the Game Birds. *Conservation Volunteer* 3(14):50-51.

Notes on Natural History: The Starling, An Undesirable Alien. *Conservation Volunteer* 3(15):10-13.

The amphibians and reptiles of Minnesota with special reference to the black-banded skink, Emcees septentrionalis (Baird). Ph.D. Thesis. University of Minnesota, Minneapolis. 398pp.

Amphibians and reptiles of Minnesota. *Proceedings of the Minnesota Academy of Sciences* 9:67-68 (abstract).

Museums of Natural History and Their Use in Science Teaching. *Proceedings of the Minnesota Academy of Science* 9:85-86.

Scanning the Natural History Aspects of the St. Croix. *Proceedings of the Minnesota Academy of Science* 9:103 (title only).

1942
Ring-necked snakes in Minnesota. *Copeia* 1942:128.

A large hognosed snake from Minnesota. *Copeia* 1942:128.

Unusual Additions to the University Museum Collection. *Flicker* 14:16.

Lake Traverse Bird Life in April. *Flicker* 14:25-27.

Wood duck Houses. *Minneapolis Public Library Museum Nature Notes* 5:94-97.

The Hungarian Partridge. *Conservation Volunteer* 3(16):46-47.

The Snowy Owl. *Conservation Volunteer* 3(17):50-51.

Notes on Natural History: Bird Flight Speeds. *Conservation Volunteer* 3(17):5-9.

The Black Capped Chickadee. *Conservation Volunteer* 3(18):56-57.

Minnesota's non-poisonous snakes. *Conservation Volunteer* 4(21):10-15. Wilson's or Jack Snipe. *Conservation Volunteer* 4(23)30-31.

The Morning Dove. *Conservation Volunteer* 4(24):6-9.

Upland Plover Comes Back. *Conservation Volunteer* 5(25):16-17.

Notes on Natural History: Hawks and Owls: A Revaluation. *Conservation Volunteer* 5(26):8-12.

Frogs and toads of Minnesota. *Conservation Volunteer* 5(27):32-36.

The Shoveler. *Conservation Volunteer* 5(27):44-45.

Amphibians and reptiles of Minnesota. *Proceedings of the Minnesota Academy of Sciences* 9:67-68.

The Farmer Tackles Conservation. Minnesota Department of Conservation. *Conservation Bulletin 4* (with Gustav Swanson, Warren W. Chase, Richard J. Dorer, Parker Anderson).

1943
The life history of the black-banded skink, Eumeces septentrionalis septentrionalis (Baird). *American Midland Naturalist.* 29:591-606.

Do you recognize Minnesota's lizards? *Conservation Volunteer* 6(33):21-24.

Another Minnesota Raven Record. *Flicker* 15:39.

Reptiles of Minnesota. Minnesota *Conservation Bulletin No. 3.* 24 pp.

Notes on Natural History: The Courtship of Birds. *Conservation Volunteer* 5(28):14-18.

Blue-winged Teal. *Conservation Volunteer* 5(28):34-35.

Notes on Natural History: The Private Live of Marsh Hawks. *Conservation Volunteer* 5(29): 14-18.

Notes on Natural History: Hibernation - The Long Sleep. *Conservation Volunteer* 5(30):37-40.

The Mallard. *Conservation Volunteer* 5(30):24-25.

Notes on Natural History: Those Puzzling Salamanders. *Conservation Volunteer* 6(31):9-12.

American Merganser. *Conservation Volunteer* 6(31):47.

Redhead and Canvasback Ducks. . *Conservation Volunteer* 6(32):26.

Notes on Natural History: Little-Known Phenomens of the Plant World. *Conservation Volunteer* 6(32):27-30.

Red Fox. *Conservation Volunteer* 6(33):17.

Nature Calendar: Go Afield in July. *Conservation Volunteer* 6(34):6-10.

Lesser Scaups. *Conservation Volunteer* 6(34):35.

Nature Calendar: August Afield in Minnesota. *Conservation Volunteer* 6(35):18-23.

Nature Calendar: Beside the Trail in September and October. *Conservation Volunteer* 6(36):6-11.

Nature Calendar: Nature's Winter Preparations. *Conservation Volunteer* 7(37):8-12.

1944
Reptiles and amphibians of Minnesota. University of Minnesota Press. Minneapolis. 202 pp.

The pilot black snake in Minnesota. *Copeia* 1944:64.

Birds at "The Brackens". *Flicker* 16:4-6.

Nature Calendar: In the Dead of Winter. *Conservation Volunteer* 7(38):36-42.

Nature Calendar: The Awakening Season. *Conservation Volunteer* 7(39):8-13.

Nature Calendar: Glimpses of May and June Wildlife. *Conservation Volunteer* 7(40):12-17.

Richardson and Franklin Ground Squirrels. *Conservation Volunteer* 7(41):44.

Notes on Natural History: Minnesota's Ace Divers, The Loons and Grebes. *Conservation Volunteer* 7(42):16-21.

Canada Lynx. *Conservation Volunteer* 7(42):49.

Notes on Natural History: Cormorants and Pelicans. *Conservation Volunteer* 7(43):40-45.

A Nature Calendar. Minnesota Department of Conservation. *Conservation Volunteer*:1-46.

Attracting Winter Birds. *Minnesota Horticulturist* 72(1):3-4.

1945
Great Horned Owl and Giant Water Beetle. *Flicker* 17:18.

Pileated Woodpecker and the Red Squirrel. *Flicker* 17:19.

Tufted Titmouse near Anoka. *Flicker* 17:19.

A Message From the President of the Minnesota Ornithologist's Union. *Flicker* 17:62-63.

Nebraska Crane Flight. Flicker 17:79-81.

Notes on Natural History: Minnesota Herons. *Conservation Volunteer* 8(44):10-16.

Notes on Natural History: Rails - Birds of the Swamps. *Conservation Volunteer* 8(45):8-14.

Notes on Natural History: Minnesota Gulls and Terns. *Conservation Volunteer*8(46):8-13.

Notes on Natural History: Those Dancing Cranes. *Conservation Volunteer* 8(47):16-22.

Notes on Natural History: The Hawks Now Protected in Minnesota. *Conservation Volunteer* 8(48):6-13.

Notes on Natural History: The Broad-winged or Soaring Hawks. *Conservation Volunteer* 8(49)6-12.

1946
Thomas Sadler Roberts – Obituary. *Auk* 63:574-583 (with William Kilgore).

Another Snowy Owl Year. *Flicker* 18:10.

Wood Ducks at the Brackens. *Flicker* 18:1-2.

A Rose-breasted Grosbeak-Cowbird Puzzle. *Flicker* 18:62.

Weights of a Minnesota Moose. *Journal of Mammalogy* 27:90-91.

Notes on Natural History: Bird Hawks, Eagles and Vultures. *Conservation Volunteer* 9(50):16-22.

Notes on Natural History: Minnesota's Large Owls. *Conservation Volunteer* 9(51):16-22.

Notes on Natural History: Minnesota's Smaller Owls. *Conservation Volunteer* 9(52):36-42.

Notes on Natural History: Shorebirds-World-wide Adventurers. *Conservation Volunteer* 9(53):36-41.

Notes on Natural History: Birds Have Housing Problems. *Conservation Volunteer* 9(55):30-33.

Minnesota's Birds of Prey. Minnesota Department of Conservation. *Conservation Bulletin 10.*

1947

Wood Ducks Versus Squirrels. *Auk* 64:621.

Obituary of Russell Messer Berthel. *Auk* 64:662-663.

Winter Golden-eye Count in Minneapolis. *Flicker* 19:22.

A Roadside Migration Study. *Flicker* 19:64-65.

Expanded Natural History Opportunities in Our State Parks. *Flicker* 19:68-69.

An Unusual Melanistic Squirrel. *Journal of Mammalogy* 28:403-404.

Notes on Natural History: Birds Have Housing Problems, Too. *Conservation Volunteer* 10(56):27-31.

What Makes Rare Birds Rare. *Conservation Volunteer* 10(58):47-50.

Minnesota's Birds of the Waterways. Minnesota Department of Conservation. *Conservation Bulletin 11.*

1948

Obituary of Ruth Eddy Keyes. *Auk* 65:342-343.

Book Review: Eddy and Surber – Northern Fishes. *Flicker* 20:25.

Roberts Bird Sanctuary Memorial Completed. *Flicker* 20:78.

Birds in Conservation. *Conservation Volunteer* 11(65):33-38.

Birds in Conservation. *Conservation Volunteer* 11(66):37-43.

Swifts and Swallows. *Conservation Volunteer* 11(67):30-36.

The Academy in 1947-1948: The President's Address. *Proceedings of the Minnesota Academy of Science* 16:4-7.

1949

Mountain Bluebird at Bemidji. *Flicker* 21:18.

Brown Thrasher Killed by Gray Squirrel. *Flicker* 21:60.

Wood Ducks Nesting in St. Paul. *Flicker* 21:61.

Unusual Wood Duck Nestings. *Flicker* 21:61-62.

Prothonotary Warbler Nesting in Anoka. *Flicker* 21:62-63.

Tentative List of Candidates for State Bird. *Flicker* 21:67-70 (with State Bird Commission).

Minnesota Record of the Great Black-Backed Gull. *Flicker* 21:63-64.

Birds in Conservation: The Thrushes. *Conservation Volunteer* 12(68):30-35.

Birds in Conservation: The Wrens. *Conservation Volunteer* 12(69):18-22.

Birds in Conservation: The Longspurs and Pipits. *Conservation Volunteer* 12(71):31-36.

A Century of Minnesota Wildlife Part One. *Conservation Volunteer* 12(72):36-41.

A Century of Minnesota Wildlife Part Two. *Conservation Volunteer* 12(73):37-22.

Nesting Season, Western Great Lakes Region. *Audubon Field Notes* 3:236-237 (with H.L. Gunderson).

A Century of Minnesota Wild Life. *Minnesota History* 30:123-134.

A Century of Minnesota Wild Life. *Minnesota History* 30: 220-231.

Birds of the Canadian Border Lakes. President's Quetico – Superior Committee, Chicago. 25 pp.

1950

A Century of Wildlife – Birds. *Conservation Volunteer* 13(74):29-34.

A Century of Wildlife - Birds (continued). *Conservation Volunteer* 13(75):38-44.

1951

Bison and Bird Remains from Ancient Peat Beds. *Flicker* 23:15-16

The Nature Hobbyist in Conservation. *Conservation Volunteer* 14(80):45-48.

Birds of the Canadian Border Lakes Part I. *Minnesota Naturalist* 1(4):10-13.

What is the Qualified Museum Person – Curator of Collections. *Museologist* 45:12-13.

1952

Guidebook to the Minnesota Museum of Natural History at the University of Minnesota. University of Minnesota Press, Minneapolis. 32 pp (with Ruth W. Self).

Cover - Flicker Version 3. *Flicker* 24(1) to 26(1).

Birds of the Canadian Border Lakes Part II. *Minnesota Naturalist* 2(1):11-14.

Birds of the Canadian Border Lakes Part III. *Minnesota Naturalist* 2(2)27-30.

Plan Your Planting for Birds Early. *Minnesota Naturalist* 2(3):33-34.

Cover – Canada Geese. *Minnesota Naturalist* 2(4.)

The President's page. *Wilson Bulletin* 64(2):66.

The President's page. *Wilson Bulletin* 64(3):130.

The President's page. *Wilson Bulletin* 64(4):194.

1953

The President's Page. *Wilson Bulletin* 65(1):4.

Night Rafting of American Goldeneyes on the Mississippi River. *Auk* 70:201.

M.O.U. Cooperative Bird Studies. *Flicker* 25:28-29 (with H.L. Gunderson and D.W. Warner).

Obituary of William Kilgore, Jr. *Flicker* 25:136-138.

1954

The Birds of Churchill. *Flicker* 26:46-58 (with Harvey Gunderson and John Jaroz).

Obituary of William Kilgore, Jr. *Auk* 71:348.

How to Cultivate Your Garden Birds. *Minnesota Horticulturist* 82:73-74.

U Scientists tell about their Trip into the Tundra. *The Minnesotan* 7(4):6-7,14.

1955

Mammal Observations at Lower Back River, Northwest Territories, Canada. *Journal of Mammalogy* 36:254-259 (with Harvey Gunderson and John Jaroz).

Where to find Birds in Minnesota: A Guide to 78 Birding Areas, Parks, and Sanctuaries. University of Minnesota Press, Minneapolis. 157 pp. (with K.D. Morrison and J. Daneman Herz).

Final Report of the University of Minnesota – Wilkie Back River Expedition. U.S. Department of the Army. 195 pp.

Comparison of the Breeding-bird Populations of Two Neighboring but Distinct Forest Habitats. *Audubon Field Notes* 9:408-412.

Naturalist on the Back River. *The Beaver* 1955(summer):9-15 (with R.J. Wilke).

Revision of Manual for the Identification of the Birds of Minnesota and the Neighboring States. University of Minnesota Press, 362 pp. (with Dwain W. Warner).

Observations on the life history of the softshell turtle Trionyx ferox, with especial reference to growth. *Copeia* 1955:5-9.

Review of The Passenger Pigeon: Its Natural History and Extinction. *Flicker* 27:126-127.

1956
Birds of the Lower Back River, Northwest Territories, Canada. *Canadian Field-Naturalist* 69:1-9.

Birds of the Minneapolis-St. Paul Region. *Pamphlet Series 1, Bell Museum of Natural History* 29 pp. (with Anne Winton Dodge, Helen Ford Fullerton, and Dwain J. Warner).

Nesting Study of Wood Ducks. *Journal of Wildlife Management* 20:16-21.

Book Review Hochbaum's Travels and Traditions of Waterfowl. *Minnesota Naturalist* 7:5.

Naturalists for State Parks. *Conservation Volunteer* 19(111):19-22.

Measurements of the Habitat Niche of the Least Flycatcher. *Wilson Bulletin* 68:47-51.

Annual Cycle of the Wood Duck, Chapter 4, pages 54-62 in *Outdoor Horizons*. T.S. Denison and Co., Minneapolis.

1957
A large spiny soft-shelled turtle. *Copeia* 1957:232.

Cover Art - Bald Eagle. *Flicker* 29(2).

Specimens of toads wanted. Minnesota *Journal of Science* 1:38.

Cultivate Your Garden Birds. *Pamphlet Series 2, Bell Museum of Natural History* 35 pp. (with Anne Winton Dodge, and Dwain J. Warner).

Book Review: Buss and Mattison – A Half Century of Change in Bird Populations of the Lower Chippewa River, Wisconsin. *Wilson Bulletin* 69:190-191.

Western Great Lakes Region – Nesting Season. *Audubon Field Notes* 11:405-407.

1958
A New Threat to Wildlife. *Flicker* 30:60-61.

Western Great Lakes Region – Fall Migration. *Audubon Field Notes* 12:32-33.

Regional Reports, Winter Season, Western Great Lakes Region. *Audubon Field Notes* 12:280-282.

Regional Reports, Spring Migration, Western Great Lakes Region. *Audubon Field Notes* 12:354-356.

Regional Reports, Nesting Season, Western Great Lakes Region. *Audubon Field Notes* 12:412-415.

Birds of the Border Country. *Naturalist* 9(3):16-17.

1959
Cover Art - Parasitic Jaeger. *Flicker* 31(2).

Cover Art - Grove Billed Ani. *Flicker* 31(4).

The Kako Moriat Painting of the Yellow-headed Blackbird. *Flicker* 31:46-47.

Short-eared Owl Preying on Pocket Gopher. *Flicker* 31:98.

Regional Reports, Fall Migration, Western Great Lakes Region. *Audubon Field Notes* 13:232-233.

Regional Reports, Spring Migration, Western Great Lakes Region. *Audubon Field Notes* 13:371-373.

Regular Report, Nesting Season, Western Great Lakes Region. *Audubon Field Notes* 13:431-433.

1960
Revision of Bird Portraits in Color by Thomas S. Roberts. University of Minnesota Press (with Dwain W. Warner and Robert Dickerman).

Cover Art – Sandpipers. *Flicker* 32(4).

Cover Illustration. *Flicker* 32:105.

Western Sandpiper Taken in Minnesota. *Flicker* 32:125.

Barn Swallow Killed by Electric Fence. *Flicker* 32:126.

A Bird Bath Count as an Indicator of Bird Population. *Flicker* 32:2-4.

A Bald Eagle Exploit. *Flicker* 32:63.

Field Studies of Hibernation of the Manitoba Toad (Bufo hemiophrys). *Bulletin of the Ecological Society of America* 41:129 (abstract).

A spiny soft-shelled turtle nest study. *Herpetologica* 16:284-285.

Book Review: Sweny – The Techniques of Drawing and Painting Wildlife. *Wilson Bulletin* 72:297-98.

1961
Factors Influencing the Distribution of Animals in an Ecotone, as Represented by the Zone of Contact of Three Toads, Bufo terrestris americanus, B. hemiophrys, and B. cognatus. *Progress Report and Renewal Proposal*, U.S. Atomic Energy Commission Contract AT(11-1)-899 (with J. Tester).

Growth, local movements and hibernation of the Manitoba toad, Bufo hemiophrys. *Ecology* 42:637-646. (with John R. Tester).

Another Hybrid Red-shafted/Yellow-shafted Flicker. *Flicker* 33:92.

Book Review: Pettingill - Penguin Summer. *Flicker* 33:96-97.

Common Loon – Frontispiece. *Flicker* 33(2).

Cover Art – Dowitchers. *Flicker* 33(2).

Book Review: Greenwalt – Hummingbirds. *Wilson Bulletin* 73:429-430.

1962
Radiation and other Factors Influencing the Distribution of Animals. *Progress Report and Renewal Proposal*, U.S. Atomic Energy Commission Contract AT(11-1)-899 (with J. Tester).

Aid for New Construction of Graduate Research Laboratories. Minnesota Museum of Natural History, Minneapolis (with L. Lunden).

Nature's Wonderland Stamp Album. General Mills, Gilbertson Co., New York. 50 pp. Worm-eating Warbler in Hennepin County. *Flicker* 34:65.

1963
Radiation and other Factors Influencing the Distribution of Animals. *Progress Report and Renewal Proposal*, U.S. Atomic Energy Commission Contract AT(11-1)-899 (with J. Tester).

A Second Minnesota Dovekie Record. *Flicker* 35:30.

Birding in the Northwest Territories. *Flicker* 35:74-77.

Albino Crows. *Flicker* 35:99.

Birds Feeding on Elm Leaf Miners. *Flicker* 35:99.

Bird Watchers Focus on Salt Lake. *Conservation Volunteer* 26(151):1-3.

American Avocet. *Conservation Volunteer* 26(151):cover.

Review: Prairie Spring: Volume VII of the Sounds of Nature Series. *Wilson Bulletin* 75:223-224.

1964
Population dynamics of the Manitoba Toad, Bufo hemiophrys, in northwestern Minnesota. *Ecology* 45:592-601 (with John R. Tester).

Winter behavior patterns of the Manitoba toad, Bufo hemiophrys, in northwestern Minnesota. *Annales Academiae Scientiarum Fennicae Series A. IV Biology* 71:423-431 (with John R. Tester).

State Parks Natural Values. *Conservation Volunteer* 27(155): 23-31.

No Habitat – No Birds. *Minnesota Out-of-Doors* 10(XX):12.

Book Review: Peterson – The Birds. *Wilson Bulletin* 76:102-103.

1965
Book Review: Austing – *The World of the Red-tailed Hawk. Wilson Bulletin* 77:107-108.

A Virgin Prairie in Minnesota pp 269-275 in Pettingill's *The Bird Watcher's America.* McGraw Hill, New York 441 pp.

Radiation and other Factors Influencing the Distribution of Animals. *Progress Report and Renewal Proposa*l, U.S. Atomic Energy Commission Contract AT(11-1)-899 (with J. Tester).

That May Wave of Warblers. *Conservation Volunteer* 28(160):51-54.

1966
Radiation and other Factors Influencing the Distribution of Animals. *Progress Report and Renewal Proposal*, U.S. Atomic Energy Commission Contract AT(11-1)-899 (with J. Tester).

Dovekie on Little Diomede Island. *Auk* 83:680.

A Double-brooded Wood Duck Record. *Loon* 38:83-84.

Book Review: Top Flight. *Wilson Bulletin* 78:327-328.

1967
Sandhill Cranes and Other Birds from Bering Strait, Alaska. *Auk* 84:277 (with David Cline) Islands of Refuge. *Conservation Volunteer* 30(185):1-5.

Guidebook to the James Ford Bell Museum of Natural History at the University of Minnesota. University of Minnesota Press, Minneapolis. 32 pp. (revision of 1952 guide).

Book Review: Collins and Boyajian – Familiar Garden Birds of America. *Wilson Bulletin* 79:127-128.

Book Review: Murphy – A Certain Island. *Atlantic Naturalist* 22(2):147.

Growing Demand Noted for Science Information. *Minnesota-Out-of-Doors* 13(2):21-22.

1968
Radiation and other Factors Influencing the Distribution of Animals. *Progress Report and Renewal Proposal*, U.S. Atomic Energy Commission Contract AT(11-1)-899 (with J. Tester).

The Strange Case of the Stuck Duck. *Loon* 40:52-53.

Letter on King Birds. *Loon* 40:56.

Minnesota Nesting of White Pelicans. *Loon* 40:100.

Ecology of mima-type mounds in northwestern Minnesota. *Ecology* 49:172-177 (with B.A. Ross and John R. Tester).

1969
Science and Parks. *Conservation Volunteer* 32(185):14.

Migratory Birds in *An Appraisal of the Fish and Wildlfie Resources of the Proposed Voyageurs National Park.*

Final Report: An Ecological Study of the Twin Cities Metropolitan Area. Wallace, McHarg, Roberts, and Todd, Inc. (not a named author but cited as a major contributor).

1970
Cover Art - Prairie Chickens. *Loon* 42(1).

1971
Francis Lee Jaques – Obituary. *Auk* 88:478-479.

Cover Art – Woodpeckers. *Loon* 43(2).

Our Disappearing Kingbirds. *Loon* 43:89-90.

1973
Possible Swallow-tailed Kite Sighting. *Loon* 45:136.

1977
Another Wintering Carolina Wren. *Loon* 49:100-101 (with Dorothy Breckenridge).

Cover Photo - Carolina Wren. *Loon* 49(2).

1979
Obituary of Whitney Eastman 1889-1979. *Loon* 51:163.

1981
Minnesota herpetology - Ecological and historical perspective. Page 1 in *Ecology of Reptiles and Amphibians in Minnesota: Proceedings of a Symposium.*, Cass Lake, MN. Elwell, L., K. Cram, and C. Johnson (eds.) 64pp.

Cover - Bald Eagle painting. *Naturalist* 32(2).

The Beginnings of Nongame Conservation in Minnesota. *Naturalist* 32(4):1-3.

Keynote Address. *Proceedings of a Symposium on Priorities for Nongame Conservation in Minnesota.* University of Minnesota pp 1-5.

1982
Cover Art - Chuck-will's Widow. *Loon* 54(3).

Chuck-will's Widow - First Known Occurrence in Minnesota. *Loon* 54:139-141.

The Remarkable Flight of the Sandhill Crane. *Naturalist* 33(4):32.

1984
Review of Wood Warbler's World. *Loon* 56:215-216.

House Finch in Hennepin County. *Loon* 56:64

Back's Great Fish River pp. 189-196 in *Flyways, Pioneering Waterfowl Management in North America* US Fish and Wildlife Service,

1987
Thomas Sadler Roberts father of Minnesota Ornithology. *Loon* 59:63

1988
Cooper's Hawk at Bird Bath. *Loon* 60:127-128.

1989
Evidence of Sense of Smell in Wood Ducks. *Loon* 61:202-203.

Another Partial Albino Chickadee. *Loon* 61:205.

1990
A Possible Jaeger in Hennepin County. *Loon* 62:233.

1991
Wood Duck Olfactory Sense Questioned. *Loon* 63:137.

Comments on Eberhard Gwinner, internal rhythms in bird migration. *Loon* 63:17-18.

1992
Hooded Warbler in Brooklyn Park. *Loon* 64:120-121.

1993
An Exciting Visit with a Barred Owl. *Loon* 65:51 (with Dorothy Breckenridge).

1994
Forward to *Amphibians and Reptiles Native to Minnesota* by Barney Oldfield and John Moriarty. University of Minnesota Press, Minneapolis.

1995
Was the Carolina Parakeet a Minnesota Bird? *Loon* 67:222-223.

1996
Moving Day for the House Finches. *Loon* 68:177-178.

1997
Dr. Breckenridge remembers a nuthatch and a 1st State Record Western Sandpiper. *Minnesota Birding* 34(2):5

Are You a Realist or a Happy-Go-Lucky Optimist pp. 1-2 in *Priorities for Nongame Wildlife Conservation in Minnesota: Conference Proceedings.*

1998
Cover Art- Wilson's Phalarope Chick. *Loon* 70(4).

Unusual Nesting of House Finches. *Loon* 70:123.

Minnesota's First Harlequin Duck. *Loon* 70:187.

Capturing River Cranes. *Loon* 70:198-199.

Greater Prairie Chickens and Radisson South. *Loon* 70:229-230.

1999
Obituary of Harvey Gunderson, 1913-1999. *Loon* 71:119.

Illustrations for other publications

Bailey and Neidrach 1965. *Birds of Colorado.* Denver Museum of Natural History. (10 color plates)

Briggs, Shirley A. 1962. Duck Stamp Designs for 1962-63. *Atlantic Naturalist* 1962 (Jan-Mar) 28-31. (B&W illustration of WJB's second place duck stamp design)

Dickerman, Robert W. 1961. New Species of Pinnated Bittern (Botaurus pinnatus). *Wilson Bulletin* 73:332 (full page color plate)

Dorer, Richard 1963.*The Ghost Tree Speaks.* Ross and Haines, St. Paul 73 pp. (12 full page B&W illustrations)

Flugum, Charles T. 1973. *Birding from a Tractor Seat.* privately published. (Cover and 20 B&W chapter illustrations)

Green, Janet C. and Robert B. Janssen 1975. *Minnesota Birds: Where When and How Many.* University of Minnesota Press. (Frontispiece - Spruce Grouse)

Kimball, David and Jim Kimball 1969. *The Market Hunter.* Dillon Press, Minneapolis. (13 illustrations (title page and chapter headings))

McKenny, Margaret 1939. *Birds in the Garden and How to Attract Them.* Grosset and Dunlap, New York (1 color plate)

Pettingill, O.S. 1946. *Ornithology in Laboratory and Field.* Burgess Publishing, Minneapolis. (127 illustrations, 3 revisions.)

Roberts, T.S. 1932. *The Birds of Minnesota.* University of Minnesota Press, Minneapolis. (10 color plates and numerous text illustrations)

Roberts, T.S. 1934. *Bird Portraits in Color.* University of Minnesota Press, Minneapolis (10 color plates)

Roberts, T.S. 1936. *The Birds of Minnesota,* revised. University of Minnesota Press, Minneapolis. (10 color plates and numerous text illustrations)

Roberts, T.S. 1938. *Logbook of Minnesota Bird Life 1917-1937.* Univ. Minnesota Press. (B&W frontispiece and 21 illustrations)

Roberts, T.S. 1949. *A Manual for the Identification of The Birds of Minnesota and Neighboring States.* University of Minnesota Press, Minneapolis. (numerous text illustrations)

Searle, R. Newell and Mark E. Heitlinger 1980. *Prairies, Woods and Islands: A Guide to the Preserves of the Nature Conservancy.* The Nature Conservancy, Minneapolis. (14 B&W illustrations)

Sperry, Charles C. 1940. Food Habits of a Group of Shorebirds: Woodcock, Snipe, Knot, Dowitcher. U.S. Bureau of Biological Survey. *Wildlife Research Bulletin No. 1* (3 full page color plates)

Swanson, Gustav, Thaddeus Surber and Thomas Roberts 1945. *The Mammals of Minnesota.* Minnesota Department of Conservation, Technical Bulletin No. 2, 108 pp. (4 full page B&W illustrations)

Young, S.P. and E.A. Goldman 1944. *The Wolves of North America.* American Wildlife Institute, Washington DC. 636 pp. (1 color plate of color variations in Wolves, plate 16 (page 34))

Living Bird (Cornell bird Lab) 1968. (color painting of Common Loon) 6:56.

Minneapolis Sunday Tribune- **color paintings**

Four Upland Game Birds
    Oct. 4, 1942
Seven Minnesota Ducks
    Oct. 18, 1942
Mass Migration of Wild Geese in State Spectacular
    April 11, 1943
Minnesota Hawks
    Oct. 10, 1943
Four Minnesota Mammals
    Feb. 7, 1943
Six Minnesota Songbirds
    Apr. 4, 1943
Birds that live in Minnesota Marshes
    Apr. 30, 1944
Minnesota Ducks
    Sept 23, 1945
Summer Residents
    May 4, 1947

The western meadowlark was a common roadside bird and one of Breck's first field sketches (watercolor field sketch) (Chapter 1, Page 4)

White-tailed buck along the Mississippi River, 1980 (watercolor) (Chapter 3, Page 31)

Plate   2

Aerial transfer of food by marsh hawks, 1965 (watercolor) (Chapter 4, Page 33)

Plate   3

Juvenile marsh hawk or harrier (watercolor) (Chapter 4, Page 33)

Plate   4

5A. Six-lined racerunner, 1986 (watercolor) (Chapter 4, Page 36)

5B. Spiny soft-shelled turtles, 1995 (watercolor) (chapter 4, Page 38)

Plate   5

6A. Pileated woodpecker and red squirrel, 1984 (watercolor) (Chapter 7, Page 58)

6B.Cardinal at the birdbath, 1988 (watercolor) (Chapter 7, Page 58)

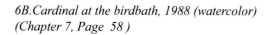

Plate 6

7A. Rose-breasted grosbeaks, 1994 (watercolor)
(Chapter 7, Page 58)

7B. Baltimore orioles at nest (watercolor)
(Chapter 7, Page 58)

7C. Goldeneyes on the river, 1945 (oil) (Chapter 7, Page 59)

Plate   7

8A. A pair of Flying Squirrels, 1993 (watercolor) (Chapter 7 , Page 60)

8B. White-tailed Deer, 1970 (watercolor) (Chapter 7, Page 61)

Plate   8

Wood duck, 1982 (watercolor reproduced as note cards) (Chapter 8, Page 70)

Plate   9

House hunting, 1983 (watercolor) (Chapter 8, Page 70)

Plate   10

Wood ducks with pickerel weed (oil) (Chapter 8, Page 70)

Plate   11

12A. Osprey, 1974 (watercolor)
(Chapter 9, Page 76)

12B. Swallow-tailed Kite, 1959
(watercolor) (Chapter 9, Page 76)

Plate   12

13A. Goshawk eyeing a pheasant (watercolor)
(Chapter 9, Page 77)

13B. Peregrine Falcon (watercolor)
(Chapter 9, Page 77)

Plate   13

14A. Peregrine attacking pheasant (watercolor) (Chapter 9, Page 77)

14B. Red-tailed hawk, 1984 (watercolor) (Chapter 9, Page 80)

Plate   14

15A. Prairie falcon harassing shorebirds (watercolor) (Chapter 9, Page 80)

15B. White phase of Gyrfalcon, 1974 (watercolor) (Chapter 9, Page 81)

Plate   15

Kestrel or Sparrow Hawk (watercolor also reproduced in limited edition print) (Chapter 9, Page 81)

Plate   16

17A. Barred owl, 1984 (watercolor)
(Chapter 9, Page 81)

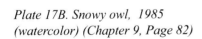

Plate 17B. Snowy owl, 1985
(watercolor) (Chapter 9, Page 82)

Plate   17

Great horned owl at sunset, 1980 (watercolor) (Chapter 9, Page 83)

Plate   18

Mobbing a great grey owl, 1985 (watercolor reproduced as note cards) (Chapter 9, Page 85)

Plate   19

Bald Eagle, 1978 (watercolor) (Chapter 9, Page 86)

Plate   20

Sandhill cranes, 1973 (watercolor) (Chapter 10, Page 91)

Plate 21

Early man at the River Warren (watercolor) (Chapter 10, Page 94)

Plate   22

23A. Sharp-tailed grouse courting, 1993 (watercolor) (Chapter 10, Page 95)

23B. Ruffed grouse, 1981 (watercolor) (Chapter 10, Page 95)

Plate   23

24A. Prairie chickens courting, 1993 (watercolor) (Chapter 10, Page 96)

Plate 24B. Spruce grouse, 1995 (watercolor) (Chapter 10, Page 97)

Plate   24

25A. Prairie Marsh Farm at Salt Lake, MN (watercolor) (Chapter 10, Page 99)

25B. Egret on elk antler at Prairie Marsh Farm, 1997 (watercolor) (Chapter 10, Page 99)

Plate   25

26A. Tundra swans over the Mississippi (oil) (Chapter 10, Page 100)

26B. Red Fox hunting a mouse, 1972 (watercolor) (Chapter 10, Page 101)

Plate   26

27A. Caribou at night (oil on board) (Chapter 10, Page 102)

27B. Chuck-wills-widow, 1982 (watercolor) (Chapter 10, Page 103)

Plate   27

Great blue heron:courtship ritual, 1981 (watercolor reproduced in limited edition) (Chapter 10, Page 104)

Plate   28

29A. Least bittern,1993 (watercolor) (Chapter 10, Page 105)

29B. Passenger pigeon, 1993 (watercolor) (Chapter 10, Page 105)

Plate 29

"Loon Family", 1981 (watercolor reproduced in limited edition print) (Chapter 10, Page 106)

Plate   30

31A. Ruddy ducks, 1963 (watercolor) (Chapter 10, Page 106)

31B. Harlequin ducks, 1985 (watercolor) (Chapter 10, Page 107)

Plate   31

32A. Mountain sheep, 1993 (watercolor) (Chapter 11, Page 109)

32B. Elk or wapiti (oil) (Chapter 11, Page 110)

Plate   32

33A. Moose, 1985 (oil) (Chapter 11, Page 113)

33B. Bison in the Black Hills (watercolor) (Chapter 11, Page 114)

Plate   33

34A. Red-breasted merganser (watercolor) (Chapter 11, Page 115)

34B.. Saguaro Cactus, 1973 (watercolor) (Chapter 11, Page 117)

Plate   34

35A. Young arctic fox, 1953 (watercolor) (Chapter 12, Page 121)

35B. Willow ptarmigan, 1953 (watercolor) (Chapter 12, Page 122)

Plate   35

36A. Willow ptarmigan chick, 1953 (watercolor field sketch) (Chapter 12, Page 121)

36B. White-eyed robin, 1962 (watercolor field sketch) (Chapter 12, Page 126)

Plate   36

37A. Yellow wagtail (watercolor field sketch) (Chapter 12, Page 128)

37B. King eider duck, 1964 (watercolor field sketch) (Chapter 12, Page 129)

Plate   37

38A. Red-faced parrot finch, 1985 (watercolor) (Chapter 13, Page 142)

38B. Frigate birds, 1980 (watercolor) (Chapter 13, Page 143)

Plate   38

Rufous-crowned motmot, 1984 (watercolor) (Chapter 13, Page 144)

Plate   39

Oropendolas with nests, 1983 (watercolor) (Chapter 13, Page 145)

Plate   40

Scarlet Macaws, 1989 (watercolor) (Chapter 13, Page 146)

Plate   41

Quetzal or resplendent trogon, 1988 (watercolor) (Chapter 13, Page 146)

Plate   42

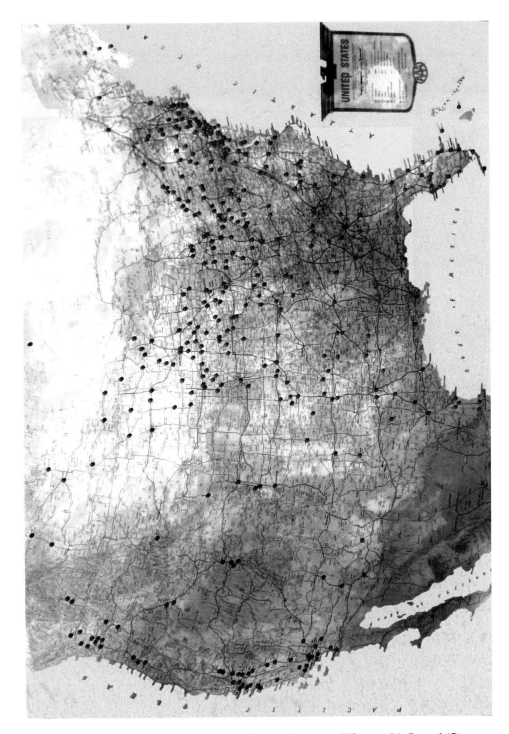

Map of Breck's travels Red – lectured; blue – lectured more than once (Chapter 14, Page 147)

Plate   43

Woodpecker plate from Robert's Birds of Minnesota ,1932 (watercolor) (Chapter 17, Page 157)

Plate   44